Tracey Ellen Maria /

RECOMMENCED

Motivation > Limitation

By Tracey Ellen Maria

Recommence – "Begin or cause to begin again"

Past Tense – "Recommenced"

Love & Best Wishes
Tracey Ellen Maria
Xx

Dedication

This book is written in loving memory of:

Jennifer McCann (Jenny)

20 April 1984 - 27 December 2012

"I believe I can fly"

&

Ellen Hogan (Nanny B)

19 November 1939 - 24 October 2016

"The bells of the Angelus call us to pray,

with sweet tones announcing the sacred Ave"

Until we meet again…

Table of Contents

Testimonials

"Tracey's book is a shining example of dignity, courage, and resilience. Her determination to be a winner burns bright on every page. God bless you." - Christina Noble, founder of *The Christina Noble Children's Foundation*

"Tracey is an extraordinary inspiration who has a strong message to share. She may not have a physical voice to express her message but she has one of the most compelling voices I have ever heard. What she cannot express in words, she expresses through her heart and radiates in her energy. She reaches people on a level that most people can't and I am confident that through this book she will make a positive global impact. This book offers hope where there is none and it shows us that no matter what challenge we are presented with, we can overcome it." – Donna Kennedy, professional speaker and best-selling author of *The Confidence to Succeed*

"Tracey's story is intriguing, captivating and inspiring with lots of great Irish humour to keep you entertained. What I loved most about the book was the little hidden gems and reminders which Tracey had for us about how life is a gift to be lived. I predict this book will be a best seller." – Stevie J, author, professional speaker and life coach.

Acknowledgments

For as long as I can remember I have always wanted to write a book; a book with an important message that I needed to share. A message of the sudden shock that can inflict anyone at any time in the course of their lives, and a message of hope that in not only facing those moments head on but bettering your situations after those moments arise is not fantasy, it is possible. This message was inside me eagerly waiting to escape onto paper. I have spent years writing bits of paragraphs and sentences, not 100 per cent certain as to how to structure my thoughts into pages, chapters, and an overall book. However, through my recent networking, I have successfully managed to find the right people to assist me in achieving this lifelong goal.

The people whom I met through my life and who have stuck by me deserve recognition because they assisted me greatly in getting to where I am today. I am forever grateful that these beautiful, kind, loving people came into my life. I wish to thank the following:

- John Carty, Brian and all the staff at the Endorphin Release Clinic in Crumlin for never giving up on me.

- Frank and Billy for all their brilliant support throughout the years and being such great friends.

- Amanda and Ian Delany for all their belief and encouragement, pushing me to make videos informing people of my message. Encouraging me to do public speaking, something that I would have previously assumed impossible and putting me in contact with other amazing people.

- Pat Slattery for being another great encourager and for making people aware of me and my story.

- Donna Kennedy for her fantastic course that aided me on how to structure my book, and much more. The time and dedication she has given to me has been amazing and again for all her amazing support and encouragement.

- Maria Kelly who ventured out to Howth with me and took amazing photographs as seen on the covers of this book, a lovely and very friendly lady.

- Michael Piercy for his assistance with my website, a true professional.

- Lesley-Anne Hogan for the beautiful piece of art she has done in the creation of my fabulous butterfly logo. I am so happy Lesley-Anne has been part of this project as she has offered great advice, love, kindness, and friendship.

- Samantha Hogan for all her support, encouragement and 'big sisterly' advice.

- Maria Hickey from Dystonia Ireland for providing me with information and granting me permission to use that information in this book.

- My team of proof readers, four brilliant and kind past teachers; who proof read my book on their own time. Jackie Pierce, Adrienne Webb, Mary Kenny, Cepta Loughnane, Breege McGee. Thank you for your dedication.

- All my special friends who I have met throughout the past few years and have been absolutely fantastic to and for me. I have waited so long to have friends such as you all and I now have more than I ever imagined: Bronagh and Karl Davidson, Sandra Pelly, Aisling Burnett, Daniel Egan, Flavia Pordominsky, Catherine Graham Kavanagh, Sinead Mangan, Beth Ahimsa and many more. I love you all very much.

- Laurie Burke for all the legal advice and support.

- Lorraine Maher for her great support and years of friendship.

- Jenny Kavanagh for introduction me to the world of networking in the first place. That one thing that you posted on FB all those years ago has made all of this possible. Thank you.

- The people who I am so blessed to have as my close family: My mam, Philomena Mooney, my stepdad, Stephen Mooney, my brothers, Alan and Dean, and my nanny and grand dad. I would not be the person that I am today if I did not have the guidance, love, encouragement, and support from you all. You have been absolutely amazing. I love you all very much.

- Lastly, my main supporter and my rock is my absolutely wonderful man, Patrick Hogan. He has been on the same path as me, meeting the beautiful people that I have and assisted me in gathering these people together to collectively help me be a success in achieving my goals. His belief in me is so strong and unquestionable. He has assisted me tirelessly in creating this book, designing my website, and my book cover. He has pushed me to do public speaking and assisted me in getting my name out there. I am so blessed to have Patrick. I am so happy that we are on this journey together so that we can grow, have fun, and make memories of constantly achieving in life together. Patrick, my love, you are brilliant in every way I admire you every day. You are strong, brave, determined, and I am so proud of you. Thank you so much for everything. I love you dearly.

I am extremely proud to have my book completed and I wish to thank you, the reader, for purchasing it. As I have said at the beginning, I wanted to share my story and my message to all who wish to know. It has taken a great deal of time to put this book together and throughout that time I have experienced writer's cramp and back and neck pain from typing one letter at a time and at a slow pace with one finger. Enduring all the frustrating moments and feeling that I will never reach the end. The commitment of having to stay in at the weekends as Patrick and myself kill each other over what is to be done next. Now, however, it is completed.

For as long as I can remember I have always wanted to write a book. This has been my goal. What you are holding in your hands is this goal. I have achieved it, with great assistance I know and acknowledge, but I have achieved it. Do not give up on your goals, especially and more importantly when the moment it gets too hard and feels impossible arrives. Believe it will happen, work on making it happen, and it will happen. You will achieve.

Prologue

"When life gives you a hundred reasons to cry, show life you have a 1000 reasons to smile" Stephanie Meyer, *Twilight*

I remember when I was a little girl, Mam would sing along to powerful songs such as Celine Dion's *Because You Loved Me.* I could see how talented Mam was and how enjoyable she made it seem, so I started practising. At the time I sounded pretty good. In fact, I thought I sounded deadly. I used to look at myself in the mirror while singing; I could not get the smile off my face. I was free, energetic and loving my happy little life. At the time, I loved getting up to mischief and trying to be sneaky about it. I once got my tongue stuck in a plastic Barbie doll's head, my stepdad had to pull it out, and I did not try that again. I would regularly act the maggot, roaring laughing, screaming, or throwing an outright tantrum. If I was caught getting up to mischief, I would act all shy and innocent, looking at people with my big blue innocent eyes...and not say a thing.

Tracey Ellen Maria / **Recommenced**

In the summer of 1996, my family and I went on a summer holiday to the Canary Islands over the last two weeks of August. It was the first family holiday abroad for us and, as such, we were all very excited. I was with my friend, the night before we travelled; she had been to Spain already and was telling me how great it was. I remember looking into the clear, black sky and staring at a beautiful sparkly star; the air was so warm and soothing. I took a deep breath in and thought, "I will be flying high in that magic sky tomorrow". I had butterflies in my stomach from the excitement.

When we left, I literally could not stop talking from the very start right to the very end. On our return, my aunt came to collect us all from the airport. My aunt asked how the holiday went. Before anyone could speak I immediately dived in. "Oh, it was great. We went to the beach, ate watermelons, and went to shows. Oh and we saw dolphins, oh and Alan fell into a cactus and he had lots of spikes all over him. It was my fault really, as I made him wave at the bin lorry and he got too excited and fell right into them. I thought it was a Bee Baw job. They had to be taken out with a pliers but he's ok now. What else? Oh, we saw a parrot show! They are very smart." I literally did not stop talking; even my mam could not get a word in. My aunt was laughing at how excited I was telling her about all our adventures. I could see that she was trying to get a word in, looking at me in the rear-view mirror as I rambled on. After a few minutes, she gave up trying and she just let me waffle the ears off everyone. We arrived at my nan's to give presents to everyone and I still would not quieten down. I just kept taking in deep breaths, talking very fast and loud as if it were my last breath. I felt that I needed to say everything. Everyone kept having to try to talk over me because I was annoying them. At this stage, my mam said, "Tracey, will you relax now? Give your voice box a break. You're overworking it". To which I cheekily replied, "No, I'm talking," which made my mam just roll her eyes then turn to my nan and laughingly ask, "Do you have a gag?"

I loved to talk; I could talk rings around me and would wreck everybody's head telling them all about our amazing holiday. And it was an amazing holiday.

****

I used to have a saying when I was a little girl. Whenever I was leaving my nan's house and skipping towards the gate, I would shout back and say, "Goodbye, goodbye, I'll see you tomorrow where I'll kiss you at the garden gate". One day, while I was writing a story at my nan's kitchen table, she said, "You know you keep saying you'll kiss me at the garden gate but you don't". My response was, "Well, that's tomorrow". It was always tomorrow until one day, before I even finished my phrase, my nan crept up behind me and gave me a big a kiss on the cheek. I was going mad at her.

"No, Nanny, you're breaking the rules, that's tomorrow." My nan would say, "But tomorrow never happens". We would stick our tongues out at each other in a cheeky manner. What were we like? I treasure those memories. They make me smile every time I revisit them.

***

When I was nine years old my stepdad had to spoon-feed me my dinner, which was a lovely cooked meal my mam had made. It had to be blended into a paste as I could not swallow properly. I was at a very high risk of choking; my food would pour down my chin and I would go into these bouts of uncontrollable coughing after every spoonful. My little arms were twisted around my neck stuck in a seemingly never-ending spasm. I felt like a baby, degraded, and sad. Missing the old Tracey deeply and wondering if I would ever see her again, the child in me was emotionally wounded and I felt like a complete failure that I could not adapt quickly enough. I could not feed myself. The energy it required to even be fed together with the length of time it took would always wear me down; I was half asleep by the time I was finished.

**

When I was sixteen years old I was still adjusting to life with a physical disability that made my day-to-day life generally difficult. Trying to do normal things like dressing, eating, and talking were made extremely complicated, due to this disability. I was very keen to travel the world. In my situation, however, I could never imagine myself doing those things, I was just fantasizing. As I was unable to verbally communicate I was full of self-pity because I found myself socially isolated most of the time. I had no friends; the only people I generally engaged in conversation with were my family. I would spend most of my teens sitting in my room…staring out the window...watching my life pass me by.

*

As I write this book I am twenty-nine years old and have experienced many more life-altering and socially isolating moments than most people I know. I have also, however, achieved many great things...things that I am very proud of. I have travelled the world visiting twenty-one countries and counting; I have seen amazing things such as the aurora borealis or northern lights and the Panama Canal to name but a few. I have gone to college and received a Diploma in Psychology and a QQI level 6 qualification in Coaching Models of Practice.

I have done all of these things not because I wanted to prove anything to anyone but because, even though I am disabled, I am not willing to sit back and accept society's definition of what I can or cannot do. I am more than my disability and I want to live my life the way I see fit.

Allow me now to tell you how I made my transformation from a healthy, able-bodied girl to a woman who has struggled most of her life with a life-altering disability; a woman who does not see obstacles just opportunities to defy expectations and stereotypes. This is the story of how my life was put to an abrupt halt at the age of eight...and how, through my unwavering determination, I ***recommenced*** my life.

Chapter 1
The beginning

"Life has many ways of testing a person's will, either by having nothing happen at all or by having everything happen all at once"
Paulo Coelho, The Winner Stands Alone

Build up to event

16 September 1996 was the day my life changed in such a dramatic way that it would end up shaping the rest of my life. I remember that day so clearly. I woke up feeling like I had a head cold. Mam gave me a spoonful of Actifed to help with the pain saying I would be ok and that it would do me good to go to school. I was eight years old and in second class at the time. She told my teacher, Ms Brennan, that I was feeling unwell. Despite Mam telling me that I would be fine I had this strange feeling that I should not go to school. However, my teacher talked me around. We were going on a school trip to a fun factory and she said it would be good, so I agreed. Looking at Mam as I left, I had this feeling of sadness in my stomach; I did not know exactly what it was. We said goodbye.

Trying to build up the excitement for the trip ahead I went over to a girl who was my best friend at the time and tried to feed off her excitement. Everyone got really excited and loud on the bus; you would swear we never got out. On the school bus, I was sitting at the front, it was a white mini bus. Everyone was screaming, singing God knows what; they were like a pack of squawking crows. I remember thinking at the time that I wish they would shut up. Suddenly the weird feeling I had felt earlier that morning came over me again. I told my friend who was sitting beside me on the bus that I thought something bad was going to happen to me. She just looked at me strangely. I asked if we could stick together in Playzone and she agreed without knowing fully as to why I was asking.

There was a massive scream from everyone when the bus finally arrived at our destination. We went in to get used to our new, temporary surroundings and Ms Brennan gave us the all clear to let loose. There was a big stampede of kids running around like lunatics and I started to get into it too, having fun. My best friend and I ran over to the bouncy castle. We were jumping around it laughing, falling and jumping back up. Suddenly, while on the bouncy castle my legs gave in and would not work. I felt paralysed, I was in such a panic, "Oh my legs don't work," I was saying to myself as I put my hands on them. I had feeling in them but I just could not control them. My friend looked at me strangely again as if to say "stop messing". She ran off and beckoned me to get up and carry on having fun. I really had to focus to get the power back. I felt I was going to fall face first, but I kept telling myself "you can run".

Slowly I felt the control come back so I pushed myself off the bouncy castle. I saw my friend at the other end of Playzone and she yelled to me that she would go around and meet me at the other side. The other children were playing kiss chasing. I did not want to be kissed by a smelly boy, so I ran for it. I was running beside another girl from my class; we were running towards the monkey ropes. I was trying to keep up with her, which I found strangely difficult. As we were climbing up the ropes that weird feeling came over me again as my body seized and would not work. I began to panic and I put my hand out for my friend to catch but she just said "no" and ran off. In my head, I was saying, "Please, don't go". Feeling my body get weaker and weaker, I started to fall backwards.

Everything was in slow motion as I listened to the distant sounds of kids screaming. I felt like I was in a movie. I thought I was going to die.

As I was falling, having no control over my body, I started to think of everyone's names. I was in a panic in case I forgot people so I said everyone's name twice, screaming them in my head as I was falling. The ropes were beginning to wrap around my legs. My head slowly hit the padded floor and I went to sleep. It felt like I was unconscious for hours but it was only three minutes. What woke me was the noise of my best friend coming down from the monkey ropes.

"Oh my God! What happened?" she asked.

I was unable to answer because I was just getting my bearings. She stood in front of me and started laughing as I can only imagine what I looked like on the floor with my legs up in the air and the ropes wrapped around them. I started crying. She panicked and got my legs out, they felt so floppy. I tried helping but I felt so useless and weak. She got me out and stood in front of me as if to say to me that I can get up now. I felt very fuzzy and dizzy. I tried sitting up first but I felt extremely weak. It was such an effort to do the simplest thing. However, with a lot of determination, I sat up, feeling very uneasy.

Soon I was surrounded by other kids. My teacher was outside looking in through the nets gesturing to me to try and get me to stand up. With every ounce of power I had I stood up feeling like I was on stilts, my legs were shaking so much. I could hear the kids whispering,

"What's going on?"

I felt as though everything was in the distance still. I could not stand any longer so I dropped to the floor but soon I got back up again. There was a bar over one of the kid's head. I saw my hand reaching for the bar but I hit her in the stomach. My coordination was all over the place and I fell back down, feeling extremely frustrated.

"What's wrong with me?"

I was so confused. My teacher knew I was finding it difficult to get out of the play area and was deeply concerned for me. She proceeded to crawl into the space to assist me. To get out of the play area she advised me to crawl behind her. It felt like I was dragging my lifeless body through the tunnels then down the slide into the play balls. At the time it was the most difficult thing I had ever done. I honestly have no idea where I got my strength from but I knew I had to get myself out in order to get the help I required. When I fell into the balls, the staff cut a patch in the wall so I then needed to pull myself through the balls and out through the newly cut hole. They were shouting at me, "Come on, Tracey. You're almost here."

I really wanted to quit as my body was screaming stop but my mind screamed louder to keep going. Eventually, I made it out. A member of staff carried me over to the seats where my teacher had put the chairs together. I lay down and rested. My teacher stuffed jackets behind my head to make a pillow. It was not exactly the feeling of lying on a bed of roses or as extreme as a bed of thorns but it was not comfortable. The seats were bar metal with metallic arms. I was propped up and was watching everyone else run around, not a care in the world. It was hard as I felt my neck had to twist to look. Ms Brennan kept giving me sips of 7-Up. To this day, I am not really sure as to why there was no ambulance called. Maybe everyone thought I had just had a fright and needed to rest.

By the time the trip was over, I tested my legs one last time; they still felt a little fuzzy and weak but I was feeling a lot better. Ms Brennan brought me to the toilet. Even though I still felt a little weird, I did not really question it. I was eight after all and I was walking again which I was glad about. I thought that was it, that the strange feeling I still felt would just wear off. Little did I know that would be the day my life would change forever!

I remember going back home on the bus where we were sitting in the same seats as before, which meant I was sat up the front beside my best friend again. My teacher kept sitting at the edge of my seat keeping an eye on me but I think it was so she could keep an eye on the kids at the back. I don't blame her as we were all a handful. I was feeling a little bit claustrophobic as I did not have much space to move. I remember turning to my friend and saying, "I told you something was going to happen." She did not really respond.

I was made to feel as if it was not as bad as it seemed and that I had put it on, in order to not get involved in the games. I know we were only kids and kids are usually egocentric, that the only person that matters to them is themselves, but I just needed recognition that what I had experienced was as scary to the others as it was to me. What happened to me at Playzone was very real and very frightening. However, I got over it. We all arrived back to our school where classes were due to finish in ten minutes but we were let go that bit early. Ms Brennan did not want to leave me stranded as she was concerned. I kept insisting I was fine, that I only lived five minutes away and I did not need to cross any main roads. But another teacher said she would drop me home. I was adamant that there was no need as I hated to think I was putting anyone out. The teacher would not give in though. She dropped me home to the courts in Ballymun. Mam's car was not outside when we arrived and the teacher said that she would wait to see my mam to tell her what had happened. However, I assured the teacher that I would be fine and I would make sure to tell my mam everything, so the teacher left.

I knew Mam would be collecting me from school with my little brother Alan and if she missed me she knew I would walk home. I waited in the garden feeling very anxious and I was dying for Mam to drive up I was not able to sit still; I was pacing up and down the court. When my mam arrived I quickly walked towards the car with a deep sigh of relief. Mam popped her head out of the car window saying she had been looking for me at the school. My brother Alan was sitting in the front seat, I leaned into the window and I started talking really fast.

> "I couldn't hang around the school. We were let go ten minutes early, and something crazy happened to me on the school trip. I thought I was going to die but I'm grand now."

I proceeded to tell Mam what had happened but she and Alan were looking at me very intensely as I described the drama I had just endured. Mam kept looking at Alan as if to say "She's not right". When I was talking I would not stop for a breath. My eyes were very open, I probably seemed 'spaced out'. As my mam got out of the car she said she would have to take me to my GP. I remember while walking to the house I kept insisting I was grand; I kept laughing. Looking back my laugh now it seemed very false; maybe it was a nervous laugh. Mam and Alan looked very scared as if they did not recognise me. As my mam was opening the hall door she said, "Trust me. Just see if the doctor can see what I can see."

I then remember looking at my refection in the hall door. It gave me a fright. "Shit!" I actually did not recognise myself as my eyes were extremely dilated. I ran into the house panicking, *What's wrong with me?*

Mam was making calls to my get my nanny to mind Alan. Alan was just standing in the hallway staring at me. I started to feel like I needed to vomit so I ran upstairs and sat on the side of the bath. I started panicking even more. My mam ran up after me. I began to get sick. Mam was rubbing my back saying, "I have to bring you to the doctor".

In between vomiting, I screamed, "Is something bad going to happen?"

Mam reassured me that she was there for me and that she would make sure I was well looked after whatever the problem was. When we went to my GP we brought an empty basin just in case. While I was in the waiting room, I made good use of the basin. Mam told the secretary that I had to skip the queue as this was an emergency so I was brought in fairly quickly. The family GP knew my mam years before I was born so he had been the family doctor for a very long time. When I went in to the doctor his immediate reaction was that I did not look right and I would need to get to the hospital as soon as possible. He did a quick check up. Mam and he both knew that something serious had happened or was happening to me so an ambulance was called from the GP's surgery.

What happened next…?

When I got to the hospital in Temple Street my symptoms had started to wear off. My eyes were not as dilated and my nausea had subsided. I was in no way as bad as I was at home or in the GP's office. When I was finally seen to, the doctors said there was nothing wrong with me so I was sent home and told to return if I was feeling unwell again. Mam and I went home feeling very confused as if we were making mountains out of molehills. In that moment, I felt relieved to hear those words that there was nothing wrong with me; I know my mam was too. I remember going to bed, recapping on my frightening day – what a very frightening day – and counting my lucky stars that I was alive and well. Mam said that I was not returning to school the next day as I needed to fully recover from the shock I had just experienced of the unknown terrifying symptoms. However, in a few days, I would return and everything would be back to normal. My 'little episode' would be a distant memory; I went to sleep with a smile on my face feeling very grateful.

The following morning, I heard my stepdad come in to check on me before he headed to work. I am a very light sleeper. I can hear the tiniest creak on the floorboards and I wake up. Nobody can get past me. I was sleeping in a bunk bed, on the bottom bunk. I could sense my stepdad squat down to my level. Suddenly, I opened my eyes wide and stared at him. From his reaction, I could tell that I had given him a fright. I could just imagine what I was like; something out of a horror movie. He asked if I was ok and I just nodded yes. He was just about to leave before I got his attention. I said to him, "Wasn't I very funny for falling yesterday?"

He laughed. "Yes, but you are ok now?"

I smiled in agreement and we said our goodbyes.

I listened to him go down the stairs and open the hall door. As soon as I heard the door close, my whole body went into a convulsion. It felt like I was having a fit of some kind as my whole body went into sporadic, uncontrollable spasms every few seconds. I needed to find a gap between them so I could make a run for it into Mam's bedroom. I stood at the end of her bed; I was in such a panic. She woke up suddenly without a word coming from my mouth to try and wake her, it was like she knew I was there and something was wrong. Mother's instincts, I suppose. She immediately asked what the matter was but she knew by looking at me that whatever it was it was serious. I fell onto her bed. My whole body kept going into spasms, every muscle tightening up and I could barely catch a breath. I felt my toes and fingers curl up uncontrollably, my legs, arms, face, and neck just kept tightening. I'd feel every muscle lock, and then suddenly I would be like a plank. Tears streamed down my face in between the spasms; I was absolutely petrified. I kept making sounds of distress.

Mam stayed with me throughout this extremely horrific event, trying her best to remain calm. Every time I thought the random spasms had finished they started again, this was an extremely daunting experience for me and went on for a good fifteen minutes. When it was finally over, I felt exhausted and barely able to move as I felt every ounce of energy had been drained from my body. I just lay on my mam's bed like a lifeless doll. She immediately rang for an ambulance. This time we would not leave the hospital till we got answers as my body's behaviour was not normal and we needed answers. My mam also rang my nanny and granddad to come around to bring Alan to school. She also called my stepdad to tell him what had happened. He was in shock as he had only seen me not so long ago. I had seemed grand and in good form, laughing at myself for falling the previous day. When we arrived at the hospital, Mam made sure we would not be left hours without being seen. My mam is a great one for getting people to move in a hurry especially when her children are the ones in the spotlight for concern. When a doctor came to assess me, my mam went through everything from the previous day until that morning. I was in line to get a number of tests done such as an MRI scan, CAT scan, and blood tests. It was strange going through those procedures at such a young age. It was very daunting going through the MRI machine and being told that I cannot move. I was assured that I was safe, that I would be able to hear everyone including Mam, and also see her through the camera. I felt ok about it after that. A few reassuring words were all I needed to hear and to know Mam was close by. I was happy about that. The noise of the MRI was exceptionally loud and equally frightening for me considering my age but I could see Mam wave through the screen and that was a welcome distraction from the frightening procedure I was going through.

After undergoing a battery of different tests, we waited around to see what the outcome was. My stepdad met us in the hospital. All the tests came back clear but we were not sure if that was a good sign or not.

Doctor's initial diagnosis

I was kept in the hospital for a number of months in order for them to keep a closer eye on me and observe me to see if my symptoms improved or worsened. Noticeable changes quickly occurred: When I smiled people would freak out. The team of doctors would surround my bed whenever I smiled because my smile had no expression to it, i.e. my facial muscles would not respond in the way they used to. It seemed like that was the main thing that was being focused on. My eyes, however, were dilating again and other symptoms persistently worsened. I would stare piercingly at people like I was reading their soul. At times I probably seemed like the little girl from the *Exorcist.* An extreme example I know but I am just assuming that is how I seemed at the time. Mam went into an awful panic around this time saying that it was not normal, asking the doctors and nurses to look at me urgently. She kept pointing at me in a panic, she was understandably very upset. The doctors kept writing down notes, not saying much just "hmm". My voice gradually weakened and faded out like a distant echo. At first, I actually could not see these drastic changes. Maybe I was oblivious to these and did not want to believe that I looked and seemed different. Ignorance is bliss, I suppose.

My body started to deteriorate rapidly in front of people's eyes and that was when I really began to notice the changes. My body kept going into spasms and stopped doing what I wanted it to do. I felt like I was paralysed, like some kind of unwanted entity had entered my body and wanted to form its own methods of bodily control. All the tests were redone because this was far from normal and the doctors knew it.

One of the mornings during my first week in hospital, I was sent down for a lumbar puncture, which basically felt like being stabbed in the spine several times. Even though the area is numbed you can still feel it. The objective of this exceptionally painful procedure (as many people know) is to take fluid from the spine and run tests on it to see if it helps the doctors diagnose an illness. Mam was there with me during this, holding my hand as I lay on my side and the procedure began. Oh my God! I had never experienced pain like it. Each time I felt the needle it was like a slow stab, but they did it so fast, I could not breathe. All I could do was scream out in absolute agony. I was hyperventilating, I was in such a panic, throwing a tantrum on the bed. The nurse roared at me, "Stop moving!"

I sobbed as I was in so much pain and did not fully understand why this was happening to me. Mam was trying to tell the doctors to stop, but they would not listen to her. I felt the pain to the extreme because I was in bad pain with my muscles already. The nurse kept saying to Mam, "Well, if she stopped moving, it would be over sooner."

My mam replied with distress in her voice, "Well, can you not see that she is in agony?"

I felt very nauseated and ended up being sick in the bucket that was beside the bed. This prompted them to put a stop to this torture and bring me back to my ward. I sobbed all the way back as if I had been slaughtered. Mam was fuming that they had not stopped sooner. They had let it get to the stage where I was physically puking before they put a stop to it.

The doctors came to their own assumptions that my symptoms were caused by some kind of trauma. Their initial diagnosis was that my mam had been neglectful, which was the furthest thing from the truth and clearly a huge misdiagnosis. It was an absolute outrage that obviously created massive shockwaves throughout my family. No matter what was going in Mam's life (and, believe me, my mam had a really tough life as she had always been given difficult challenges to face and any challenge she was given she faced head on and battled through it) one thing was for sure she would always protect her children to the ends of the earth. She would go the extra mile for us. For that nasty accusation to be made was extremely uncalled for and I do not see any member of the modern healthcare system making such an assumption without tangible evidence today.

The social workers got involved almost immediately after my being 'diagnosed' by the doctors. A social worker, Mr S, was dealing with my case. As a young girl, to me, he was a huge beast of a man with glasses and not very attractive either. He believed I was so bad physically due to a bad mental breakdown, and that I was suffering with post-traumatic stress disorder. He claimed that there was no way back for me; saying that, in his expert opinion it would be more beneficial for me if I were placed in an institution. He had said to my mam, "Well, there is therapy for Tracey and then there is 'therapy' for Tracey".

He made a quotation gesture with his fingers while saying that last part to give the impression he meant it sarcastically. He then suggested that I be put into a care home. Mam felt so insulted that she picked up a chair and ran at him but managed to remain calm enough to stop herself from throwing it at him.

"How f****** dare you," she roared. She was spitting venom at this stage. "All I want is to find answers. The last thing I want is to see my daughter put into one of those homes. Those homes are for children whose parents cannot take care of them; who do not give a f*** about them," she screamed at him in rage.

His answer only added to Mam's already burning anger. "Well, we would have her in an isolation room anyway, away from those troubled type of children. She would not see them."

My mam was beyond seeing red at this stage. "No f****** way. My daughter does not deserve that!"

A short time previous to this, my mam had suffered from a serious illness herself and she had almost died. How she got the strength to keeping fighting to protect me from those types of places combined with the doctors and the on-going court case with my dad I will never know. The doctors claimed that the fact that Mam was very sick for so long could have also contributed to me getting sick as I lacked "parental stability" for a while. The doctors kept looking at my mam as though she should be locked up for not looking after me properly. She felt so frustrated, she felt like she was fighting a losing battle. However, throughout all the allegations and accusations she kept her will and determination to fight. A different social worker took over from Mr S after a number of weeks and her name was Ms A. She tried to offer an alternative solution to the drastic ones offered by Mr

S: more in-depth counselling to get to the bottom of my issues.

The doctors came down on my mam like a tonne of bricks and even dragged my stepdad into their 'theory'. I was put into my own room with CCTV cameras to monitor my every move, to see if I changed and to see how I reacted around my mam. It even got to a stage where a twenty-four-hour nurse was put in with me when my mam or stepdad visited. It was degrading for Mam and myself that I was not allowed time on my own with her. She was not even allowed to assist me in the toilet; a nurse was always in the background. I was distraught. I was going through a really frustratingly difficult time not knowing what was going on with my body, combined with the doctors in their indisputable wisdom taking away such an important person from me, my own loving mam. I felt isolated as I could not have time by myself with any of my own family. I remember the first time waking up to a jolly nurse right in my face.

"Hello!" she screamed.

She was so close to my face that I could smell her breath, which stank. I was definitely awake then. I am the type of person (like many) that hates anybody being in my face – I hate feeling anyone invading my space – so when I heard I would be given a twenty-four-hour nurse I understandably felt very anxious about it.

That first morning I was definitely off to a good start; yeah, right! When I turned around in bed thinking, "Ah here!" The nurse just stood there asking if I wanted a shower. She was getting my shower stuff ready but there was no way I would let a stranger assist me. I would not cooperate with her one bit saying that I could manage. But I really could not manage. At this stage, my voice was so low and weak that it was like a whisper. I only wanted my mam to help me but that was not allowed. The nurse was nice, a bit overpowering at times, and was just too happy. I ended up upsetting her because I did not want her to help at all, I was so stubborn. When my mam came in the nurse said I was being extremely difficult and I was uncooperative. Mam talked me around and asked the nurse if she would try to assist me again. The nurse agreed even though she knew she was not getting anywhere with me but she still had to be there to keep an eye on things.

Shortly after that, a new nurse took over, which made it harder for me as I was just beginning to like the first one. I felt if I started to take a liking toward a particular nurse and started to feel comfortable with her assisting me that she would then be removed, which I believe affected me psychologically long term. That second nurse was a real battle-axe, really strict. She looked like a principal from the olden days, the type that would not think twice about giving you a few beatings if you acted up. She had short tight blonde hair and a face on her that would raise the Titanic only to sink it again. She would not take any nonsense from me, which made the situation more stressful.

An incident that really stands out in my memory and serves as a good example as to the extremes the nurses and doctors went to in keeping my mam away from me unsupervised was when the doctors decided they wanted a urine sample from me. I knew this was going to be quite difficult for me to do without some assistance. However, I was determined to try as I did not want the nurse's help. There I was in the toilet trying to pee into a plastic cup which is a rather challenging feat when your arms do not work properly. I tried to relax my arms to get them to work for me. I was in a panic. I heard my mam through the bathroom door, which was comforting for me. Finally! Someone who I felt comfortable with to aid me in my predicament. She had just come into my ward. I came out and signalled to Mam that I needed her assistance and I did not want the nurse's help hence the reason I had tried to do it on my own. Mam was in quite a panic at this point as she knew I genuinely did need help but she knew that she could not provide me with this as there were no cameras in the bathroom and she would be 'killed' by the nurse if she was caught. She was stuck between a rock and a hard place. However, the nurse was not there so my mam decided to take the chance and help me. When she and I emerged from the bathroom we had hoped that we had acted fast and did what needed to be done before the nurse arrived back in the room. But the nurse was standing outside the bathroom looking very cross with her arms folded. She gave us such a fright as we never even heard her come in; we both felt like we were in school and had just committed the world's greatest crime. The nurse stood for a moment glaring at the two of us in silence. My mam broke this uneasy silence. "I just sorted Tracey out, she wanted me to help".

The nurse laid into my mam roaring, "What do you think you are doing? You know the rules. How dare you go behind my back!"

This, in turn, caused my mam to lose her cool and she snapped back, "My daughter needed my help. She couldn't do it on her own."

Mam was understandably fuming. The argument between her and the nurse went on for a bit until eventually, Mam walked out and on her way out said that she'd had enough and was putting in 'a formal complaint' about the attitude of the nurse and the ridiculousness of these 'rules'.

Most nights, I would cry myself to sleep but I had to try being quiet while I was crying so as the cameras or nurse would not notice. I would not open up to them. I felt like their prisoner and I was not going to allow my captors see me cry. I remember being in my enclosed room, which felt like a cell, sitting on the bed in silence. It was so quiet I was able to hear the other children and their parents in the public ward beside me. I could peep through the tiniest cut in the curtain that separated me from that ward. I really wanted to be there instead of this tormenting isolation ward feeling like I was on Big Brother. I used to run off on the nurse and hide to hang out with other children. The nurses would give out stink to me when they caught me in the end. I was a child, though, and I wanted to explore and have some type of fun in that hell hole.

A new nurse took over after a while and I took to her immediately; she was a young girl, I would say in her early twenties. She had black hair and her face was full of freckles. She looked a bit like a grown-up version of Little Red Riding Hood. Her name was Helen. She had a lot of understanding and was very compassionate toward me. I felt she was more like a good friend or big sister to me than a nurse just doing her job. We would go to the hospital garden and at times she would give me jockey backs around and we would have a bit of a laugh. Some weekends I was allowed go home although I still had to be accompanied by a nurse during these home visits and Helen was the nurse who would do the weekend visits with me. My family did not mind though because they all took to Helen. She was not like the other nurses. My mam and stepdad were always bringing us out on walks; I cannot remember ever sitting around during my childhood.

The importance of getting out and about has stuck with me and my brothers. That weekend I remember going to St. Anne's Park in Raheny, which is a lovely park full of tall trees and hills. Alan and I would run around the trees playing childish games. I was like a little T-Rex all hunched over, my arms and hands were twisted to one side, and my body was disfigured. However, knowing I' be going home at weekends kept me going, so I did not give it much thought.

I was just happy to be out of the hospital and around my loving family. Helen walked with my mam and

.stepdad in the middle of the park while they chatted about how disheartened they were feeling. Helen understood and empathised with them. Whenever I had to return to the hospital I did not mind as much because I felt that Helen was looking out for me and she made me feel more at ease. She would let me mingle with the other kids and I started to form good friendships with them.

I began to feel happier in myself. I even started fancying a guy. I thought he was gorgeous. Black wavy hair, tall, broad shoulders and kind of tanned. He was about four years older than me. His brother was in there too and he was a year older than me. He was a ginger and he was mad, always messing, slagging and giving the nurses plenty of headaches. He gave light laughter to the general pessimistic mood that was felt by all at times in the hospital; he was truly loved so much deep down by all. Both brothers had cystic fibrosis as did many.

I knew a girl in the hospital who suffered with this horrible disease. She was such a beautiful girl and her name was Caroline Mahon. Her smile would brighten up a room; she would have been about four years older than me as well. You could tell by looking at her that she was a genuinely caring girl who truly idolised and loved her family and all the good people she had around her. Caroline was also from Ballymun and Mam got to know her mother not just from the hospital but seeing her around the area. Caroline's mother had two sons who were younger than Caroline. They also had the disease. They all went to the same primary school as me, St Joseph's in Ballymun. There was a shared bond between all given the similar situations. Both Caroline and I were going on different journeys yet came from the same background.

At one stage the doctors had told Mam they suspected that I had a brain disease and that I would be dead within six months. They advised her to bring me home in order for me to enjoy my final moments. It was as blunt as that. This obviously made my mam sick with worry. However, one thing that moments like that prove is that doctors do not always have sufficient knowledge to make the correct diagnosis as, clearly, I am still alive and well. There was no way I would die so young. I had lots I wanted to see and do and while I did not have a clue as to how my life would turn out my mentality was to keep on going.

I was only eight years old when my life changed but I had a strong belief that I would pull through. I acknowledge that I am extremely fortunate to still be here as there are many children who are not so lucky. I believe that I am alive today so that I can share my story and experience with whoever cares to listen. I have experienced so many truly terrifying moments at such a young age. However, I have also experienced many positive moments that I am grateful for. Even though I had a strong, fighting mentality there were still moments when I was full of hate and anger asking, "why did this happen to me?"

I could not see a justifiable reason for what had happened. I was also under the illusion that I would wake up one morning and find myself being 'normal' again. However, after months of this self-deception, there was no sign of the old Tracey coming back. I realised I needed to fight hard and grow up fast. The eight-year-old inner child in me was not ready to suddenly grow up but she was there to help me get through my situation and enjoy the fun stuff I would experience in my life. Thanks to that little girl I got through the most difficult parts of my life with a smile on my face.

A few months into my stay in the hospital the doctors wanted to do another lumbar puncture seeing as the previous one had been unsuccessful. This time they said they would sedate me. Mam straight out refused though, "There is no f****** way you are putting my daughter through that again! I don't care if she's put asleep; it's too much distress on her! I am warning you! No, and I mean no".

They said that they would not do the procedure if my mam was telling them not to and then they started being nice to her, "You go home and get some rest. Tracey will be fine here".

When Mam left, I was suddenly whipped out of the ward. I had no idea where I was being taken but the doctors seemed to be in a hurry. I quickly realised I was back in the same room where the dreaded lumbar puncture took place. I was told to lie on my side and I was injected with the sedative. A nurse was sitting in the corner and I smiled at her. Her attitude was vile.

“Close your eyes,” she told me in a blunt manner.

I remember thinking, “I wish my mam was here to hold my hand.”

It was very sad that I was a little girl and I felt like I was being experimented on. I got no love or affection from the nurses and that made me even more terrified.

I went to sleep with this dreaded fear and when I woke up I felt paralysed. My spine felt very heavy and sore. I was still heavily sedated when I was wheeled back to my ward; it felt like I’d got a smack from a bus.

Two days previous to that, a mother and her two kids were brought into the hospital because their house had caught fire. The youngest girl was two and the eldest was about seven and they were in the ward when I came back. I was still heavily sedated but I remember seeing the seven-year-old girl and her little face still black from the smoke. I remember the look of concern on her face. “Oh what happened you?” she asked.

As I lay in my bed, the sedative started wearing off and I felt very scared and fragile. The little girl kept looking over and asking if I was ok. I tried to smile at her. All I wanted was my mam and stepdad. I was craving some loving attention and that soothing reassurance that everything would be ok. Suddenly, my stepdad came in and my heart sank. He walked into my ward and I literally started to ball my eyes out. He did not realise why; he just thought I was upset; until he got closer and saw that I was not moving. He also saw that I looked distraught and he asked what was wrong. I cried and indicated toward the nurses with my eyes. The little girl came over and told him that I was brought back looking very sick. My stepdad ran out to the nurses' station immediately. From my bed, I heard him laying into them.

The little girl stayed with me until my stepdad came back. That little girl was like my guardian angel as she was with me all day, looking out for me, sweet little thing. When my stepdad came back into the ward he was still fuming after hearing I had had another lumbar puncture especially after my mam warned them not to. He read me a story; I kept trying to sit up to see the pictures. My stepdad sat with me until it was lights out and visiting time was up. Mam was spending time with Alan at home. The nurses and doctors would not know what hit them the following morning; it was like the calm before storm. My stepdad was just the beginning.

"When she's mad: even the demons run for cover."

- Jordan Sarah Weatherhead.

Surviving the trauma of prolonged hospital isolation

I recall one of my earliest memories: I had a collection of dolls and in my head, they were my children. I had one in particular that I had a stronger connection to. I remember clearly that I got the doll when I was four. I was in the wax museum with Mam and after our visit, we went into the gift shop. My mam said to me, "I'll get you a new doll."

She showed me two dolls on a shelf that were the same except one had a red bow and the other had a yellow bow on her dress. Mam asked which one would I like. I remember I went to point for the one with the yellow bow but suddenly changed my direction and pointed at the red-bowed one, so my mam bought her for me. I called her Jenny. She was a small doll. Her body was soft but her legs, arms, and head were plastic. I remember that at the time I loved her so much. I felt very happy. I grew my collection of dolls and I would spend hours talking to them. They would be all lined up at the end of my bed and I would tell them which one I would be bringing out with me that morning. I got so much comfort chatting to them. I love to see little children loving their toys; inanimate objects such as transitional objects are very important for a child's development.

A few years later my aunty brought me home a doll from America. On the box, it said her name was Jenny. She was a bit bigger than the smaller Jenny that had been bought for me by my mam so I kept them together. I pretended they were long lost sisters. I brought little Jenny into the hospital with me, I had a closer bond to her and felt in my kid's mind she needed me but I am sure it was other the other way around, I needed her. I felt less isolated with her around. I think I had the bigger Jenny at home to watch over my other dolls. One day I was in the ward and I had Jenny on my bed. I went somewhere and when I returned Jenny was not there. I panicked, looking all around me. My lip started to quiver. Then, I noticed a girl in the ward throwing her up and down and swinging her side to side like a baby. I immediately got a nurse's attention, which was difficult for me so I had to make sure I made good eye contact. The nurse understood and she got my doll back. This was just the first time that girl took my doll so I had to hide Jenny but the girl always found her. I was annoyed but realised that the doll must bring that girl comfort and that little bit of happiness that she gave me.

Eventually, I decided that Mam should take Jenny home as I needed to be strong without her. I knew one day Jenny would go permanently missing and besides I was trying to impress that guy I had a crush on. I had to say goodbye to Jenny and reassure her that big Jenny would look after her. I felt like more of me was being taken away; first, my body, then something that helped me so much through childhood. I realise now, however, that this was my first step toward young maturity. I had made a conscious decision to "put away childish things" and face my situation in a more grown up way.

I am currently in my late twenties and I still have Jenny and little Jenny;

it is good to have a bit of your childhood, especially the ones that gave you comfort through tough lonely times. Now, mind you, they do not look like they did all those years ago, especially little Jenny; she looks like she has been dragged through a ditch attached to a tractor. She meant a lot to me though. When Mam took her home that time, she was extremely smelly; there was that instantly recognisable hospital smell off her. My mam had decided to put her in the washing machine and her eye fell out. Mam panicked. My mam and my nanny, Peggy (my stepdad's mother) brought Jenny to the doll's hospital for a new eye. Jenny had to stay overnight; it cost my Mam €20 at the time. As if my mam had not enough on her plate on top of bringing my doll to the hospital. That is Mam though. She knew how upset I would be and she did not want to add to the trauma of what I was going through at the hospital with my own health.

I was eventually put into a public ward that just happened to be the one the guy I fancied was in. He was directly across from me. Through the first night I spent in the ward, we were staring at one another from our beds without a word. The tension was electric and magical and we then fell asleep gazing at each other. The next day he came over to me and started giving me "the look". A nurse was beside us tending to a patient next to me. He said, "That was incredible last night". The nurse overheard and asked, "What happened last night?" to which he replied, "Oh, me and Tracey just connected," and gave a cheeky grin.

This feeling rushed over me and I thought, "Oh my God, he likes me too." He would come over and read to me at times. I felt blessed he was even taking time for me. Anytime he smiled at me, or even if he was around me, I felt fireworks were going off in the distance. How dramatic! It kept me going though; it kept me distracted from my reality, which was nice.

First signs

Prior to that day at Playzone, there were no clear signs that I was not right or that I would ever experience anything out of the ordinary, and as far as my family and I were concerned I would live a healthy, happy life. That being said, I was a slow learner. I was fifteen-months old before I learnt to walk on my own without depending on the furniture as my safety net but this was not because I was slow. I was just late at developing the necessities required in walking, i.e. balance and reflexes. Anytime I went to fall, I would not automatically go into a sitting position; I would just fall backwards like a plank of wood.

Mam was concerned for my safety and told her GP who explained I had delayed reflexes. He said that my mam could train me to get my "signals to connect" and that this would improve my reflexes. He advised her that anytime I began to fall that my mam should hit me in the stomach with the side of her hand really fast and that would build up my instinct to lean forward as I fell backwards.

Mam felt uneasy at the idea of having to hit one of her children. However, the GP advised her to try it every time she saw me about to fall. He said that eventually, it will make me sit when I began to fall. My mam decided to try it after debating the morality of what she had been advised and it actually did start to register with me after a while.

In our garden in the courts, there was a big tree. My brother and I use to run around it, chasing each other, laughing our heads off. I would run with my elbows tucked under my arms and my hands would be so unnaturally floppy. People would think that I was just playing, that I thought I was like a little bird flying around. Nobody gave much heed to it; I was very happy and that is all that mattered.

My cousin Jenny getting similar symptoms

As time went on, my mam noticed sudden changes in the way the doctors were treating her. This change started to develop instantly and out of the blue. They were now attempting to be overly nice towards her, which was very strange and confusing after accusing her of those terrible allegations for such a long time. They were asking Mam if there was anything they could do to help her in assisting me; they asked this in such a lovely manner. How can people treat you like you are such a bad person one minute, pointing the finger and making accusations at you, and then suddenly being that nice? Mam who was understandably confused asked them straight out what was going on.

"One minute you're blaming me for neglecting my daughter and now, all of a sudden, you are asking if I would like any assistance in caring for her?"

The doctors said, "Well, we have recently found out that that one of Tracey's cousins, Jenny McCann (from my dad's side) is appearing to show similar symptoms to Tracey."

The doctors put two and two together and gathered that there was a high possibility that it was a genetic disorder that ran in my dad's family. Jenny was being seen by doctors in Our Lady's Hospital, Crumlin. It was around Christmas before we heard about this officially because during that period of time there was no real contact between us and that side of the family. It was the October after my incident at Playzone that Jenny got struck with this mysterious illness and from what we could gather the symptoms were extremely similar.

My mam and dad's marriage had ended a few years before my incident. There were custody battles between them for my brother and I, and this went on for years. It stressed my mam out so much as she felt she was hitting brick walls at times. It was hard, however, Mam never gave in. She had a justifiable reason for ending her marriage; she knew that it was the right thing to do. I do not want to go into the reasons because there are some things I wish to keep private. All I will say is that it was the best decision for all concerned. I believe everything happens for a reason; there was a lot of conflict between the two families so at that time I did not really know any of my cousins from my dad's side. Mam did what she did for the indisputable love of her children and for that, I am eternally grateful to her.

My mam decided to visit Jenny in Crumlin Hospital despite all the battles she had endured over the past number of years with my dad. Mam wanted to offer her support as she knew Jenny was on a tough road that would not get any easier. She wanted to be there for Jenny's mam also, to offer her support and an understanding that most people would not be able to provide. I am sure it is not a nice thing to watch your child go through that while feeling so helpless. As a parent, you need to be strong for your child and it helps a great deal if you have strong support behind you. When she visited Jenny in her ward, Jenny was lying on the hospital bed; her whole body was like a plank of wood even her facial muscles. Her hands were locked at her side. Mam looked into Jenny's eyes and could tell that she was so scared; that look of terror was so real to her.

Mam can remember Jenny as a little girl, not a bother on her. I also remember Jenny visiting us when we were young. We would go up to my bedroom and play with dolls; we'd be yapping away and having great fun. I also remember seeing Jenny on her First Holy Communion Day. That day we did the exact same thing as always, went up to my bedroom to play. Jenny had gorgeous long red hair and she was so angelic-like. We were all very fond of her. Her brother Stephen and her mam, Carol, are nice people. It was a shame we could not get to know them properly and keep in touch at that time with everything going on. This did not mean we stopped caring, though, and I am certain the same would be said by them about us.

Once Mam had seen Jenny like that it really hit her. She had just received the reality check that whatever this genetic disorder was, it was real and would be a massive life changer for all concerned. And so my life with this disease known as dystonia and all the struggles involved with it began.

"Just because something devastating has begun,
does not mean it is the end" – Tracey Ellen Maria

Chapter 2
Dystonia

"It's not our disabilities, it's our abilities that count"
Chris Burke

What is Dystonia?

'Dystonia is a neurological movement disorder in which a person's muscles contract uncontrollably. The contraction causes the affected body part to twist involuntarily, resulting in repetitive movements or abnormal fixed postures. Dystonia can affect one muscle, a muscle group, or the entire body. The movements may resemble a tremor. Dystonia is often intensified or exacerbated by physical activity, and symptoms may progress into adjacent muscles.[i]

Dystonia generally develops gradually. Exceptions include Rapid-Onset Dystonia-Parkinsonism (which may develop over days or hours) and the acute dystonic reactions associated with certain antipsychotic drugs.'

- Dystonia Foundation[ii]

Who can get it?

Firstly, there are many different types of dystonia and these can all be subcategorized into either primary dystonia or secondary dystonia. They primary dystonia types are generally passed on genetically whereas secondary dystonia can result from *'external factors e.g. a reaction to antipsychotic drugs. Part of the neuroleptics class can cause a form of dystonia known as tardive dystonia. Other external factors that can cause the onset of dystonia or dystonia like symptoms are:*

- *Physical trauma*
- *Exposure to toxins*
- *Environmental factors*
- *Other related disorders*

With regards to other related disorders causing an individual to show dystonia symptoms the main disorders are Wilson's Disease and Hallervorden-Spatz Disease.' (Dystonia Ireland Information Leaflets)

While there are many different types of dystonia and the symptoms can vary just as much as the form of dystonia the individual has, unfortunately, the type I developed is very rare. It was discovered a number of years ago that there are only five families with this type in the world. They say the younger you develop dystonia the worse the effect it will have on the individual's body. I was just eight years old when it developed so, realistically, I was inevitably going to feel the full brunt of this condition. However, from day one, I did not give in and accept what I had been diagnosed with. I pulled myself forward believing this would not be my life.

The reason I have dystonia is because it genetically runs in the family, on my dad's side. Six members of the family, including myself, have this disorder. However, I believe there could have been more over the generations. When he was twenty-one years old, my brother Alan decided to go for a genetic test to ascertain if he carried the dystonia gene or not. The doctors at the time did not think it was a good idea so they tried to dismiss him in case the outcome of the test was not good and he could not handle it. Alan has great inner strength and I believe the not knowing would have been more of a killer on him. He was planning on moving to Australia and did not want the possibility of having this disorder hanging over him and being uncertain as to whether it would come on suddenly or not while he was abroad. If you get tested and it comes back positive, there is a chance of it taking effect between the ages four to sixty-four.

Alan got his results on 16 June 2011. He was twenty-one and was planning to go to Australia that September. He got his results over the phone and it was great news; he did not carry the dystonia gene. I was sleeping downstairs in my bedroom at the time. I heard a big commotion upstairs between my mam and Alan. They both sounded very excited and relieved. I heard my mam say, "Go down and tell Tracey." I then heard Alan bomb it down the stairs, jumping down the last step. He knocked on my door and he came in. My mam followed him down. He told me that he just got a call to say that he was clear of dystonia. Mam indicated for him to go over and give me a hug. I wrapped my arms around him without any hesitation and I began to cry. I cried because I felt so relieved and happy for him that he was never going to be struck down with this horrible condition; that he could just go about his life and enjoy it freely, without it hanging over him. I also felt very unlucky in that moment and questioning the heavens, asking, "Why me? Why is Alan in the clear and I was unlucky enough to be given this challenging life?"

Upon reflection, I suppose it was my destiny to walk this challenging path. How I walked down it, though, was entirely my choice.

Different types of dystonia and the variations of the effects of Dystonia

As mentioned there are many different types of dystonia and each type carries with it its own effects on the body. Below is a list of the most common types and the ways in which they can affect an individual.

- *Early-Onset Generalised Dystonia: This form of dystonia is characterised by a twisting of the arm/hand or leg/foot. This is the most common form of genetic dystonia.*

- *Dopa-Responsive Dystonia: There is generally some form of difficulty in diagnosing this form of dystonia due to its similarities with cerebral palsy as it causes the individual difficulties in walking. It usually starts in childhood or adolescence.*

- *Paroxysmal Dystonia: The individuals who have this form of dystonia would generally have brief attacks of dystonic movements and or postures. They would return to a normal relaxed posture between episodes. The episodes themselves can vary in length of time and severity.*

- *X-Linked Dystonia-Parkinsonism: The only known cases of this form of dystonia are on an island in the Philippines called Panay. It is more common among the men on this island and is generally focal i.e. it only affects one part of the body.*

- *Myoclonic Dystonia: This is a less common form of dystonia. An individual with this form would have lightning-like movements or jerks and could also have muscular contractions and postures of dystonia.*

- ***Rapid-Onset Dystonia Parkinsonism:***
  The reason I have highlighted this form of dystonia is because this is the type I have. *It is a rare hereditary form of dystonia that affects the limbs, balance, swallowing and speech. It causes some or all of these to spasm and or seize up. As the name suggests it can take full effect abruptly.'* - Dystonia Ireland Information Leaflets

There are many other forms of dystonia; the above few are just a small example of the various genetic types of dystonia that are classed as primary dystonia.

Does it hurt?

Before I begin to put into words the extent of pain I was in when I first got 'hit' with dystonia that fateful day at Playzone, allow me to put it into context for you to enable you to have a better understanding. Have you ever written something that took an enormous amount of time to write? Have you ever written for such a long time that eventually you get what we all know as writer's cramp? Do you remember that pain in your wrist and fingers as you tried to continue writing through the pain? Well, did you know that this very common side effect to overworking your wrist muscles is actually a form of dystonia? Now, I want you to imagine that you are eight years old and that you are experiencing a much severer form of this pain except it is not just in your wrist or fingers, it is in your arms, neck, legs, feet, toes, and even your face.

At first, I was in so much pain with this condition, it was unbearable. My body felt like it was in this constant massive cramp. I felt as though my muscles were going against me. To make matters worse, my right side was affected more and I was born right-sided. Now, all of a sudden, my right side had very little control. Because my right side was affected more, I had to retrain my left side to write, type, and eat.

I have often seen people try to write or eat with the hand they were not born to use, they find it extremely difficult and some cannot do it at all. They can only try for so long and then have to revert back to their natural side because it does not feel right to them. It is too awkward and weird for them. I had no choice except to retrain my left side, which I will admit was stressful and annoying at the beginning. Now, however, it feels like I have always been left handed. Both my arms just wanted to wrap around my neck, my hands kept twisting to one side. It was so uncomfortable and exhausting. I felt like all my muscles were in a constant work out and not working fully for me.

Try to keep your arms up and twisted around your neck and see how long you can do that before it starts to hurt.

That's the feeling I had with my arms on a long term basis. If you are not lucky enough to be double jointed and you pull your finger right back, it can be excruciating because fingers are not meant to be held back that far for that length of time. Try holding your arms up until they start to ache and then try keeping them up even longer, through the pain. The release you feel when you can let them down, without any restrictions, means that you definitely will not get an urge to put them up again. However, because my arms were constantly locked around my neck I did not have that comfort of choice. At the very beginning, my arms were constantly twisted and every muscle ached. My posture was also affected, which contributed to the intense pain I was going through. My right shoulder kept coming forward and my face muscles were always tense. It was full-time agony. I also looked very discoloured; as pale as a ghost. The majority of the time I felt very enclosed with no release in my body whatsoever. It was like I was being suffocated by my own body.

Every night, Mam would tuck me into bed, I was always in hysterics with the pain. She would try to massage my arms to help them relax. Even in bed, I never got a break from this torment; my arms were still up and shooting pains all over my body. The pain was in my legs and feet; there was no escape. I found trying to lie on my side was nearly impossible but at times I had to in order to put pressure on my right hand to relieve the pain. That was the worst pain of all. I also found that my body was very sensitive to things, like the weather. If it was windy outside, it would feel like I had no skin protecting my body. This sharp sensation cut through like a knife and a shooting pain went through my teeth like someone had their nails scraping down a blackboard. I could not have dreamt of having a power shower as that would be torture to my body. I could not even touch my own skin without getting a nauseating feeling; it was an extremely horrible sensation if I touched myself, even by accident. I got in the habit of grinding my teeth because the horrible sensation did not seem that bad if I clamped my mouth closed, strange as that may sound.

Is it fatal?

'In the overwhelming majority of people with dystonia, it does not shorten life expectancy or result in death. In very severe generalised dystonia that affects many body areas, there can be problems that arise secondary to the dystonia that may cause life-threatening conditions. However, these instances are quite rare and usually treatable. Dystonia does occur as a symptom of many degenerative diseases, some of which do impact mortality, but the dystonia itself does not shorten life span.'

- Dystonia Foundation[iii]

As explained above, dystonia is not fatal. However, I know all too well, from two cases within my family, that this disease ultimately contributed toward their deaths. One of these was my cousin Jenny who had dystonia for most of her life and who died a number of years ago. She faced it head on though and her strength inspired many people. I feel in Jenny's case that if the dystonia had not diminished her physically as much as it had then she would have been strong enough to fight the sickness that ended her life and she quite possibly would be still with us today.

Her father passed away years before. He was never officially diagnosed with dystonia as there are no signs of the disorder in a person's body when they pass away; the dystonia dies with the individual. His wife now knows, however, that he did, in fact, have it.

Retrain

After the correct diagnosis of dystonia was made, a rigorous retraining of my physical body began. The work involved with this was extremely testing for me. I had to relearn every single aspect of living from scratch. I had to find new ways to do things that I, along with every other able-bodied person in the world, had come accustomed to and as such had taken for granted. I began to retrain my body and taught it to keep moving on and not to give up even in the face of the inevitable pain that awaited. The first things I got working early, in my new life, were my legs, thankfully.

My arms were tough; I was always afraid that I would break them as they were very tight. I retrained myself to eat on my own, shower on my own, and dress myself to an extent. I still needed a lot of help, though, for this; more for the upper part of my body. Socks were difficult to put on; it was difficult to get my thumb out. I can manage better now thankfully. Whenever I was going out by myself, it was hard at first. It made me feel very independent, though, so I wanted to. At times I did struggle at things like getting my bus pass out of my bag, paying for stuff, and carrying bags – dependent on the weight of the bags, of course.

Not only did I have to retrain physically but mentally too. I had to keep pushing forward to become stronger in my way of thinking. I do still have obstacles that I need to face on a daily basis. That is life, though. All I can do when faced with those obstacles is look at it objectively and ask, "How can I find a way to overcome this?" It took me a very long time to fully feel a sense of belonging; socially, I mean. I took each day as it came, learning everyday how things could be improved. In the events after that day, I fell into my own trapped world, not knowing how to communicate. I did not even know what to say as my mind felt blank. I could not grasp conversations. It was only after the conversations had ended that I thought of things I could have said. It was too difficult to keep the focus required to engage in conversations. I had to retrain everything, even my social skills, many of which rely on facial expressions, which are difficult when your face is in a never-ending spasm.

My muscles were constantly working, even when I was relaxing my muscles were tense. The energy required to do simple things could be more based on my mood.... If I was tired, hungry, stressed or being rushed then it became harder to do things. Eating was and still is, at times, so exhausting. When I reach the stage that my arms ache, I cannot even swallow properly.

Healthy eating was and still is, important to my retraining programme. I find that the healthier foods help my muscles relax more and I have more flexibility. Drinking alcohol affects me too as it causes muscle tension and diminishes my mood.

One of the most difficult things to deal with was the mess that I was making when I ate. To this day, I find that if I am tense, then I'll make more of a mess. I realise, however, how much I've come on; ***a mess can be easily cleaned up***. For me, if I become aware of people staring, it makes it harder to go about my day. It makes me more tense, which draws even more attention to me, but I found that if I keep doing what I am doing and don't mind anyone, the better I am. I found out very early on that the more I do things, the less challenging they become for me. If there is a day that I feel tense and I know that I am going to struggle more, it is easier to say I will just stay in until I am more relaxed. I found early on in my life with dystonia that it is important to overcome all obstacles and to face the world head on. The more I conquered something, the easier it became.

I did feel like I was on this road alone, even though I had my close family right there beside me. Whenever I think of those days I spent retraining myself, both physically and mentally, it makes me so grateful to have a family like mine. They aided me through some tough times. They helped me along at the beginning and then gently let go so that I could live my own independent life. To be honest, I do not think I would have made it through any of this without my family;

they made the whole terrifying experience of what happened to me bearable, and to them, I am eternally grateful.

And Finally

At times, I walk with my right arm sticking out and leaning over on my left side. If I am stressed, overworked physically or overtired, my body gets tense and it takes a longer time to readjust and move. I have to fill my mind constantly with positive thoughts to help my body relax.

There are times when I am really tense and it feels as though my body is working completely against me. I try to hide this as I don't want anyone to notice and pass comments. No one can really understand fully as they are not experiencing it. I suffer a lot with back pain from muscular tension.

Over the years I have made great progress with feeding myself. I have my own ways of achieving this, which may look odd to others. I eat everything with a fork and the fork does the work that my tongue struggles with. I can eat chocolate or biscuits with my hand; I have to tilt my head to one side but these foods are small enough for me to manage.

I cannot pick up a sandwich, take a bite, and then get it between my teeth to chew it. It requires too much effort and is too dangerous as there is a higher risk of choking. My epiglottis, the muscular flap that lies within the throat and acts as a 'gate' blocking the windpipe during swallowing, has more of a delayed reaction than most. This means that I have to be careful while eating and drinking because I am at a higher risk of choking. Fluids and bits of food can go into my lungs and cause me to have chest infections or pneumonia. A number of years ago it was suggested that I eat only blended foods. I tried this but found it very annoying and reverted to the normally prepared food. Thankfully, I have never had any severe chest infections and hopefully, I never will. I have to take my time eating, be very careful, and not worry.

If I am aware of anyone watching me eat, I cannot manage doing anything that I normally can do. Often, they will dive in and try to assist me, which is so frustrating. When this happens, my muscles tense up and I look more disabled, especially if I am eating. I am aware that I can get food everywhere but I would rather make a mess while enjoying my food and not have people wipe my face while I am eating unless I am really stuck. I can grab the napkins myself when I am ready and in a more relaxed manner. I know people try to help but the truth is they are not really helping at all, they are just making me more anxious and I end up making a total mess of what I am doing.

As I have said, I cannot use a knife, fork or take a drink in the normal way. At times I cannot grip anything with a fork and my way around this is to lean my head down to scoop the food into my mouth with the fork. I also require a glass, which can only be half full and has a handle in order to take a drink. I find people sometimes stare at me when I am eating and drinking. They look at me as if to say, "Be careful. You'll knock stuff over. People are looking."

This is my way of eating and, unless people have first-hand experience of the challenges I face doing this simple task, then their input is not required.

"I am not dystonia, I am much much more!"

- Jenny McCann

Chapter 3
Family

"With families, there are heredity ailments that, we may inherit, such as life defining disabilities; and there are also values and characteristics that we can obtain, such as love for our fellow man, honesty, being law-abiding, and, the ability to remain positive and focused on achieving our dreams"

- Tracey Ellen Maria

Sticking together

Families can come in many shapes and sizes with many different types of internal relationships forming. However, a family that sticks together and laughs together through thick or thin can be very rare. I deeply appreciate and love my family for being able to do just that.

Mam

Mam is a very powerful and inspiring woman to me and anyone who crosses her path; she constantly goes from strength to strength. I, personally, do not know any other person who has gone through all that she has and has still managed to have such an incredible sense of humour; she really is a fun person to be around. Her attitude is and has always been, 'if you cannot laugh at yourself then you are not living. We are all given tough challenges to face but we still must get on with it'. In other words, perseverance with a smile.Mam would never give in, she is not a quitter and she will keep at it while smiling to the very end. She is truly brave and wonderful, a woman with the biggest heart who just wants the best for everyone and for everyone to get on and be grateful for every single person in their lives. She does not hold grudges or criticise anyone in a malicious manner. She is such a good and decent person.

Her personal strength and courage

Not everyone can see Mam's wonderful and caring traits. Throughout the years, I have seen how some people have suddenly turned on Mam, cut her out of their lives completely, or just blanked her. There is no legitimate reason for doing this; Mam has never gone out of her way to maliciously hurt people. The one thing I will say about her is that she does have a tendency to say it how it is, which I love about her. She is very open and honest. The problem is that a lot of people do not like to hear the truth.

When Mam has had enough of their negativity and their persistence in not making the relevant changes to rectify their situations, she tells them in an extremely honest way to get a grip and retake the reins of their lives. When she hears people moan about petty things, it also drives her mad as she knows everyone's problems are big to each of them but when you do nothing to change and instead would rather delve into self-pity, it's extremely frustrating to her. Mam cannot stand that self-pitying attitude.

She does not go around suppressing her thoughts because that would only make her ill; she is a worrier by default. It was difficult for her growing up as she had many challenges to overcome; these have helped her to evolve as a person, though. Over the years, Mam has got stronger and now values herself much more; she now knows that she does not need to take negativity from anyone. Mam had always put herself last and has helped many people; she constantly offered her support and sometimes got none in return. Here are some of the amazing challenges she has faced head on with her head held high and her sense of humour still gleaming through. Some of these are prior to me being diagnosed with muscular dystonia.

Mam is an amazing woman. Not only did she go through the shocking and dramatic events that happened to me she also fought custody battles with Dad, her own illnesses and having to deal with the ridiculous accusations thrown at her by the doctors, nurses and social workers regarding her treatment of me. She did all of this so tenaciously and that shows true strength.

Mam's illnesses

In 1995, my mam was struck down with a serious illness. She had not been feeling well for a couple of years and she was always visiting her GP. Her GP kept telling her she was feeling this way due to stress because, at the time, she was going through an annulment which was not an easy process. The Pope himself had to grant permission because, at that time, divorce was illegal in Ireland. I remember when she was twenty-eight she got very sick; she was so thin and weak, which was very scary to see as Mam had always been at a healthy weight. Mam is a tall woman measuring around 5ft 8 and at the time when she was at her sickest she weighed only seven stone; her bones were almost protruding through her skin. She would lie on the couch going in and out of sleep, she was that run down; she would put cartoons on for Alan and me.

My nanny, granddad, and stepdad kept encouraging her to go to the hospital but Mam refused saying that she had too much fighting to do. Her deeply concerned family advised her, however, that she had to look after herself or she would be no good to anyone. She truly was in so much pain. Between my nanny, granddad, and stepdad they would look after my brother and I. Mam finally agreed, telling her solicitor to rearrange the court dates as she did not want anyone to know she was that sick or they would make it more difficult when she went into hospital. The doctors were fuming that my mam had let her health decline so much and that she did not seek help sooner. After she had undergone an MRI scan the doctors informed Mam that she would need a hysterectomy. This was due to what had showed up on the MRI, which was a string-like substance, and resembled a bracelet according to the doctors at the time. She was in absolute agony. How she lasted as long as she did without been looked after properly amazed the doctors. At this stage, Mam was actually screaming with pain; she asked the doctors quite dramatically to put her out of her misery. She went to the Coombe Hospital because they primarily look after women there. The doctors gave her as much pain relief medication as possible to help her better deal with the agony she was going through. When the doctors told Mam that she needed a hysterectomy she was distraught because she was only twenty-eight and was adamant that she was going to have another baby. She wanted my stepdad to have his own child with her as she saw how amazing he was with us. The doctors, however, were insistent that she get this procedure done telling her that unless a miracle happened, that's what she would need to save her life.

She told us that before her operation while she was just about to be sedated that she was saying in her mind, "I know I am going to have another baby". The doctors told Mam she might not even survive as she was that sick and fragile; it was a high-risk operation on a very thin, weak woman. Hearing those words, Mam thought, "No way! I have too much to do on this earth!" During the surgery, Mam woke up while already cut open. She sat up and asked if they were finished. Later, she said she just remembered seeing a doctor point at her and then she was back in 'Noddy land'. The doctors had discovered while operating that the issue was not her womb at all, it was, in fact, her bowel, which was infected. They had to call in for an emergency doctor from James's Hospital; he flew over in a helicopter, which was unusual. After the operation when Mam was coming around, the surgeon told her that her miracle had happened and that they did not have to take her womb. Then he smiled at her.

It was not the case that Mam could have the surgery and then be sent home. They had to send off a piece of her bowel to be analysed so as to see what had caused the infection. When it came back (again it must be something in the family, for very rare conditions) it turned out that Mam had bovine tuberculosis (bovine TB). She is not one to mope around and, because of this determination she got her strength back, slowly but surely.

The story that makes me still laugh to this day is the Guinness story – allow me to explain. When the doctors realised that Mam had bovine TB, this meant that rather than them removing her womb they had to remove part of her bowel. They also removed one of her ovaries because it was stuck to her bowel. After the operation, the doctor told Mam she would need to eat lots of meat and drink some Guinness as she needed to build up her iron levels. Mam took it up wrong though and assumed the doctor meant that this would have to be done straight away. So, she got in contact with my stepdad and got him to bring a few cans of Guinness into the hospital. This was in 1995 and at that time there was this particular Guinness ad out with a guy dancing around with a pint of Guinness to a catchy tune…Mam could not help herself. As soon as she got the cans she imitated the ad, dancing around the ward singing the song. Everyone was in stitches laughing until the matron (chief nurse) walked in and berated Mam for drinking on hospital property. Mam had not even taken a sup of the Guinness yet, though, as she was too busy messing around. She tried to explain to the matron that she was acting on the doctor's advice but the matron explained that he did not mean to start drinking it while she was still in the hospital!

When the day finally came for Mam to leave the hospital, my stepdad collected her. She says she felt very strange when she got out because of the time spent in there as a patient. She had also lost a lot of weight and needed to build herself back up. She was so frail that it took her extra time and effort to do the simplest of things like going up a flight of stairs. She even went through a bit of depression due to the struggles she had readjusting to normal life, which she had to do rather quickly as she was due to go back to court for the custody battle with

Dad for my brother and I. This court case went on for a number of years with both Mam and Dad fighting their corners for custody, which Mam ultimately won.

Line dancing queen

While Mam was in hospital, her sister and sister-in-law would visit her and sometimes they would drop in on their way to line dancing, which they had only started a few weeks beforehand. This inspired Mam to get involved in line dancing as well. She was adamant that after she got out of the hospital she would join up. She kept to her word and started a few weeks after getting out of the hospital. She had started to take part in line dancing mainly to build up her morale, self-confidence, and physical fitness as the hospital stay had taken a lot out of her. My stepdad even bought her a cowboy hat to help encourage her to take part in it, which took place in a pub, in Fairview, called Millers. The first time she went, she wore the cowboy hat and white jeans and the other people assumed that she was the teacher when she arrived because no one else was wearing a hat. When Mam started dancing a few of the men started laughing because she could not put one foot in front of the other. They were muttering while everyone was trying to learn the dance; this was very off-putting as line dancing requires a lot of concentration. One of the guys started to slag Mam off saying, "Look at your one in the white trousers" and laughing, adding that she looks like the teacher but she can't put one foot in front of the other. Mam is quite feisty so she left the floor and walked over to the men, like someone from a John Wayne film, in her hat and trousers. She was fuming with them for laughing at her. They were sitting against a wall so when Mam got to them she put one hand against the wall and was face to face with them asking if they had a problem. Everyone in the room gasped. The men stood up and left red-faced. She would not let it damage her confidence; she always faces her problems head on. When Mam got home, she filled me in on what had happened and I knew from that moment on that she was getting back to her old feisty self. She progressed in the line dancing over the following months to the extent that she and three other women took part in the All Ireland Line Dancing Competition that year and came second.

My mam had felt for some years that she had lost her identity. Her life was more stressful than fun with those hardships she had experienced. When she joined the line dancing and became a pro at it, I knew that was what she loved and it brought her an unbelievable amount of happiness, fulfilment and, most importantly, it gave her the identity that she had lost over the previous years. She grew up loving her line dancing. Some people hear of line dancing and think of a bunch of "auld wans" in a line, dancing to hillbilly country music. Line dancing has improved dramatically over the years to accommodate the more modern music. It has very different genres in it now such as Latin American, waltz, and salsa, and people dance to all the well-known charts songs. That being said, some of the stuff would be country-themed but you have to please everyone, I suppose.

Throughout the years, there have been many fancy dress nights and Mam loved them; it was a great way for her to express herself. She is such a character. She took great time in getting her costumes perfect and thinking 'outside the box' from conventional costumes. I remember one time she dressed up as a cow; the cow suit was black and white and had big udders at the front. She put a pillow down her top so she looked fat and the udders stuck out. She wore a little cow hat that had little ears and fake eyelashes. The line dancing was in the Spa Well in Tallaght, which meant she had to drive down the M50 from our house in Ballymun. This was when that motorway had a toll bridge. The person who worked on the toll bridge looked at my mam strangely while giving her change to her. Mam just smiled, fluttered her eyelashes and said, "I'm off to a fancy dress". When she arrived at the Spa Well she walked in, really excited only to find she was the only one dressed up. Everyone stopped, turned and stared at Mam when they saw the ears flapping as she walked in. The teacher roared, "Here she comes, the aul cow!" Mam stood with her hand on her hip saying that she thought the fancy dress was that night. Everyone informed her that it was on next week and called her a Wally. They were falling over laughing. Mam said "awh damn it, I don't even have spare clothes, ah sure fu** it! I'm still going to enjoy my night!" Everyone roared, "Woohoo! Go on, ya mad cow!" She was scarlet. Nobody could look at or take her seriously for the rest of the night.

Nonsensical and creative

Mam has a great tendency of saying something that does not make much sense. To her, however, it does and she cannot understand why everyone is struggling to comprehend what it is she is saying. If we all laugh at her silly comment and repeat it back to her in the hope that she will see how confusing it sounds she will just laugh and say, "Well, you know what I mean." There are times when I am walking up the road and I spot Mam driving towards me. She will begin doing these hand signals with one hand and big lip movements leaving me somewhat confused as I have to figure out what exactly she has just said to me within that split second of me glancing as she drives by. Later on, she might say did I get or do such a thing, to which I have to say no, as I have no idea what she is talking about. She then insists that she informed me while driving past me in the car, in that split second that I saw her.

She is naturally very creative. When we were growing up she would make puppets out of my stepdad's socks; they were cool. I remember for the "female" sock she would sow big red lips and big black eyelashes onto the sock. She and Stepdad would get behind the sofa and make up a story with the puppets, which was great fun. She made all of our Halloween costumes; I am not just talking about throwing a sheet over us, having two circles cut out for eyes, and bang, it's a ghost! She would put more effort in. One year, Alan wanted to be Batman, so Mam got an old sheet dyed black. It came out dark grey but it did the job. She then cut out the mask from a cereal box and painted it the same colour. She had a black overall suit that she used to make grey underwear from the material. It was fantastic. Alan was so happy. I wanted to be a fairy so she dressed me in white and used netting from a curtain to create a cool skirt. She then cut out wings from a big piece of cardboard she had and painted them white, which were then tied onto my arms. With my face painted white and with large pink cheeks, I looked like a beautiful fairy. Mam is very creative in her house as well; sporadically, she gets these great ideas. She has her house looking amazing and different every few months. She takes great pride in everything that she creates.

Her love for her family

Mam had always wanted to have a third baby with my stepdad. The operation a few years previously, however, had left her with just the one ovary and even that one, along with her fallopian tube, had been severely damaged by the TB. The doctors also made her aware that due to the TB operation, twelve inches of her small bowel had had to be removed, which meant she was unable to absorb certain vitamins; this would limit the chances of having a healthy child. She put herself through tough procedures to try to get this problem rectified if possible; she was told by the doctors that these procedures had proved to be unsuccessful. They told her to just accept the outcome of the results and be grateful that she had two children already. Mam felt dejected and guilty that she could not give my stepdad a child of his own. My stepdad did not get too upset about it, he saw my brother and me as his children anyway and if it was not meant to be then so be it, he would get over it. Mam and my stepdad are such amazing caring parents. There are so many people out there who can get pregnant so easily and half of them would not compare to Mam and my stepdad. Some children are not shown the proper amount of love and affection required in helping them develop into healthy people, they are left to fend for themselves. The children that are brought up in abusive environments, whether it be physical, sexual or mental abuse, or who witness their mother, father or siblings go through these forms of abuse can be so damaged psychologically, it affects them in some cases for most of their lives. Some of the parents who witness this torment that their children are going through are at times too afraid to just walk away with the child, until, in some cases, irreversible psychological or physical damage is done. Mam would never stay in an abusive environment for too long; she would put her own life at risk to make sure her children were safe and happy, even if it meant everyone turning their backs on her for leaving. She would always stick to her guns, no matter how difficult it was. She knows what is right and what is wrong. This kind of loving, strong-minded person deserved to be given another chance to be a mother again, to be able to enjoy a baby in peace without all the problems that she faced when my brother and I were growing up. She did her best with us, and an outstanding job she did, I must say.

During the summer of 1998, Mam and my stepdad were due to go on holiday with Alan, Mam's brother and sister-in-law, their son and me. A week prior to our holiday, my auntie who had started working in a crisp factory met a woman who claimed to be a fortune teller and that she did 'readings' at house parties. My auntie asked Mam if she would like to organise a party and they could all have their fortunes told. Mam agreed, saying it would be a fun get together. She then said it to a few others and they were all on board to have their fortunes read. It was arranged for the weekend before we were due to go away; Mam got a few snacks in for the party. My auntie arrived with the lady who introduced herself and asked Mam if she could set up in the kitchen. While she got everything in place, Mam said that she would go in first and report back. The fortune teller told Mam lots of stuff but also probed her with questions to assist her. Mam was not giving anything away, though, just replying, "yeah" while eating a packet of crisps. At the end the fortune teller had one last thing to say to Mam, that she was going to have another baby. This prompted Mam to erupt with laughter. "Ha! That's where you're wrong! I can't have any more kids! I looked into it and the docs said I can't." Mam explained a bit to the fortune teller and then left the room. When she went back, all her guests were waiting in eager anticipation to hear how she got on. Mam said, "She's a load of crap!" trying to whisper. She then pointed at my auntie who got embarrassed when the spotlight was put onto her saying that the fortune teller was rubbish and a waste of time. To which my aunty replied, "Well, I heard she was good". Everyone asked Mam what made her think that the fortune teller was so bad? "Well, she was saying a lot of true stuff at first and I was thinking, how did she know this but I didn't want to let her think she had it right, then at the end she throws out that I'm going to have a baby boy! That's when I said you're wrong, I can't have any more babies." Everyone was surprised. I think Mam felt a bit disappointed; it was something she wanted alright, however, she was accepting the reality that it was not going to happen. The night carried on and they all still had a great time. That Monday, Mam visited her sister and my cousin; she was not feeling the best at the time. They were joking with her saying that maybe she was pregnant. Mam laughed. "Wishful thinking." They advised her to get a pregnancy test, just to rule it out for sure. My cousin walked to the pharmacy across the road and got a pregnancy test. When she got it Mam began to take the test; they were making boiled eggs, at the time, for their lunch. When Mam came down the stairs, after she did the test, she placed it between the boiled eggs, which were in egg cups; they had a chat while waiting in anticipation. Then, after the specified length of time, the moment of truth finally arrived. My mam lifted the pregnancy test and stopped for a moment in shock. The test had come back positive. Mam could not believe it and thought it was a mistake. She got my cousin to get a couple more pregnancy tests from the pharmacy. However, all the tests had come back with the same result as the first. "Do you need any more indications that you are pregnant?" my auntie asked. The realisation hit Mam that this was happening. "Oh dear, I'd better make an appointment with my GP, just to confirm." The other thing that hit Mam was the way she'd spoken about the fortune teller. My auntie told my Mam not to worry about that, she needed to inform my stepdad straight away of the amazing news that she was definitely pregnant. Mam broke her heart laughing, she could not stop. She was in hysterics. Then came the moment when she had to call my stepdad at work to say that the fortune teller was right. "I'm pregnant! I must have done about four tests and all have read positive!" My stepdad went silent. He was shocked to hear those words as he never thought he would hear them. He was quiet but I am certain that, on the inside, he was happier than any words could express. Mam went to her GP and, yes, her wish had come true, she was, in fact, pregnant despite being told it would be impossible. To say she was over the moon would be an understatement. She told her GP that she and my stepdad were due to fly out that week on holidays but that would be impossible now. The doctor said, "Well, what's meant to be is meant to be. It is a miracle you even got pregnant in the first place, so, if you stay or go you could lose the baby either way." Mam decided to go and hope for the best as it would possibly be the last holiday for us as just a family of four. When we went, she blew out like a balloon and only one skirt fit her the entire week. We all had great fun and that holiday remains clear in my memory.

When we came back, Mam went to the doctor to get a test to see if the baby was ok and the baby was still alive and well, so Mam was relieved. She went line dancing up to the very end and every week while there she would say that she was in labour and get my stepdad to bring her to the hospital. Everyone would be wishing her good luck and then the following week she would arrive back to line dancing still pregnant. When it was finally time for the baby to arrive, it turned out she had to be induced because the baby was too comfortable and was not budging for anything. She was induced on the 17th of March 1999, St. Patrick's Day. She wore green eye shadow and had green ribbons in her hair. Looking dazzling she said, "I'm ready." By the time it was all over she was not looking so dazzling anymore. The eye shadow had run down her face and her hair was in a mess. She said it was all worth it, though; her little boy was finally born, weighing seven pounds eleven ounces. Both Mam and Stepdad could not have been happier. They could not wait for Alan and me to meet our new baby brother, Dean.

Mam and Stepdad are always bickering at one another (as most couples do). You could say they have a love/hate relationship. Over the years they have been compared to Mary and John from the TV programme 'Father Ted'. In some ways, I can see the comparison as they do generally seem to bicker among themselves. The one thing I will say with regards to this comparison, however, is that they would NEVER physically harm one another. They just bicker, which I am certain is a common thing among all couples who have been together for twenty-plus years. They are both open-minded people who make a great couple and they are excellent parents to Alan, Dean, and me. I find it funny at times when they have their petty arguments because they are both so strong-minded that it is like a tornado and a hurricane clashing; neither of them will concede to the demands of the other. They are very good at giving each other a good telling off and are equally good when they team up and berate anybody else who needs it.

They have got better in recent years; they have worked on their listening skills and used different approaches. I find it very funny seeing them make up when they eventually decide to. Mam still has that face on her as if he is still in the dog house; this would generally be followed by a number of days of silent treatment. Mam is very stubborn when she knows she is right; she will not give in, and she always has to have the last word. The one thing I will say about my mam is that she does not make empty threats; she always follows through on everything she says. An example of this would be the time when Mam and Stepdad were arguing and Mam said that she was going out to get a job. She'd had enough of not being able to help provide for her family, that she was just a cleaner in the house. It was evening time so Mam rang her friend and asked if she could go down to her for a cup of tea. My stepdad thought she was just going out for a cool down. Off she went and when she came back she said she would get a job. She said that her friend's niece knew of a job going and had offered it to her own mam while my mam was in the house drinking her tea and chatting. Her mam did not want it and before her friend had even finished her sentence, Mam jumped in saying that she would take it; she did not even know what it entailed. I think she just wanted to prove my stepdad wrong. She was told that the job was working in a sex shop, part-time. She came home looking like the cat that got the cream. My stepdad was relaxing on the couch when she arrived home looking very smug and told him about the job. My stepdad's reaction was an instant,"What the hell! Of all the jobs, this is what she gets. This would only happen to her." He did see the funny side though.

Mam always acts like this mad person who would do anything when in fact she is actually a private, shy person underneath it all.

While Mam worked in the sex shop, I would collect my brother Dean from primary school and we looked after one another. It helped me to grow up and learn responsibilities.

Going back to the hospital after the doctors made the correct diagnosis of dystonia and after knowing that my sudden illness was not brought on by Mam being neglectful, the doctors were terrified Mam would sue them. She had every right to after those awful accusations but she wanted to move on despite the hurt they had caused our family. The doctors offered to help with anything she needed or wanted. She told them that she had her eye on a house around the corner from her mam's. She loved that area; it was full of semi-detached houses. The house in question was a corner house that had a big side garden. She wanted to move on from our old housing estate and make a fresh start. There were too many bad memories in the old house.

Every day, Mam would visualise herself in that new house and tell her dad that that house would be hers. Nobody else saw it as being possible because everyone wanted that house. It was lovely and the back garden was huge. It was the only garden in the estate that was that big. Mam continued visualising her house and speaking her ideas for it aloud. Everyone thought she was off her head; that she was building herself up, only to be let down. She did everything that she possibly could to make sure she got it. She was pregnant with my brother Dean at the time. The story of Mam's determination not to concede to other people's impressions of a vision of something you know you will obtain is the best example of the importance of positive attitude and dogged determination not to give up on your dreams. She got the keys to our new home in October 1998. I will never forget, for as long as I live, that look of accomplishment on her face. We all moved into the house and Mam had Dean the following March. There, we created wonderful memories; we have had our ups and downs like most families, slamming doors out of frustration and anger but there were plenty of belly laughs too. Even though I now know that leaving the old house in the courts was the right choice, it was still tough on me leaving the friends that I had grown up with, and all the lovely neighbors who became family friends throughout the years. Even though we moved just literally round the corner we did lose that connection with those people, which I missed.

When Mam envisions something clearly, she knows that she will obtain it; she has always put this down to her ability to 'manifest' things. I put it down to her determination and motivation to achieve what can be perceived by others as impossible. I did not realise at the time, but this was the first time I had ever witnessed a person achieving a goal that no one else sees or believes to be achievable. This was to be yet another important life lesson taught to me by Mam. Even though we both had severe knocks that might mentally cripple most people both Mam and I are a rock for each other, and because of that fact we have, and can, overcome anything.

Her new-found love and respect for herself

Mam is your typical Irish woman; she loves a good bargain and, my God, can she source out unbelievable bargains. People are sometimes shocked. A number of years ago, she attended a wedding and people were commenting on how great she looked and saying that her dress was fabulous. Mam replied, "Oh, thanks very much. It was a bargain. I got it in the flea market for €5." Mam could not help but brag about how cheap she had got it while throwing shapes around. My stepdad gave out about her suggesting that she say that she got it in a high-end shop and put more value on herself! Mam is always delighted to show she can get something stunning in the last place anyone would expect.

Mam has gone through extremely bad and testing stages where she felt suffocated by self-pity and was very low and bitter. However, she did not like who she was becoming and she made sure that she rectified her situation by taking action. She had a very good reason to feel the way that she felt prior to taking action. However, she worked very hard on herself and was determined to become better day by day.

Before her making this self-declared necessary change, Mam felt that if she was a different and better person then that would appease others; she would feel more accepted and encouraged for being that transformed person. To this day, however, certain people do not fully understand Mam because she can come across to those who do not know her as being strange. She is very expressive and always speaks her mind. I would not change her for the world. I have learnt a lot from her over the years. She has always believed that it is very important to have fun and not take life too seriously. Mam always encourages everyone she has befriended along the way in making sure that they stay true to themselves, and that they enjoy and are grateful for the life they have.

When it comes to being given any input contrary to her beliefs, nobody on this earth can tell Mam what she can or cannot do, especially if it is something she has her eyes set on and that would assist her with being her independent and creative self. She gets so much pleasure, happiness, and therapeutic satisfaction from being able to design her home freely, in her own different style, and she loves to release her creative side. One time, there was a bit of a debate as to what wallpaper to get for the kitchen. Mam had this idea of doing something completing different. She had a vision of the finished product and thought that it would be fabulous. My stepdad was not having any of it as he wanted to go plainer. Mam was telling him that he was boring and is he not willing to be a bit adventurous? She questioned whether he trusted her saying that it would look great. Besides, if it did turn out wrong, it was not the end of the world. It could be redone. All she wanted was to wallpaper the kitchen differently from the norm. My stepdad tried his hardest to talk her out of it but she felt that he was preventing her from expressing herself. They then went into the 'no talking' stage. Mam would be in the kitchen cleaning intensely while my stepdad would be in the sitting room watching TV. "How dare he say I can't get a certain wallpaper. Who does he think he is telling me what I can and cannot do?" In the end, Mam got her way, the wallpaper went up, and the room was exactly how she envisioned it.

Loving and respecting one another

Mam and I have had, and still have, a number of clashes over the years. We are so alike in a lot of ways in our stubbornness with backing down. A number of years ago, I felt trapped because I felt that I could not express myself around Mam, and let her see the real me. She would annoy me because I could never get a word in with her, or she would always run around feeling that she had to take on the world. If I was ever doing something independent from her, she would automatically go into panic mode, which made me feel as though she was being very controlling. There were moments throughout the years that we would quite literally be on the verge of strangling one another; we would call each other every name under the sun and were so bitchy towards one another. However, I am sure that we are not the first mother and daughter to have had those moments. My stepdad was always at the 'butt end' of these clashes and always had to try to sort it out. Eventually, we did get beyond that and learn to respect and love each other, but, my God, we were vile to each other. It took both of us to work really hard on ourselves to become better and treat each other in a proper manner. I always grew up with Mam there protecting me, which she did amazingly. However, it was the letting go part that she struggled with. She always feared that if I did anything wrong that the social workers would come down on her; a fear that she had understandably acquired over the previous years. It was difficult for her to let me go out into 'the big scary world' to learn how to find my own way and go on my own journey. However, I had said to her many years previously, as cruel as it may sound, that she was more disabled than me because I have done more in my life up to that point than she had, despite my disability. That made her think hard, but ultimately she knew I was right. She acknowledged that my proactive mindset was putting everyone else to shame. Over the years, following that comment from me, our relationship and her trust in me grew stronger, and we developed a better understanding of one another. I am so happy and proud that Mam retook control of her life. She now travels around Ireland and the UK regularly with her good friends, all of whom love her for the wonderful and fun person that she is.

Mam just recently decided to go back to school as she was never able to enjoy school while growing up due to bad bullying that she suffered and feels that she had no chance to develop herself educationally. She has always wanted to go back to her education and eventually work towards something that she would love to do in her life. She is now taking the right steps towards achieving that dream. She has always put her kids first and dealt with her challenges head on. She has so much potential and can be or do anything that she wants to; she has a great deal of life experience behind her and that ultimately acts as motivation for her to succeed.

I believe that she deserves everything that she is seeking due to her commitment to me and the needs of others over the years. She is, in my view, not only a 'super mam' but also a 'super woman'.

My Stepdad

> *"A best friend is the only one that walks into your life when the world has walked out."* – Shannon L. Alder

The story of how Mam first met my stepdad is a rather typical story of a man who falls for a woman, irritates the hell out of her until she decides to go out with him, and then unknowingly falls for him. It was just as unexpected for her family as it was for her. It was St Stephens's Day, 1990. Mam had gone to a neighbour's house for a party, which she had not been going to bother with at first but her friend kept hounding her so she gave in. This was the time in Irish society that perms were fashionable for women and almost every Irish women thought they were gorgeous due to this 'fad' when, in fact, they looked like they had a bird's nest on their heads. I have seen the photos; I know what I am talking about. That particular night, Mam rushed over to the party with her hair looking like she'd had bed hair for days. She did not bother with make-up and she was still in her PJs which only Irish people do and can to some extent get away with doing. She is a good-looking woman, but when she went to the party like that, she looked like she had just woken up. My stepdad came into the party with his mate. He spotted Mam and he kept asking who she was. He sat beside her most of the night and was more or less sitting on her lap gazing into her eyes. Mam kept telling him to leave her alone. He kept asking her out. She, as honest as she is, kept calling him a weirdo.

Despite her many attempts to dismiss his advances, he would not give up on her and eventually, she gave in. She realised he was a decent and caring man who would be very supportive of her, my brother, and me. From all the funny stories they had from day one, I knew they were a perfect match; they connected so well.

My first impressions of him were that he had this lovely energy about him. He had long straight hair that covered the length of his back and had a moustache. He was very thin, wore skinny jeans that were always too short on him. He wore white socks with black shoes and a denim jacket; he genuinely looked like one of the Bee Gees! He walked with a stride, flicking his hair about. He thought he was very handsome. He was a real poser and still is to this day. He loves himself; no harm in a bit of self-love.

As time went on, weeks turned to months, months to years and he and Mam started getting serious. He made me feel safe and so loved. We also developed a special bond; he used to bring me out to the zoo, which I loved. I treasure my memories with him growing up. I admire him so much due to the fact that he was a young man who took on the role of looking after two children that biologically were not his own, although I know that this technicality is not given much attention now. He took on so many responsibilities and supported Mam throughout all the drama that was going on in her life; the court case, going through a marriage annulment, her getting seriously ill, and then, to top it all off, me getting sick also. My getting sick caused years of challenges for me, my family, and my stepdad. At any point, he could have walked away freely, but he chose to stick by us all and for that I and my entire family are grateful.

Over the years he has had many different hairstyles as a way to express himself. He has lost his long hair style and ditched his moustache. During his early years, he was very proud of that moustache but, as soon as everyone began mocking him saying that it made him look like an eighties porn star he made the decision to finally shave it off, which did, in fact, knock years off his appearance.

My stepdad is a naturally loud individual and, as such, you can hear him before you see him. He loves to have music blasting from his car as he is driving. His preference would be UB40, The Script or at times radio talk shows. He will blast the music so loud that I do not know how he can actually hear what the radio is actually playing, and nobody has a clue how he can still hear perfectly and has avoided doing any serious damage to his eardrums. His own mam wears a hearing aid as her hearing is terrible so you have to repeat everything. You would think he would have learnt by now to reduce the level of noise coming from within the confinement of his car but, no. Even with his eighties look long since gone; he knows how to live his life on the edge.

Up the Dubs! – My stepdad loves the GAA

For the past number of years, I have gone to watch the Dublin GAA matches in Croke Park with my stepdad. There would also be a large number of other family members along but some of them stopped going for one reason or another. My granddad Tommy, who is my stepdad's father, would accompany us to almost every game, without fail. As the years have gone by, however, and he has got older, he finds it hard to walk long distances. He is in his eighties, so it is understandable. Mind you, he can still dance you off the dance floor at parties. He is always the first to get going on the dance floor and has never lost his dance moves. A lot of elderly people who get up to dance tend to stay in the same spot while barely swaying from side to side, but not Tommy. He takes over the whole floor, swinging other family members around. When Tommy went to the GAA matches, it was easy to tell that he loved it. I loved it too when he came because it meant spending time with him. He is a very funny man to be around. Now it is just my stepdad, my fiancé, Patrick, and I who go to the occasional game. My stepdad will always try to get us tickets for the big matches on Hill 16. I personally do not follow GAA or any sport; I do, however, love the happy and positive atmosphere at these events, and enjoy the fun. The main reason I get so much enjoyment from going along to these events is that I really enjoy spending time with my family. In recent times, my brothers have occasionally come along and we may also meet someone who we know along the way, and they might tag along with us.

During the many years of attending these events, we would always go to the seating section of the stadium as Tommy was not able to stand for long periods of time. However, now that Tommy does not attend we now preferably go on Hill 16, which is a standing area. My God, if it is a popular game like a quarter or semi-final, and we are not on that stand a good few minutes before kick-off or throw-in as it is known in GAA, we will be faced with a serious predicament. We can be squashed in between a large number of bodies stuck on the steps of the stand. This can cause a bit of a nightmare when people are walking up and down because we have to grab onto the person in front of us and hold onto them for dear life. Even though we do endure this nightmare, the fun had is still worth it. The deafening roars from my stepdad add to the atmosphere for me. He is so passionate and loves the banter. A few beers in the pub, a match at Croke Park, and having a good time with fun people; this makes my stepdad's week. Seeing him smile makes it worth all the hassle we face while on 'the hill'.

My stepdad has endured many of his own struggles and stresses in his lifetime, but he got through them all. The stress he has gone through during the week in the build-up to the match instantly disappears and is replaced with the anticipation and excitement of the match at hand. His face turns red as if his blood pressure has gone through the roof and the veins in his forehead look as though they are ready to pop. During these moments he is screaming intensely. I can get more entertainment from watching his reactions. It is good for him to have something, aside from his family, to feel passionate about.

His hidden affections for the family pets

My stepdad has formed a close bond with the family dog, Sam, a collie that the family got two years ago when he was eight weeks old. This has left him open to being teased by the family because when we had our previous family dog for over seventeen years, whose name was Buster, my stepdad would not bat an eyelid towards him. If he did pat Buster you could easily see that the dog was terrified. My stepdad never publicly showed any affection towards Buster; I personally think he did not want anyone to see that he had a soft side to him. However, when Buster passed away a number of years ago I am sure that he was secretly saddened. Seventeen years of such a lovely and funny dog who suddenly passes away can have an effect on anyone, even a man who gives off such a masculine demeanour. When the family got Sam soon after Buster's death, my stepdad could not hide his emotions; it was like he had received a new child and he instantly fell in love. He was delighted to have made a new "buddy" in Sam.

My stepdad has had many friends over the years that let him down; he was a good friend to them all and would do anything for anyone without hesitation. Life just moved them all apart, I suppose. Everyone in his job loves him and looks to him for advice. They are always asking him to do little jobs as favours because they know he will get it done correctly, promptly, and without hesitation. He is more than happy to help out in any way that he can. Some of the people that he called good mates took advantage of this behaviour and then dropped him when it suited them. I can tell that this, even to this day, has got to him and affected his confidence. It demonstrates that it does not matter who you are, or what age you are, we are all in need of good, loyal, and supportive friends, aside from our partners and/or children. They say that a dog is a man's best friend, and in my view, this is very true. They appreciate our love and provide us with their own unconditional love. They are very forgiving and are always happy to see us. My stepdad appreciates Sam and loves bringing him for his walks. At times, I go with him when I can. Sam, like most dogs, loves a ball to be thrown so that he can chase it and release some of the large amounts of inner energy that he has. He loves having the freedom to run and we do get such a laugh from watching his excitement. Through walks with Sam in the park, my stepdad has met other dog walkers and they now have a good chat. There is one gentleman whose name is George and he is there on a seemingly daily basis with his little dog Pip. If my stepdad and I are out walking Sam in the park, we will always be guaranteed to catch up with them. Sam will spot Pip first and run over excitedly. When they first met, Pip was just a little pup and Sam would lie on his back to let Pip jump all over him. Every few minutes during these times Sam would twist and turn in all directions because he was so happy, his tail would be hopping off the ground with excitement. Due to all his moving around he would get himself tied up in Pip's lead. Both leads would be wrapped around both dogs legs, and trying to unravel the leads while the dogs were still playing was great fun. Both dogs have lots of energy already but, when the two of them are together their energies are multiplied. It is funny witnessing Sam getting into that state; it seems apparent that dogs have more appreciation of the littlest of things. Over time we have got to know them both properly and we usually find George sitting on one of the benches within the park while Pip plays around him. We always stop for a chat. It is amazing how you can meet extremely friendly and nice people, all from within a local park while walking the family dog.

If it was not for Sam then my stepdad and I would not have met this man among other equally nice people. It has given my stepdad yet another social outlet that he is happy to have. There was hassle involved in getting Sam in the first place and finding where exactly his seller lived. He was down in Offaly or somewhere around that area. My granddad Billy drove Mam, my brother Dean, my nanny, and me down to collect him. It was like a family day out looking for his location. It was a lovely dry day in May and we stopped for tea on the way and used that stop as an opportunity to ask for directions. When we arrived, the little pup we saw was the last of the litter. He was so cute and tiny. We put him in a box and placed it on Dean's lap; he fell asleep while Dean was stroking him. While we were thinking of names to call him on the drive home and debating as to what name suited him, we came up with Sam. All the effort endured in finding Sam made us feel like giving up and going back home but, we kept on going, and it was worth it. I believe Sam brought us some luck and brought with him another unexpected gift for my stepdad, his loyal friendship.

Unbreakable bond of love and support

Due to the close bond that my stepdad and I share, most people assume that he is my biological father. Even though this is not true, I do not see him as just being my stepdad. He has been there from the beginning and has been supportive to all of us along the way. He is the father figure that I look up to and have always turned to. He has been supportive and helpful even during my moments of stubbornness when I refuse to talk about what struggles are going on in my life. I eventually come round, feeling safe and knowing that I am not being judged; his words of wisdom are very comforting to me. There are times when he does not say the right thing to me and this makes me somewhat angry. However, I eventually realise that all he is attempting to do is offer me some solutions to the problems I am faced with. I feel comforted in the knowledge that I can talk to him about anything and he will listen and offer some form of advice. He does not expect me to take his advice, however; I always have a choice, and I am respected enough by him to be allowed to make my own decisions. His motto is 'Learn to be responsible for your own actions. For every action you make, there is a reaction that comes with it, so think wisely.' At times when dejected, I try to be supportive of him too, just like he has been there for us over all those years. I love spending time with him as it is great for us both. It is great for him to have an ear to bend if he feels like ranting about any particular problems that he is faced with. During these moments I will use my phone to communicate my support to him, and I see a slight glow in him as he realises people are there for him also and that it is not just him offering positive suggestions towards dealing with a negative situation.

I am certain a number of the readers of this book will be somewhat surprised to discover that he is not my biological father but, in my eyes, he is and has always been my dad. Blood is not everything. It is testament to his love and commitment that he has stood by and supported Mam, my brothers, and me throughout the many difficult years that we all faced together. In my opinion, he is a man to be admired and a man to be respected.

"It's not about being a blood relative and, as such, feeling an obligation, it is about being there since day one, giving endless love, support and happiness. That is what has mattered the most"

– Tracey Ellen Maria

My two brothers

Alan

My brother was born in August 1990, two months premature. He was originally supposed to be called Anthony, after St Anthony, the patron saint of lost things but Mam changed her mind and called him Alan Anthony. Prior to his birth she and some members of the family, including my stepdad, went camping. Mam was pregnant with Alan at the time but she was not expecting the baby to arrive until October. On one of the mornings, while camping, Mam felt sick and decided to get some fresh air. She proceeded to crawl out of the tent, while still half asleep, and was met with a large pile of cow manure at her doorway. On seeing this, she screamed and woke everyone in the camp site. This sudden shock triggered her to go into an early labour; this early labour was also triggered by the stress that Mam had endured in the previous months. She was brought quickly to the hospital where Alan was born instead of in a field surrounded by cows and onlookers! When he was born Alan was five weeks premature and weighed six lbs. three ounces. He had breathing problems so they decided to keep him for seventeen days in the hospital. Mam and my stepdad made the daily trek back and forth twice a day to feed him and look after him, which was hard work as they also had me to care for. I was two-and-a-half at this stage so I was obviously a lot to manage on my own without them having to look after my brother as well. But, they managed to keep everything balanced nicely.

When Alan was finally discharged from the hospital and came home it was very exciting for the entire family; everyone was anxious to meet the newest member of the family. Alan and I became very close from the get go and he became my little buddy. Having a new brother in my life was very exciting for me and was indeed a blessing, and Mam and my stepdad were very happy with their two children. They both made great parents as they spent so much of their time with us, constantly making sure we were both happy children. Mam used to put us on the sofa during the day while she would make up her own dance show along to the *Dirty Dancing* soundtrack. She would dance exactly how they did in the movie, which was very entertaining for Alan and me. I remember a few times while performing her dance, she'd spin and slap her hand off the door accidentally. Even though she was in agony she managed to contain herself from blurting out bad language. Another funny and entertaining thing that she did was the robot dance around the sitting room to a weird sound track, which would have us in fits of laughter. She was so serious while doing this and very focused; I think she loved it, to be honest. While our lives were full of drama, even prior to the dystonia, both Mam and Stepdad were full of fun, laughter, and happiness due to their refusal to fall into a depressed state.

I remember one day when Mam had the pair of us ready to go to playschool. Alan was not long home from the hospital and Mam was still trying to get used to him being home. Alan had his hat and gloves on and was in his pram. Mam and I were walking to the playschool, which was twenty minutes away from our house; it was called Tir Na Og. I loved going to that playschool to meet all my friends. I was walking along a wall while Mam held my hand. I used to do this every day, and I would always jump off at the end for her to catch me; this was always great fun for me. When we arrived at the playschool one of the teachers came to the door to greet us and asked Mam about the baby. Mam's face dropped as she suddenly realised she had left Alan at home, in his pram with his jacket and gloves on, in the hall. I proceeded into playschool while Mam waved goodbye with a look of hidden panic and concern on her face, masked by a faint smile. I then saw her disappear like the road runner from the Looney Tunes. By the time she made it back into the house, Alan was still sitting there with sweat pouring out of him while he slept in his pram. We all laugh about it now.

Growing up with Alan was a fun adventure; we have so many wonderful memories together. He was my first proper childhood friend. I use to torment him and he would equally annoy the hell out of me but deep down we truly loved each other. We made each other laugh, smile, cry, and want to murder one another. The reality was that for me, he made my childhood so much better and I would have been lost without him, and his cheeky grin.

Doll drama

I had a large collection of dolls, as I have mentioned, with Jenny being my number one. Alan became a bit jealous, which he admitted to me years later. He had a green monster teddy that he started to treat exactly as I treated Jenny. He would throw him up into the air and catch him, and then hug him intensely while saying "my green monster". He did this to attempt to make me jealous of 'his green monster'. He would make cheeky faces at me and stick his tongue out while saying this. Despite his attempts, however, this did not faze me in the least. He would watch how I treated my dolls and then proceed to do the same with his teddy. If he went outside to play and left his teddy sitting on his bed I would tell him afterwards that I always bring my dolls out with me and they have great fun and then ask why he did not bring out his green monster teddy. I would wind him up even further by saying that his poor teddy was alone while he was out having fun. Nothing beats winding up your younger sibling. God love, poor Alan, I really made him feel bad about that. The next time he did bring him outside, however. Before we knew it he was back in the house like lighting, crying his eyes out. The other children were picking on him and trying to take his teddy off him. Of course, I'd known this would happen, and I had this evil laugh that I was trying to contain. Alan roared at me to stop laughing at him. Mam shouted at me also to stop laughing, which I denied while hiding my victorious grin.

As I was getting older, I moved on to playing with Barbies. I had two Barbie dolls and one Ken doll. I started making a great background story to these three dolls. The two Barbie dolls were sisters and the Ken doll was with one of them. I needed a man for the other doll because she was fed up of being single. She had a few guys, but nobody was Prince Charming to her. Alan had an Action Man, and I used to sneak into his room and borrow this toy, and he became the Prince Charming for the sister doll. When Alan copped on his Action Man was gone, he went berserk, even though he hardly played with him. In the story that I had made up for my two female dolls, Alan's Action Man was an army man that always had to go away suddenly. Then when the time came that he had to completely disappear because Alan wanted him back and I could not get away with taking Alan's Action Man anymore the sister was back to square one, single again. I then came up with an elaborate idea that the sister seduced her brother-in-law. This was not how I wanted the story to pan out, but, thanks to Alan's whining, I had to improvise.

I was so cruel to Alan that I even told him his green monster teddy did not want him anymore, that he had told me that he wants to stay with me because he does not like being thrown up in the air. I began moving the teddy around during the night while Alan slept. I would position him in different places; even outside my own door at times, and then the following morning I'd tell him that his teddy was trying to escape to be with me. This, understandably, made Alan cry his heart out while making me laugh endlessly. When Alan informed Mam that his teddy did not want him anymore and told her what had happened I got in a lot of trouble but it was worth it. Every Saturday and Sunday morning, Alan and I would race down the stairs in our attempts to be the first to grab the remote control for the TV and put on our cartoons. During these moments we, like many siblings around the world, would nearly kill each other trying to get to it first. The funny thing was that we would both watch the same cartoons; it was just the whole competitiveness of getting to the remote first.

My favourite memories with Alan

While we were growing up, our bedrooms were right next to each other. My bed was close to my bedroom door and Alan and I would have conversations every night without fail from the comforts of our own beds, which was nice. Mam and my stepdad had to keep shouting at us to go asleep because we would be yelling from our rooms. I came up with a seemingly devious plan, which I assumed at the time was ingenious. When we got tucked into bed by either Mam or my stepdad and they had retired to the living room downstairs, one of us would sneak into the other's bedroom and climb into bed to have a conversation about random childish things. We would then sneak back into our own beds before we fell asleep. One of the times, Alan did manage to fall asleep on my bed, but I just let him be. He looked so peaceful until he began drooling over my pillow and snoring and then I kicked him out. I honestly enjoyed those lovely times together.

I can hardly remember a time when Alan did not have a huge plaster taped across his forehead, he was always jumping off walls, racing against teenagers from our estate on his bike. He has done so much damage to himself over the years from stupid things such as crashing into walls, falling off walls, etc. Mam tried her best to keep him safe in the garden but there was no talking to him. He wanted to be outside the confinements of safety and be adventurous, a rebel without a cause. He loved being in the courts within our estate away from the view of Mam who watched carefully to make sure that he was safe; he was a fearless daredevil. To me, he was 'a punchy thing', really cute, but well able for anyone, and I adored him.

Our bond is still strong

To this day, I enjoy it when Alan and I bond together and make time for each other. We have both got into fitness because we realise the importance of looking after ourselves. We recently took part in a 5k 'fun run' in a local park. I will admit that he is fitter than me, and I kept at my own pace and stuck with it. As it turned out I was not too far behind him in the end. He wanted to record our time on his stop watch, but it was not working on the day. Either way, however, I know our times were not too bad. Personally, I did well and I did not stop going throughout the whole run. This was an achievement for me considering I had not done a 5k in such a long time. I felt that it pushed me on having Alan there; I refused to walk it, and let myself down, as there was still a bit of that sibling competitiveness there. In the end, Alan finished before me, but I was happy that I finished it and had fun with him along the way. It was a truly great achievement for us as a family unit.

I deeply love and respect my brother, Alan, as he assisted me in a lot of ways while I was growing up prior to and after the dystonia diagnosis. Even though he is my younger brother by two-and-a-half years he has been a rock of encouragement and support for me, and just like his near-namesake St Anthony, he has been one of the people who has helped me find what has been missing ever since I was eight years old.

Dean

The day that I heard Mam was pregnant, after putting herself through numerous pregnancy tests, I felt so relieved and happy. I was relieved because this had been achieved despite being informed that she could not get pregnant and I was happy because I knew how much Mam and my stepdad wanted to have a child of their own together. Their dream had finally come true. Also, I felt happy because it was something for the entire family to be optimistic and excited about after the previous years of drama we had gone through; it was a much-welcome distraction from my own struggles. I could not even begin to imagine the full extent of feelings that Mam and Stepdad felt. As I was ten years old by then I was more than aware as to what was going on. I felt excited witnessing Mam as she went through this experience; she was getting happier and transforming on a seemingly daily basis. Watching her stomach grow and seeing her gleam from ear to ear with happiness added to my own excitement.

As the months went on, I was listening to him inside her stomach and feeling him kick. I knew a little miracle was forming inside Mam. When she went to get her first scan done both she and my stepdad wanted to know if the baby was a boy or girl but the maternity hospital could not confirm this because the baby always had its back turned, which meant they were not able to make an accurate confirmation. Mam and Stepdad decided to leave it and let it be a surprise. However, during one of the scans a few weeks later the hospital were able to confirm to them that it was, in fact, a boy. I remember looking at one of the scans, and his big wide eyes. He still looks the same, and he was and still is very expressive through his eyes. Mam experienced many false labours in those nine months of pregnancy and even had a few while attending her line dancing, but she'd return to line dancing the following week, still pregnant.

The 'miracle' arrives

The day came when it was decided by the hospital that Mam needed to be induced because the baby was not budging. Alan and I stayed with our nanny and granddad. That evening my nanny received a call from Stepdad informing everyone that the baby had finally arrived safe and sound. I remember going to see him for the first time. When we arrived we saw our stepdad first and could tell that he was happy; he was grinning from ear to ear. When we arrived at the ward, I walked apprehensively into the room. Mam had just finished dressing the baby.

I could tell immediately that she was very happy with her new bundle of joy; her face spoke a thousand words. I was in amazement and awe looking at my new brother. For a baby, he was surprisingly tall. The whole time Alan and I were there, the baby was constantly yawning and stretching; I could only assume that was due to all the hard work he had endured coming into world. Mam told Alan and I to sit down, and when we did she gave him to me to hold. His eyes were still closed. I was laughing out loud; he was prefect and I thought "my gorgeous new baby brother". I was engrossed holding him and taking his tiny hand in mine. Alan was beside me leaning over and kept asking excitedly if he could hold him. But I did not want to let him go. I fell in love with him. I remember feeling so thankful in that moment and I vowed that I would be the best sister that I could be to this little mite. Then I kissed him and smiled. I felt my heart opening up in that moment, and then I passed him to Alan. When naming the baby, Mam and Stepdad were stuck between two names, Patrick and Dean. In the end, they decided on the latter.

Growing up with Dean was the most fun experience. He was so intelligent and witty that he made me laugh on a daily basis. They say that laughter is the best medicine and Dean certainly provided us all with plenty of that. He had in his head that he was a member of the Garda and would constantly scoot around on his go-kart armed with a notepad and his handcuffs; he would harass the neighbours and make his 'arrests'. Dean also has a number of allergies that he developed while growing up. His biggest and the most dangerous is to nuts and fish. We only began to get to properly know Mam's neighbour Madeline thanks to Dean. He began playing with her granddaughter and that developed a connection between our families. Dean and Madeline's granddaughter were only two weeks apart in age and they became the best of friends. During the early years of Dean's life whoever he played with, Mam always had to inform their parents of his allergies, most importantly the nuts. Even though Mam knew that Dean was smart and well able to inform people himself, she did not want to risk it. He was very sensible when it came to his allergies so much so that if Madeline was making chips for them he would keep checking with her to make sure that there were no nuts in them. It did not matter how many times she told him no and that they are just chips which only have potatoes in them, he still refused to believe her and wanted further proof, saying that he had to be very careful as he could die. He would be so serious when saying this and Madeline would be holding in her laughter at how level-headed he was at such a young age. Usually, it is the other way around with the adult telling the child to be careful. Madeline would then have to open the chip-pan up for Dean to inspect himself and give his approval. Madeline admired how grown up he was and how he took his allergies seriously.

Moments like that make me laugh, even to this day. It makes me appreciate my younger brother Dean for bringing the most important gift of all with his 'miraculous' arrival at a much-needed time in our family. I have so many wonderful memories of him growing up. Every day that we were growing up together, without fail, Dean made me laugh. There are many more funny memories that will stick with me forever, one of which was the time that I picked him up from primary school while he was in fancy dress. He was dressed as a soldier. I was going out that night and I had to get him to go to the off licence with me on the way home. We really confused the cashier that day. Dean was so small, and he had a loud voice while trying to explain to the cashier that the drink was for me and that I was over eighteen. Another funny story was the time we were in a shop together and Dean was teasing me by saying that I fancied the store manager. To this day, I cannot help but laugh at that.

Dean was born with many of his own health problems, but each day he has overcome them. Dean has an amazing ability to, for the most part, understand exactly what it is that I am saying. At times, he has had to work as a translator between other family members and me. This again is testament to his patience, firstly, and secondly, to the closeness of our sibling bond.

Just under three years after the dystonia diagnosis, Dean brought with him the 'miracle' of laughter back into our family, and this was something we all had assumed was never going to be seen again. Not only did he help me on a personal level, but, he also physically assisted me with putting my furniture together in my apartment. He helped me in many ways over the years. A great and welcome support. I love and appreciate my brother Dean for being able to light up all of our lives in the darkest of moments.

Keeping the family bond strong

My family and I still have a close bond and this is due in some part to the bad times we have shared together. Mainly, however, it is down to the many moments of happiness and laughter we shared. We all took part in a 5k obstacle fun run in the summer of 2017, which was a great laugh and proved how strong a bond we all still have together.

Other Family Members

Aside from Mam, Stepdad and my brothers, who have all been great support to me throughout the years, these other family members also deserve mentioning as they were always there being supportive to me.

My granddad William Marsh known as Billy, who is Mam's dad, has always seen and admired the effort that I put into keeping myself healthy and fit. I love him so much. He is in his late seventies and for as long as I can remember he has always worked hard. He was in the army for a number of years and served overseas. He then went to work with his sons doing attic conversions. When he retired, he made the decision not to just sit around for the remainder of his life. He still actively looks for work, whether it is doing odd jobs in his house or in other people's houses, like his daughters'. It is not easy work he wants either: he will climb on roofs; work on electrics, and even service cars. He has his own house looking lovely and he loves to see other people's houses and gardens looking well too. He would put a lot of people who are only half his age to shame. He goes mad if he sees anyone sitting around as he feels that there is no need. He recognises the importance of keeping active as this keeps your brain ticking over. He looks at me with great pride as he remembers how bad I was, and he thinks it is great how I always walk everywhere. He knows that one day I will train myself to talk again; he encourages me to keep practising. He is always there offering me lifts to help me out. I do not always take him up on them as I do not want to feel that I am taking advantage of people when I know that they have their own lives.

My nanny has been just as supportive of me throughout the years and we have a very special bond. If Mam is busy then she is always there to help me without any hesitation. As both she and granddad only live two doors away I will pop over and she will give me a hand out. While I am over there we both have a laugh together and she will tell me her news. She will also sing to me at times; she does not let her singing voice out to be heard by others but, she should because it is great. She needs to believe in herself as to how great she is and I believe that she should be out there, singing her heart out. Her favourite songs to sing are *Somewhere Over the Rainbow*, *You Are My Sunshine* and *Anything You Can Do, I Can Do Better.* My nanny and I always hug whenever we meet as we have great fun squeezing the life out of each other, then we laugh when we can breathe properly again. She did not have an easy-going life either, and like most, she had complications along the way, but she persevered throughout all of these. She has gone through many health problems in her life but she is a great woman and has amazing inner strength. She keeps herself going by walking everyday with granddad and they both look and act amazing for their age. She loves her fashion and keeping herself looking well is important to her. She is amazing and I truly admire and love her dearly.

My nanny and granddad on my stepdad's side are also absolute troopers, and I admire them so much. They work so well together and they are a real couple because even though they give out about each other a lot it is just a bit of banter between two people who love each other. It can be so funny being around them and witnessing their petty arguments; you can see the love they share underneath. Since day one they have made Mam, Alan and I feel welcome and part of the family, which was lovely for us. It was the same with Stepdad's brothers, sisters, nieces, and nephews; we were welcomed in by all, and we felt a lovely family vibe. I love them all; they are so understanding of me and have involved me in everything. They love to see us all when we call up to visit them. My nanny is so tiny that we have to bend right down to hug and kiss her. They are both great for their age and are amazing. I admire them and love them both.

My grandparents on both sides of the family always speak highly of their children and their grandchildren. They recognise all their struggles and are proud of all their accomplishments.

"Having self-belief in accomplishing your dreams can start at home; when you are surrounded by love, encouragement and support from a young age, you will always find success" – Tracey Ellen Maria

Chapter 4
Stepping back into the real world with dystonia

"Be on your guard; stand firm in the faith;
be courageous; be strong." – The Corinthians16:13

I believe that I had, and still have, this inner power to not only face this situation head on but to overcome it and defy expectations. When the diagnosis of my life-changing disability was made, neither my family or I fully realised the challenging journey I was about to begin.

After being in Temple Street Hospital for so long I really wanted to return to my primary school. Twenty-six weeks of constantly being examined and the absolute boredom from within my isolation ward was a true test on my patience. I could go home at the weekends during the twenty-six weeks; however, it was a kick to the gut for me when I had to return to the hospital again after Mam's lovely Sunday dinner and the comfort of being surrounded by my loving and caring family. I got very low. Mam and Stepdad kept encouraging me and tried to keep me positive by saying it would not last forever. This brought me only a small comfort, however, during those times when I'd realise I was back for another week of isolating boredom. Being in hospital for so long and being surrounded by really sick children, I knew that I was very lucky in comparison as what I developed was not life-threatening. Hearing about other patients who I knew that had passed away or seeing children with extreme illness such as Rett Syndrome, I really felt sorry for them more than I did myself. Seeing them just lying there unable to do anything except smile occasionally to show that they can hear and were still responsive was upsetting to me. They would constantly stare past you, lost in their thoughts. God love those poor children; I would find myself thinking, "What kind of life were they born into? A life where it is a struggle to even breathe." After each gasp, they would not know if they could make it to the next breath. What kind of a life is that, when you cannot enjoy your life or anything it has to offer you? This was difficult for me to comprehend as I knew what it is like to be a child imagining being free and living life like a "normal" child. I would often find myself thinking "all those poor children who suffer badly, were they put here just to struggle?" Every person on the planet is born into life with a purpose, whatever that purpose may ultimately be. I am sure those children brought so much joy to their families' lives despite all the pain that surrounded their situations. Some families only have those certain people in their lives for a very short time. However, in that time they realise that their "little gifts" had made such a change to their lives and made them into better people. I did not feel that I belonged in that hospital; if anything, those children thought me to grab life while I am still healthy. I wanted to go home to my own normal environment. Even though I knew the other children at home would not see me as normal it was a risk I wanted and needed to take.

Going back to primary school

Prior to my returning home, Mam was attempting to arrange for me to go back to my old primary school as she knew I was ready and willing. I wanted to get back into the swing of things but this fear kept coming over me about how the other children would treat me. I did not allow those thoughts to hinder my determination to progress towards normality, however. Succumbing to that fear would mean I was not living my life how I saw fit and by my standards, but by the standards of others. Even though I was still quite young I knew in my heart that going back to my own comforting and familiar environment had to be done, even if it meant the other children would make me feel different or possibly ignore me. I had a strong determination in the face of predicted adversity. I assumed that they would be talking and laughing behind my back, slagging me by impersonating my appearance straight to my face. These were all the fears that I had as to how I would be treated. However, I had to get beyond those negative thoughts and focus on why I wanted to go back even though I was expecting to be treated differently. I also knew that they would eventually get over it and see that I was the still the same Tracey underneath. I was determined to grow up like others and to get my education like them.

It was my Communion year when I returned and I wanted to make it, like the rest of my class. Due to spending just over half a year in the hospital excluding the times when I occasionally came home for an odd weekend, I had missed out on a lot of preparation for my Communion. I even missed the preparation Mass for the ceremony as I was getting a test done and the doctors would not let me go. I was raging and quite upset. They had arranged for me to go to a different class for the preparation Mass a week after my own class had theirs. Mam and I sat at the back during this. The other children kept looking back saying "there's Tracey". At the time I remember feeling that I was the one they were to see. I felt like the unwilling main attraction. The teacher had to keep gesturing to them to turn around and listen to the priest. I had not been seen by the other children since that faithful day in the Fun Factory and this was a number of months into the following year so I assumed that they would be surprised to see me. I had no friendships or connections with anyone in that particular class and was missing my own class and friends deeply. Even at my young age, I was aware that what I was doing was the right thing by putting myself back into a mainstream school. Mam knew this too and encouraged me every step of the way despite the fact that others were telling her that I should be going to a special school. Mam, however, was never deterred by those people and kept on her path with an unstoppable force. That is the biggest lesson that I have ever learnt from Mam and one that I have persistently and successfully achieved in doing myself over the years. Nothing is ever easy at first. However, once we persist on our course we will get the hang of it and then, ultimately, fly at it every time.

On my first day back, I stood outside the classroom while Mrs Brennan and Mam were talking inside. I peeked into the class and again heard the other children whisper "There's Tracey". I was a mixture of emotions. I was excited, worried, and anxious but ultimately happy that I was returning to my normal routine after the extraordinary ordeal that I had endured. I felt positive about it and ready to take on the challenge. My arms were still up in a contorted spasm, and I had to keep telling myself to bring them down. I was still retraining my brain at this time to help me to deal with these spasms. Mam told Mrs Brennan that if my arms go up that she was to remind me that I had to focus on relaxing and retraining my brain. The first few days were very daunting but I soon got back into a routine; the other children just accepted the person I was, which was such a relief to me. At that age, they were too young to have a proper understanding as to what was wrong with me. We did not have the mentality to question it, it was just accepted as the way I was and besides, we all just wanted to have fun. I did not communicate with the other children at that time as I did not know how to. This was not important at the time because I could still smile and show that I was still aware of everything and that my hearing and mind were not affected. At times, though, I knew I went into a daydream and looked like I was on a different planet. I still took everything in though. I admit I can still drift off and think of something else even these days.

When it happens to me nowadays, and even back then, if someone asks me what they've said then you can guarantee that most of the time I will know. Back then, and for most of the years afterwards, I did live inside my head. Even on the rare occasions if it happens nowadays, I know that it is a just habit due to years of social isolation I endured as a teenager. Back then, I found it difficult to be engaged in a conversation as I found it exhausting trying to look interested when I did not know how to communicate. With the assistance of the teachers and the other children in the school, I was able to begin to communicate via my eyes. Because my teachers always kept eye contact with me and did not talk past me I always felt included. This rubbed off on my school friends too, which I was delighted with.

"Tracey is still Tracey"

I used to go for special classes, which were facilitated by a teacher called Ms O' Callaghan. In these classes, which at times were done on a one-to-one basis I learnt reading and she also always made sure that I was keeping up with the rest of my class. She was a lovely, kind, and considerate woman. I could not feed myself by then but she had no problem feeding me. That type of consideration is rare and I am really grateful to her for that to this day. We were in her private class and occasionally there were other children there who had learning difficulties. They never passed any judgement; the odd stare every now and again but they were just children. I was so happy with the support that the school gave me as it made the transition easier on me. To be honest, I must say that I adapted and reintegrated very quickly back into the school routine. Mam and my family were all delighted that I had gone back.

There were some people who tried to put Mam and me off the idea of me going back to the same school. They tried to bring up the day in Playzone as an example of what went wrong; that I was left there when I should have been brought straight to hospital. Looking back on the situation now, I know an alarm should have gone off and an ambulance called but the school knows and realise that now. Hindsight is a great thing. Besides, that school could not have been more supportive of me and my family following that day. It would have made Mam and I bitter if we had held any resentment toward that school; we did not want that. Besides, the fact remained that I wanted to go back to that school for the few weeks needed and make my Communion at the end with my school friends. And I did!

Senior class

When I was going into third class, which was located on the other side of the school and dubbed "the senior side", the teachers were a bit concerned about the big move as they presumed that the change would prove too much for me. It was not really an option for me to repeat second class as I had started school at the age of five and was already the eldest in my class. I did not want to be the eldest again, nor did I want to be stuck behind while my friends went into another class and what seemed like another school. All the teachers on the senior side of the school were told about me and were all fully aware of me and my situation. Mam believed that, with the right support, I could do it and that I could adapt to the new change. It would not be the first time that I'd had to adapt to change and this one would not be as daunting as the previous one. I would be with my friends and I could grow up in a more comforting surrounding than if I was stuck behind. In the end, I was thankfully allowed to follow my friends into third class. After the summer holidays, I began my journey into the unknown world of third class. It was strange walking through the big yard and looking over at the junior side of the school. I remember thinking that this is a new beginning and that I could get through it. Mam was slowly walking behind me, smiling, and I assume feeling somewhat proud at my transformation. I saw my class friends and I felt a buzz of excitement. We all were jumping around in nervous anticipation at what lay ahead, and we were all so happy to be making this seemingly huge transition together. I remember laughing faintly to myself as I entered the unknown with my friends by my side as Mam stood behind us, waving me on, and wishing me well. I smiled back at her. As I walked through the doors and down to class, I remember feeling overwhelmed. I was extremely proud of the fact that I was here, in a mainstream school, with my friends. When I considered how my life could have turned out if it was not for the courage of Mam, my family and myself. I was grateful at how far I had come. I still had a long way to go, but the progress I had made up to that stage made me fully aware that I was on the right track and heading in the right direction. As young as I may have been at the time, I knew from that moment on and with absolute confidence that I would make it. It may take a bit more effort for me but I would make it. In that moment I felt so brave and strong. I entered my new classroom, which, to me, looked huge. We all had our own individual tables and as I stood at mine preparing to take my seat I remember thinking to myself in joyous anticipation "Bring it on!" After my first day in third class, I skipped out filled with happiness and joy. Happiness was radiating from me. Mam was equally as happy and told me how proud she was of me.

One day while I was in third class, Mam and I were told that there was good news. The school had applied on my behalf for a grant from the Department of Education for a laptop for me to use in class as writing was not an option. That laptop proved to be a great stress-relieving tool for me to use throughout the rest of my time in primary school. The support given to me by all the teachers was amazing. When I got my laptop it made life a lot easier for me and I managed to settle in quite well. At the time the teachers' main concern was about me going out to the yard on breaks as they were afraid that the bigger kids would knock into me and cause me to have a nasty fall because I could not protect myself with my hands. I, however, still wanted to take that risk; there was no point in being cooped up inside wrapped in cotton wool, and I knew that I would have gone mad. I needed fresh air too;

it was as vital to me as it is to anyone else. My close friends were asked by our teacher to stay with me and keep an eye on me to make sure I was safe, and they did. I will admit that when I went to play in the yard, it was tough; it was like being in the middle of a soccer match without a ball! The lads would all run around from every angle. I did feel a bit uneasy and had to constantly avoid being crashed into. A number of times, I honestly did feel very nervous, but I still went out.

One time, in particular, one of my friends suggested that we ask the teacher if we could stay in because I was getting myself worked up and did not feel safe outside. I also think my friend wanted to stay in too. When we approached the teacher and asked she wanted to know why. She felt the reason we were giving was an excuse and she encouraged me by telling me that I was doing really well. She encouraged me because it would become harder if I did not go out now. The next day I might feel the same again and then all my good work will be gone. She told me to ignore those distressing thoughts. If it got too much for me, I was more than welcome to come in but just see how I felt first. Hearing those words actually lifted me and they have stayed with me throughout all these years. I stayed outside with a clear message in my head that I repeated to myself over and over again "Is feidir liom!" I did not want to go back inside. From that moment onward, I persistently kept going outside for yard-break. She was right, it did make me stronger. I was ready for the lads each time. My confidence increased exponentially. I fully recognised and was proud of the fact that I had come on leaps and bounds. I became much more relaxed because I felt happy and I was treated the same. My own unique sense of humour came out. I got very messy during the outdoor breaks. I use to get other members of my class into a voluntary headlock. They loved it. I think they loved the fact that I was interacting more with them and they could sense that I was coming out of my shell more and more on a daily basis. I even started making the slightest of sounds and began attempting to make those sounds into words. I could only say "home", I think from spending such a long time in the hospital that I had consciously retrained myself to say that word first.

School choir

Even though at the time I could not speak, I was put in the school choir in fourth class. The teachers presumed it would be good to help rebuild my confidence more and ultimately it would help me regain the use my voice again. My fourth class teacher was also the choir teacher and she was the type of teacher you did not want to get on the wrong side of as she would let a roar at you if you even attempted to cross her. While she was very strict underneath her hard exterior, she was a truly lovely, considerate person who saw great potential in all her students. She saw, and to some extent, allowed me to see that there was more to me than just a disabled girl struggling to get by. She knew that all I needed was a bit of encouragement from others. She knew that all I needed was someone to see and believe in my capabilities. She also knew I needed that push and tough love, and that is exactly what she gave me; to her, I am grateful for that. I cannot truly remember the moment I joined the choir. I just remember being in it one day and that it became such a huge part of my early schooling routine. I loved being a part of that choir. We would practise twice or maybe three times a week. For the lead up to communions, conformations and school shows, we would practise every day after school. It was great to be involved in a social group. I grew back into myself in my final few years in primary and it made my transition back into normality that more bearable given how well I was treated.

Fourth class and beyond

My little brother Dean was born while I was in fourth class. I remember Mam collected me ten minutes earlier one day because I had a hospital appointment. She was outside the class room knocking on the door and one of the pupils opened it. When the teacher realised who it was, she beckoned Mam to come in. Mam was cradling my brother in her arms; he was about two weeks old at this stage. Of course, when she entered all the girls went into "Aww" mode. My teacher made her way over to Mam and began doting over him. The next thing, there was a stampede of children all up surrounding Mam to see my brother. My friends were waving at me as if to say, "Come on Tracey, look at your baby brother". I was scarlet. Mam looked over at me as if to say, "Sorry, Tracey your brother is taking up all the lime light". At the age I was, having Mam come into my classroom with a new baby, made so embarrassed I just did not know where to look. It was and still is easy to tell when I get embarrassed. Believe me, it was not the first time and certainly will not be the last time that Mam took over a situation and embarrassed the life out of me. That was due to the fact that Mam always presented herself as "Tracey's mam" and she assumed everyone in the school knew all about me. Mam made it her business to get her and me out there, to be known and instantly recognised. Every day after school when Mam would collect me, the minute that I would see her I would have an obvious smile from ear to ear like the Cheshire cat. I would then try to act like I was not smiling by turning moody. The things we do to disguise our happiness all in the avoidance of embarrassment. I smiled whenever anyone I knew collected me, be it my stepdad, nanny or granddad. I think the reasoning behind it was that I got shy and embarrassed if I sensed that they were watching me from a distance as I approached them. Looking back on it now maybe I subconsciously felt that I was being judged to see if there had been even the smallest of improvements in me and that caused me to smile in response to the nervousness of the situation. All I knew for certain at the time, though, was that I could not walk with a straight face if I knew they were watching from a distance. There were even times when I would break into spontaneous laughter for no apparent reason. I would crack myself up. This random physical response would occur even if I had just had a really bad day and came out with a face on me. I could not keep that angry head on me while walking towards Mam or whoever was there to pick me up on that given day. My lip hangs down intensely when I am upset or fed up so anytime Mam drew attention to my face this would always prompt me to laugh. I knew she was right. You have to see the funny side to life too, in my opinion, and as such, I do not know how in all the years I have been on this earth that whenever I have felt upset I have managed to avoid tripping over my lip.

The fact that from third class and beyond I could feed myself independently was an amazing accomplishment. I still could not eat in the classroom with the other students, however, as my confidence while I ate was still extremely low. There were numerous occasions throughout my early schooling years where I would go all day long without eating or drinking in front of the other students in my class because I was self-conscious about the fact that I ate very differently from others. I would appear sloppy and I knew that I made weird noises while I ate or drank. I would not have coped if anyone made a comment and looked at me differently; it was better for me to avoid that awkwardness altogether. The teachers came up with a solution and allowed me to eat my lunch in the staff room with a friend. This worked out great for me and I was able to relax more and enjoy my food. I was also permitted more time to eat my lunch because the teachers were aware that it took me longer to eat in a safer manner.

Mam always made me my lunch, sandwiches cut into little squares small enough to avoid choking but large enough to get my fork into. At the time I felt like Lord Muck sitting in the staff room on a large comfortable chair with an equally large table in front of me to put my lunch on. I felt comforted once again by my surroundings. The support that was offered to me by the school was incredible. I finished fourth class successfully and my teacher at the time told me that she was sad to say she would not be teaching me anymore but that she was very happy to know that she would still be working with me in the choir, which was still benefiting me greatly. I had found my voice again and was now able to express myself thanks to that choir.

When I was heading towards fifth class I felt as ready and as eager as I had at the beginning of every school semester. My brother Alan had started in third class when I started in fifth class. I would see him in the yard and he would be waving with his silly grin on his face. I would get all embarrassed and go the opposite way from him trying to pretend that I did not know him and that we were not related.My teacher in fifth class was equally as brilliant as the previous one. She was very knowledgeable with regards to technology and I.T. and was very keen on exploring what different technological devices there were available to help me communicate. She attended many of my appointments with Mam and me to demonstrate her interest and offer us her full support. She was such a great, caring, good-natured person who believed I would inspire so many people by my sheer determination to not give in or give up. I remember on my last day in fifth class – she was moving to a different job closer to her home – she told me that it was an honour working with me and that she was grateful at how much she had learnt from me. She also told me not to focus purely on the things that I could not do or things that I struggled with like putting my socks on. She told me that she'd still be in touch by sending me the odd email and keeping me updated with how her new job was going but that she had not come across anyone like me. That was nice to hear.

I remember the day I heard who my sixth class teacher was going to be, I was walking home dreading that coming September and hoping that the summer would drag on a little longer. He was in his mid-fifties and I remember hearing stories about him that made me think if I thought my choir teacher was loud and if the stories were true then this man would put her to shame. He used to stand at the entrance trying and succeeding in catching the late arrivals to school. He would let a roar at anyone who dared enter the school a minute over the beginning of class. His face would go purple from roaring so loudly and as punishment, he would give a tonne of writing, which was known as a scale. You'd have to write 'I will not be late' fifty times and sometimes more depending on how late you were.

I would be occasionally late by about seven minutes at most and if I missed the line I would panic. At times I would try to sneak in as the teacher would be distracted dealing with other pupils. I remember one time he caught me. I tried running but he let this massive roar that stunned me and stopped me in my place. I was scared stiff and when I faced him he initially did not realise that I had a disability, he just let rip at me. I could see his face turning purple while he was standing over me. My immediate reaction was to cry obviously. All of a sudden he turned into a gentle giant and he got all embarrassed as he realised I was the disabled girl. In that moment I saw underneath that he was actually gentle and considerate. However, when I discovered that he was going to be my teacher for my last year of primary I was honestly distressed and thought that I would not enjoy it as much as the previous years. I continued to enjoy my summer break regardless. The summer breaks from fourth class onwards were a bit different to the previous ones as I now had another little brother and he added to the fun. It meant a great deal more to all of us having that little addition to keep us all busy and entertained. When it came towards the end of that summer prior to me entering sixth class I had built up an immense nervousness at what lay ahead. I remember thinking that I would not cope with my last year, not with him as my teacher. The fact that he was a very stern man whose preference was to be referred to as "sir" or "master" as opposed to "teacher" was understandably very concerning for me. I was also getting quite distressed as I thought he would not understand my needs. I was terrified that I would fall back after all my hard work and the incredible steps that I had taken to get this far. Mam knew that I was worried about this and she told me not to get too upset saying that my new teacher might surprise me.

The day arrived when I had to return to school. All the other pupils were laughing; however, I sensed that was more out of nervousness rather than happiness.

When all the teachers came out to greet their new classes I got the first glance at my new "master"; he was smiling while walking out with a teacher. He then faced us, his new class, and almost instantaneously transformed into a drill sergeant as he told a number of the pupils to stand up straight while making his inspection of us. In that moment my heart was in my mouth. I sat at the back of the class because I needed to be located beside a plug socket for my laptop. I was situated beside a number of the classes 'messers'; I, on the other hand, was not one of them. I positioned myself at the rear of the class for two reasons: firstly, because I required the plug socket and second because I liked observing the rest of the class.

Throughout sixth class I felt that I had to be on my best behaviour for my new teacher. Even though I was not capable of making much noise the saying "watch out for the quiet ones" sprung to mind and I had to tread carefully. The main reason I was happier sitting at the back of the class was to avoid the feeling of being in the lime light. I had a tendency to jump sporadically every few seconds due to the muscular condition and I did not fancy the idea of anyone witnessing this as I knew it would cause them to laugh at me. I looked like I was being electrocuted when these non-intentional moments occurred.

Sudden noises also caused these 'jumps' and as such I would subconsciously pre-empt events that could cause loud and sudden noises that would cause me to jump without any noise ever occurring. I would get myself anxiously worked up because I was on edge. Due to the dystonia, my reflexes had become chaotically sensitive. The teacher had become aware of this so whenever he wanted to roar he would hold his breath and look over at me and say, "Tracey, I'm going to raise my voice".

As time went on, I had become used to him and I eventually did not jump as much when he roared. It was like I had built up this immunity to his random loud and scary outbursts. A few comments were passed by the other pupils as time went on such as, "You don't jump so much anymore, Tracey. Are you getting better?" They assumed that it was part of my disability, which to a certain extent it was. However, it was also due to my initial nervousness of the teacher's random roaring. As I said, though, I became harder and more accustomed to his roaring. This did not mean that I was getting better though.

After a while, I realised that once again Mam had been right. My teacher was not bad at all and was actually a real gentleman with a heart of gold. I also realised that he had to roar so that the other pupils knew he was in charge and that they remained calm and quiet for him while he taught. There were some little gits during my time in that school who would talk back very cheekily if they were not kept in order. I grew very fond of that teacher. There were five rows towards the front of the class and more or less every row was taken up by boys and girls. The boys in front of me would have the occasional farting competition with each other; kids will be kids, I suppose. I, understandably, was quite revolted by this disgusting behaviour and would occasionally turn green with the smell. They could knock a horse out. Not all the boys were involved in that childish, disgusting act thankfully but the boys who were thought it was the funniest thing ever. Whenever my teacher noticed this carry on he would have an understandable look of disgust on his face.

Towards the end of sixth class, my confident side started to bloom. A friend of mine was sitting across from me and we would pass sly notes to each other every now and again. By that stage, I had taught myself to write with my left hand and this form of communication with her proved a great way to retrain myself in handling this new-found skill. The teacher would at times have maths sums up on the blackboard and he would randomly pick a pupil to come up and solve them. A number of times he got me up, which I dreaded because I was and still am hopeless at maths. However, I would always just wing it and try to guess the answer. These random events of attention equipped me with the confidence required to get up in front of my peers and I carried this confidence with me throughout the rest of my school years. I also started to develop a liking for boys. Being around certain boys sent these feel-good tingling sensations down my body.

Fancying someone was seen as a requirement and if you did not comply then you were deemed a "weirdo". There was this one boy who I told everyone that I fancied but I actually did not, I just said that I did to fit in. I saw him a number of years later and I wondered to myself what had I been thinking. To a certain extent, I had even convinced myself that I did fancy him. I remember one time in particular that he was not in school and the teacher had our end-of-year photographs that he was handing out to everyone. The teacher asked if there was anyone who could give the boy his one. I was half tempted to rob it and keep it for myself but if I was caught I would never hear the end of it.

The slagging I would have got would not have been worth it.

Despite my understandable fears at the beginning of sixth class, I actually ended up having a great year and finished on a confident high. I felt happier and more mature; I was willing and ready for the next challenge, secondary school. Again, I thought to myself, "Bring it on!"

Holidays

During the school holidays, my family took my brother Alan and me on great days out. We spent a lot of time with different aunties and uncles on Mam's side. We would play with our cousins who are in my age group. We created some lovely memories despite me having to adapt to the new and different Tracey. While I was still in shock at what had happened to me even after all that time, it was never expected that I would fully get over it. I did understandably get fairly emotional at times, but I was never allowed to wallow in self-pity over my situation. Mam and my stepdad always encouraged me to have fun with the family as the previous few years had basically been hell for us all, including Alan. He was always in the best care during those few months of drama. He has never admitted it but I know he was really affected by what had happened to me as well. Prior to it happening we had been such a normal family; living our lives having just returned from our holidays, going back to our routines when suddenly his big sister is causing mischief and telling tales. Then the reality hits that this is serious; all of a sudden she cannot speak and her body is twisted. He is obviously fully aware of the situation now but back then he did not know what was going on. I suppose that made two of us.

Alan and I never spent a day inside or at home as we were always out and about. On a number of occasions, we were even brought on a little trip down to the country for a nice family break, even if it lashed rain, which, in Ireland, is quite common. We did not care, however, we actually had more fun. One minute the sun is splitting the trees and the next minute the rain is belting down. We all would try to run to dry shelter while laughing, with snots and dribbles all over our faces, Alan, our cousins and I. We would get absolutely soaked to the skin. Mam and my stepdad would hold my hand and Alan's while we all tried to run together. At the time I could not grip properly with my hands so they would hold onto my jacket and as we all ran, my legs would lift into the air while I tried to keep up. It was great fun. At times when the rain was really heavy and I was struggling to keep up, my stepdad would scoop me up into his arms and carry me. We would all be huddled under a tree that provided us with the adequate shelter we required until the rain stopped. Moments like that are the very definition, in my opinion, of living a happy life despite whatever drama has been thrown my way. Making great memories and feeling the freedom and the happiness with my family. A lot of the time, we spent our holidays in Wicklow as we all collectively love the mountains and nature. Personally, I found it very healing and grounding. My family were with me and, as such, to me, my surroundings felt like a home away from home.

I was brought there for my Communion photographs as they served as an amazing backdrop to my day of celebration. My aunt, uncle, and cousin came too. It was such a beautiful day and there were some lovely photographs taken of me and the mountains. Instead of a traditional veil, I wore a rather unique-looking white lace hat. I wanted to be different and to stand out with regards to my clothing because I was aware that I was not like everyone else anyway. Why attempt to blend in? I am still like that to this day and Mam is the same. We do not like to blend into the crowd because we recognise the importance of expressing our own self-identity. We are all born in our own unique ways with our own unique likes and dislikes. Even still, people try to conform due to the fear of drawing attention to one's self. It can be easier for most people to just blend in; I realistically had and still have no choice but to stand out. It is something that I now, however, am grateful for even if there were some teething issues in the beginning. Despite my physically deforming disability, I stood out not solely due to that disability but due to my own willingness to dress a bit differently to the norm. That willingness not to conform along with the assistance and support of Mam contributed greatly towards me having a day that I thoroughly enjoyed and most importantly, controlled.

Despite Mam and Stepdad's struggles with money throughout the years, they always kept the attitude that they were not going to let that small fact determine their or their family's enjoyment of life. They could have just allowed us to play outside on the street because that cost nothing. We did occasionally play outside but that was after we had spent a few hours out in a park or at a beach, etc. The other children on the road use to remark that we were always taken off somewhere. Mam and my stepdad would always take us somewhere; even before they had a car, we were still brought on days out using public transport to get there and home again. It did take longer but to them, that was not seen as a good enough excuse. We created great memories as a family.

As the summers approached their end and September would be nearly upon us again I had always got a new uniform since I'd be growing as children do. I'd also get new books and stationery. It would make me feel ready each time. I was always nervous but I knew I had to face it one way or another. Over the summer prior to me entering third class, I had become a bit better. I had learnt to feed myself again, which was a brilliant achievement. My hands and speech needed to be worked on, however, I was making progress in the summer months and I knew that I would get there eventually.

Secondary school

When the time came for me to make the major transition, from primary school to secondary, Mam and I were met with the same obstacles as we were when I'd gone back to primary school all those years previously. Mam, however, had every intention of me going to a mainstream secondary school despite all the negative comments that were being thrown her way. It was not only about finding a school that would accept a disabled girl like myself but one that could accommodate me in an adequate manner and provide me with the much-needed support I required. Whenever Mam was expressing her feelings and concerns to certain individuals she found that instead of them being supportive with words of encouragement, the responses she was met with echoed the ones from previous years when she'd attempted and succeeded at getting me back into mainstream primary school. Naturally enough, these comments were disheartening to Mam, but they equally acted as a challenge to her to disprove the people who collectively had little faith in both her and me. Mam was determined to find the right mainstream school for me. She still saw me as the same old Tracey; not once did she concede and agree with those negative comments. Mam had always wanted and still wants the best for me. Her intuition told her that a special needs school would not be the correct path for me to take. Not that there was anything wrong with special needs schools, they do a great job and for certain individuals are the correct school for them given their needs and requirements. For me, though, they were not the correct school because I required a mainstream school to keep me on my path. Thank God Mam saw my inner strength and knew all too well that I had the ability to manage it.

A New World

As it happened, I got offered not just one secondary mainstream school, but three, in fact. They all accepted my application and were happy enough to take me on. Mam and I felt that the school that my primary school friends were going to was not for me. Not that there was anything wrong with the school it was just that our instincts told us that was not the school for me. My sixth-class teacher from primary school was concerned when he heard that I was not going to the same school as my friends that I had grown up with as he felt that I would fall back. However, Mam and I understood that it would be very tough in the beginning for me but again she believed that I could manage. Equally, I felt ready for a change myself and I was excited about the challenge ahead. I knew that I was a bit "mad" to make such a drastic change but I felt ready for this and the whole new life experience.

The school that I chose, in the end, was a mainstream school in Finglas. Driving past the gated perimeter of the school I noticed that it was surrounded by a beautiful garden. On the day of my interview for the school, I left all the questions up to Mam to ask. I was going along with her feeling about the school and the staff. Not that I allowed her to make the ultimate decision because that was left to me. I had a very strong positive vibe from the school and had every faith that this would be right for me. As the school was located in Finglas, I felt that was another positive too. Everything about it felt right to me and I had every faith that I was making the right decision. The school even had "faith" in its name which is quite common in Ireland but it felt like a sign to me at that time. I could see myself walking through the corridors and doing well in every aspect. While we were at the interview I was feeling as nervous as hell. I realised that come the end of August I could be starting in this huge school. Everything seemed much larger to me in this place compared to the little primary school I had just finished. I met with the principal, the resource teacher, and the guidance counsellor. I saw other teachers as we passed through the corridors. I met with the people who worked in the office who were all very nice and made clear their desire for me to attend that school. They told me that they would offer me the support I required. That school had never before had a student with a physical disability like mine and they made me feel that they were open to taking me on. They wanted to teach me and also to learn from me, which made me feel wanted. I got an intensely warm feeling in my heart and my head was screaming "yes!". I smiled graciously knowing that I was in the right place. I acknowledged the difficulties I would face with coming from primary into a new school and being in a new environment surrounded by new faces. However, as always, I was ready.

During that summer break, Mam and I had gathered the essentials I required for my new educational experience; things such as new stationery, a new school bag, and a brand new green uniform for the school I was to attend. I was a bit concerned about my uniform as the shirt had lots of buttons as did the skirt. At the time, I normally wore a tracksuit, which was far easier for me to put on and a lot more comfortable. However, I was moving up in the world and had to accept that in order to do so I had to look respectful and dress in a more appropriate manner. Mam always helped me to get dressed every morning and then always drove me to school. On my first day, I tried to ignore the unhelpful negative thoughts that I had swarming around in my head. I had a severe knot in my stomach from the nerves, as I wondered how the other students would see me. Would they accept me? Would they slag me and talk about me behind my back? Would I be left by myself, without any friends? Would I feel awkward? Would I make nice friends? I was hoping everything would work out for me. All I wanted was to be treated the same and have fun, to be able to create great friendships, to grow in education, and in confidence. I knew that these entirely new experiences I was about to embark on could improve me mentally, physically, and increase my confidence in a way that would make it go through the roof. There was no point in me trying to answer these questions before I had even begun my journey. I acknowledge that it can be extremely tough for anybody starting off in a new secondary school. However, I can tell you that experience is multiplied when you are the only student attending the school who has a visually obvious disability. I know that I am not the first disabled person in history to attend mainstream school; however, I knew that I was the first disabled person in history to attend *that* school. This knowledge, although frightening to me at the time, made me feel like a brave pioneer. I was ready and eager to explore my New World.

My first day

The day finally arrived that I would commence my secondary education. Mam smiled when she saw me in my new uniform, telling me to go out and visit my nanny and granddad. That was the tradition within our family. Nanny and granddad only live two doors away from us and they love feeling included in these kinds of occasions. When I called over to them I had my face pushed against the glass on the hall door with a grin on my face. I could hear Nanny.

"Here's Tracey, look at her face."

She flew down the hall, opened the door, and her first reaction was, "Wow! Don't you look beautiful?"

She gave me a big hug saying how proud she was. Granddad came down the hall still chewing on his breakfast and he stood admiring me. Nanny took a few photographs while my granddad stood in front of me and said, "I'm delighted for you. Starting secondary school, you have come a long way. You should be very proud of yourself and thank God for your mammy. A great mammy she is; always fought for the best for you. You are both really great people."

I was delighted by those comments from my granddad. Nanny took some photographs of me in the garden. When it was time to go they waved and said, "Good luck, you'll be great. Just be your beautiful self."

As I walked into the school for my first day I became very self-conscious moving through the crowds. But I was not alone in my nervous despair as I sensed that everyone else was in the same boat. We all collectively felt equally nervous and awkward. I was shown to my class and I anxiously dived onto the nearest chair and sat at my desk resembling a quiet, terrified mouse. The noise from the girls was surreal. Nobody copped onto the fact that I was disabled until my tutor came, introduced herself and proceeded to the roll call. Of course, when it came to my name being called out I did not speak. She was about to mark me absent until she looked up and saw the distress in my eyes.

"Oh, are you Tracey? Yes, sorry."

I just nodded and assumed the class must have thought in that moment that I was just shy. We were only in a few hours but I could not wait to go home. I knew that as time went on it would become easier. However, I felt I had done enough exploring for the day. I did obviously keep going back to that school; I was not permitting my own fears to get in the way of me succeeding in all that I had achieved up to that stage.

Sandra, my personal assistant (PA) and First School Friend

The school had accommodated me with a laptop and also thought that it would be helpful for me if I got a PA to provide me with that extra help that I required. The woman who the school had sourced for this role was a very kind woman who I eventually befriended. She assisted me with putting my coat on and taking it off and setting up my new laptop in the different classes among other things. She was a much-needed extra support to me. Her name was Sandra and while she was a bit older than me she was not so old that it made it awkward for me to communicate my fears with her. She was very concerned for my well-being and would always listen to me if I had difficulties in any and every aspect of my life. She was lovely and I could tell straight away that she was a positive person to be around. She had a great sense of humour and we bonded so well because of that. She was very fond of Mam because we all had a shared sense of humour. Mam and I loved her strength and how considerate she was towards me. As it turned out, Sandra had a fairly complicated life too that had certain similarities to Mam's and mine. She had endured a lot of hardships and struggles too and she had first-hand experience at how difficult it was to fight for everything in order to get where she wanted to go, and more importantly to be heard along the way. She could relate to a lot of what Mam and I had been through and saw Mam as a true warrior. We knew that she would go to the ends of the earth for me and it showed in how well she looked after me while I was in that school. Sandra became great support and we connected so well that I saw her as my friend. In fairness, she was just as tough on me as Mam was. It was the tough love approach, but she was great. She made the initial transition for me to secondary a lot easier because for the longest time it felt as though she was my only friend. I was honestly delighted to have her with me during that otherwise seemingly difficult time in my life.

I use to spend my school years sitting among the quiet girls as they were better behaved and kept to themselves. I felt safer in the knowledge that none of them would give me any hassle. They were girls who put their heads down and got on with their learning. Some of them were girls from my own class and the rest were from other classes. There were other girls who attended that school who were the complete opposite. They strove for attention by acting tough and answering back to the teachers. They would not back down and would constantly give the teachers and other students a tough time. They would make it their job to slag off the quiet ones by calling them "swats" and "goodie two shoes". Those girls were loud; they were constantly up to some form of devilment and would buy and sell you because when it came to it you were always deemed inferior to them. You were a "nerd" for wanting to learn. The funny thing was that when it came to knuckling down and getting the work done they always did whenever they felt pressured to; they were all very bright underneath. In my opinion, there is nothing wrong with having a strong sense of self-assurance. However, when confident people become more confident by pushing other people down and making a nuisance of themselves by being a disruption to others, then I believe that their confidence is masking their own inhibitions. I persisted in hanging around with the quiet girls. Sandra encouraged me every step and she made sure that I got in with them and mixed with them. I could not rely on just Sandra to be my friend as she did not stay with me during each class.

My teachers were equally very helpful and supportive of me. They would give me class notes as opposed to me trying to type fast and keep up at the same time. The struggle I would have had to try to listen while simultaneously being able to type what the teachers were saying during the classes. I would make sure that I took note of key words that the teacher had said in order to help me reflect back on my lesson at a later time. Sandra was only with me in the classes for a few brief minutes before class began and that was only to assist me in setting up the laptop. She knew by my timetable when she was due back to help me move onto the next class. I always felt awkward when Sandra was in the class helping me because of the reactions from some of the other girls who treated me as though I was different. They would always start rolling their eyes up anytime Sandra entered the room. I became aware of this and it was a major blow to me because I knew and respected Sandra's reason for being there. I always felt as though they were looking down on me and felt that I was getting special treatment. One time I overheard one of them say that she wanted a laptop while Sandra was setting mine up for me. The tone that was used when that sentence was said made me feel then more than ever that I was seen to be receiving some form of preferential treatment. I tried to tell Sandra that I did not need her as much; she understood that I had become concerned what others thought. She advised me to try to ignore it. Another time Sandra actually caught them laughing and passing sly comments about her and me while she was there. She had her back to them while she was setting up my laptop and she immediately could tell from my reactions that they were laughing at me. Sandra saw the distress in my face and began mouthing, "It's ok, ignore them."

When she had finished setting me up she was just about to leave quietly but she could not leave without saying something to them. She was walking towards the door when she suddenly turned and said to the girls, "I just give Tracey a hand. Don't be treating her differently, get to know Tracey for Tracey. You should be helping the girl not making things harder for her. Disgraceful."

The girls immediately tried to deny it but Sandra just replied, "Do you think we were born yesterday?"

I was in the back of the classroom sinking into my seat going redder and redder. In that moment the teacher came through the door and asked if there was a problem. Sandra looked at the girls, "No, there's not, I was just leaving."

In that moment I did not know where to bury my face. I was so scared these girls would be waiting for me after school to give me a hiding.

I was panicking leaving the school. I stuck my foot out and did a James Bond move around the wall. I was in a sweat. I saw Mam parked outside and I broke into a power walk to get to the car as quickly as I could. When I got to the car I dived in. Mam was startled saying that I looked like I was being chased. I was breathing heavily and looking around in a panic but I had worked myself up and it took me a while to get back to a comfortable state again. When I did, however, I let out a huge sigh of relief. The next day I went to school as normal, still a bit on edge. All the girls greeted me but not in a fake way; it sounded genuine. I wondered if I was in the right room, thinking that they were warming me up, then they'll hop on me unexpectedly. No such thing occurred, however, and they were a bit friendlier. We were not buzzing buddies from that moment or anything and I still felt really awkward but, there had been a change. Those girls never really came to terms with someone like me; I was always going to be a bit strange to them. How would they involve someone like me in their mischief? It also did not help the fact that I was from a different part of Dublin. For some strange reason, Ballymun and Finglas girls do not mix well. I was grateful for all Sandra had done for me. She defended me when I needed defending and spoke up for me when I could not. She was a true friend; my guardian angel guiding and supporting me along my early transitioning struggles.

Blending in with the 'quiet' crowd

Throughout most of my secondary school years, it was always my preference to hang out with the other quiet girls as it was easier for me to blend in with them. I always felt like a sheep in sheep's clothing so there was no point in me pretending that I was anything different. I ate my lunch in the class with the other quiet girls as I knew there would be no judgement made and it would not have favoured me to isolate myself away in my own secluded room for lunch. I needed to feel comfortable eating around other people again. In secondary school, I had more freedom during lunch breaks and I had the option of hanging out in other classes within the same year as myself or going outside into the courts for some fresh air. We were not permitted to leave the school, which I did not mind as it saved me the pressure of leaving my essentials lying around and the added pressure of not being given enough time to eat my lunch. I was more than happy with the rules regarding lunch as it meant that I could relax in class and enjoy my food. I was the only one who always had my lunch in a lunch box as it was easier for me to manage and kept my sandwiches intact. If I had them in tinfoil they would have been like mush by the time I got to eating them and then I would have added to the mush by trying to remove them from my bag. I found eating with the other girls was fine and I was delighted that I had chosen this option. I felt if I had attempted to make friends with the other girls instead of the quiet ones I would have found it difficult trying to be accepted and I did not want those girls influencing me in any way. There was a place in the school that some of the girls and I would go to during our breaks for some quiet time and we would send out our good intentions for the future.

I had chosen to take nine subjects but the teachers thought it would be best that I drop a subject in order to guarantee that I would be able to keep up with the rest of the classes. I decided to drop Irish; I'd been good at it in primary school and I knew the basics. I knew and acknowledged that this language was part of my natural heritage but I was also studying French and I had started enjoying that more. The French teacher, on the other hand, was a 'screamer'. Thank God that I had built up an immunity to that type of teaching method in fourth and sixth class with my primary school teachers. As it worked out, the fact that she roared and was tough on us actually helped me because it made me study harder and French became a very enjoyable subject for me. It was strange that I was good at a language considering I could not verbalise. As I was not able to do the oral part of the exams for French my situation was explained to the Department of Education and I got an exemption. Also, instead of me doing Irish I had a free class and used this to catch up with my studies. My resource teacher became very helpful to me and assisted me with my English and anything else where I needed assistance. She really was a lovely woman who I became very fond of over the years. She, like so many others who entered my life at this time, was a great support who knew and acknowledged my full capabilities regardless of the fact that I was part of the quiet crowd. She looked beyond my physically limiting exterior and saw a girl who was more than capable of learning and living a normal life.

The end of my first year initiation

When my first year in secondary school came to an end I was glad and proud of the fact that I finished it in one piece and I deemed all my misguided worrying inaccurate. I began to think that second year would not be as hard because people are already prepared, they know me now.

First year was an ice breaker, not just for the students but the teachers. It was a learning experience for them too.

The summer breaks were longer at secondary school and as such, it felt like I had not been in school in ages. When I went back for second year it did feel like I had to start all over again, to an extent. It was nerve-wracking again for me but I knew what to expect. On my first day back, I began to see the familiar faces arriving. Sandra met me at the office and she was among some of the office staff to welcome me back. They all began to laugh. I felt happy to be back as I knew I needed to continue on this journey. I knew there would still be difficult times ahead but I felt that they would become easier to deal with in time. Sandra told me to go to my classroom and get settled in. I looked at the notice board, worked out from that where my first class was and I made my way there by myself. It was a weird feeling entering the class again; I looked around to find somewhere to sit. I saw the quiet girls almost huddled together in a corner of the room and took my seat beside them. The other girls were still the same. Nothing changes, I thought. Even though I still felt like an 'odd ball', I knew I would get used to it. Again, I got on with things and knuckled down. I started developing confidence as time went on and each day became easier.

Second year

When my second year came around I had befriended a lady who worked in the school office who also took on the role of supervising at the lunch time breaks. I found her to be a great laugh. She also had the responsibility of catching the late arrivals to school. Daily, she would stand at the main door and if anybody showed up late for school she would stamp their journal. My journal was full of late stamps. I would not be that late but even still, she would just tease me because I would come in acting all shifty while giving the impression that I assumed I was on time. She was very friendly towards me. If Sandra was not in then she would help out during free classes. I got to know her as a person because of the assistance she provided me. She had a great sense of humour and always had funny stories to share with me. I would be in fits of laughter most of the time spent with her. I knew that it was great for me having those types of lovely people to assist me along my way and keep me smiling in the process.

As is the norm in secondary school, I took a number of subjects, the most interesting of which being science. However, I was struggling to pass any of my exams in this subject. My science teacher became concerned as he knew that it would not be long before the Junior Certificate came around for me. I was getting extremely frustrated with my lack of progress on the exams front because I wanted to do well. The teachers all knew that I was struggling with this subject and one of them, in particular, offered to give me help. She wanted the two of us to work around her timetable and mine. She insisted that we do one-to-one sessions to try and conquer this dilemma. I was a bit nervous about meeting her on this basis as I automatically had this self-limiting thought about how we would communicate. I sat in a little room that was allocated to me. As I got to know her I could tell that she really was such a lovely caring person who wanted to assist me in any and every way possible. She broke science down to a level that made it easier for me to understand. I felt delighted with the assistance and with the fact that I was starting to understand my favourite subject. I was also delighted at the fact that I was easily understood by her, especially after my previous limiting thoughts. She worked patiently with me; she also saw and believed in my potential. There were days that she would get me to do IT-related things that helped me greatly in improving my skills in this field. Maybe she saw me being extraordinarily reliant on technology in my future life and knew that I needed to learn early. She was in charge of designing the school leaflets and one day she came into the class and asked me if I wanted to assist her with one of the leaflets. I delightedly agreed and she and I designed the leaflet on her laptop. Being a part of something gave me a great feeling. When we had finished it she made sure that at the back of the leaflet I was mentioned as one of the designers. She wanted the other teachers, students, and parents all to know that I was a part of the designing process for this leaflet; she wanted to get my name out there. She was always encouraging and supportive of me and was always full of praise. One day she came to me with an idea that she knew would really test my confidence. She asked me if I would be interested in entering the Young Scientist Awards with one of my friends who I had connected with at that time, one of quiet girls. She was also such a lovely person and had a very caring nature to her. The teacher was really excited for me and knew that it would be good for me to get myself out there. My friend was very interested in starting this project with me when it was put to her. It was not just a case of saying, "Yes, we can," and be done with it. There was plenty of hard work involved. Luckily, all our hard work paid off and we were accepted by the Young Scientist Awards Committee. For the project itself, we decided to highlight the importance of having a good breakfast in kick-starting your day. This project was called "Does breakfast improve your performance?" Personally, I was delighted to do this project as I recognised the fact that I could not perform properly without having breakfast and to actually get the figures to support this knowledge would be pretty cool. It worked out that for our 'test subjects' we had asked sixth and fifth years to volunteer. The live test involved all of our volunteer subjects arriving to the school one morning and doing some fitness, and then we got them to try to write an essay. Some of the volunteers were advised not to have breakfast until after the test so that we could get good results. To assist with the physical element of the test the teacher brought in a dance mat that her daughter had and we got the volunteers to use it.

This test took a lot preparation in the build-up but it felt great having our own big event to organise and it worked wonders for my confidence. At that moment, I felt as though I had properly taken my first step back into the real world by putting myself out there with my friend by my side and in a normal environment. My teacher was amazingly supportive and was with me every step of the way.

At that time I had a little digital organiser that I used to communicate with others. I also found that my speech was beginning to improve, even though I still would not speak in public. "One thing at a time," I thought. Being a part of the Young Scientist Awards was a truly amazing experience. I was so grateful to that teacher for putting me forward, believing in me and most importantly seeing beyond my struggles because, in that moment, I felt much happier in school. I finally felt that I had an inclusive role to play.

Third year

On entering third year, I felt much more capable and equipped for all the dynamics of change that I was enduring. Again, I sat with the quiet girls as I had done previously. As time went on, I began feeling as though I was being more accepted by the other girls in my year. I was placed beside a girl who I had never really spoken to before as the teachers wanted everyone to move around and build up new friendships so as to be confident with and around new people. The girl who I sat beside, was a lovely girl who I became very fond of. I noticed that through her I began making new connections. Eventually I even started to visit this friend and have sleepovers. I was happy that I had made new connections and I recognised the importance of creating those new friendships. I was also aware that just because I had these new-found friends that did not mean that I could dismiss my old friends. Everyone added a certain element of happiness to my life and it was important for me to make sure that I stayed loyal to all of them.

With my confidence blossoming daily, I began feeling more comfortable in using my voice to make sounds and attempting to develop those sounds into audible words. I only attempted this with Mam initially, though, because I still felt extremely self-conscious making the effort around other people. I use to record my voice on tape. I honestly did not like how I sounded but I knew that by recording I could work at it and learn to like that part of me. It was, after all, part of my new identity. It was a big step for me and as I listened back over the recordings I felt two things, disheartened but also very proud that I had taken that step. I then took an even bigger step by replaying it in front of Mam and my nanny. Then one of my aunties came in to listen too. The next huge step that I needed to take occurred when I gave a recording to one of my new friends. I felt at the time that I was taking a huge risk as I did not know her that well and I was concerned that she would pass it around and tease me, but she did not. She was a bit taken aback at my trust in her and told me the following day that she listened to it at home and felt very touched and emotional listening to it and that she had tears in her eyes. She was grateful to me for allowing her to hear me talk, something that she had previously assumed I was unable to do. I got brilliant support throughout third year and again I felt that I was improving on all aspects of both my schooling and social life. The Junior Cert was quickly approaching and the school had arranged with the Department of Education that I be given extra support in preparation for the exams. I was allowed my own space in a room with Sandra to use as extra study time and it worked out amazingly. In the end, I did really well in the exams and felt very proud and relieved.

Fifth Year and Sixth Year – *Finally Feeling Accepted*

As some of you may know, in Ireland's second-level education you have an option to do a fourth year called transition year or skip it and go straight into fifth year. This is optional only and in certain schools, mine included, so I opted to skip transition year. As I was entering fifth year I immediately noticed that it was a different system because everyone was preparing for leaving school even though there was still sixth year and the leaving certificate to go. The buzz of excitement became immediately apparent to me and it was contagious. Even though I too was excited about what the future held I was also a bit concerned about getting through fifth year. I felt as though it would be like starting all over again. I had only started feeling included and having my own independence towards the end of third year. On my first day in fifth year, I remember feeling very overwhelmed. I truly felt in that moment that I was back to square one again. This was because, from fifth year onwards, in half of my classes I was placed in with girls who I did not know. I told Sandra that I thought I would need her, now, more than ever, because I was feeling very anxious. Sandra told me not to worry and that I would get into the swing of things again. Some of the classes had many loud students in them. There were a few quieter students but they were just as loud as the others when they wanted to be. I remember one day during a class the other students were being very disruptive and the teacher told them that everyone would get detention. This meant that we were all going to be held back after school, which, of course, caused mayhem because some of students, myself included, who were not involved, were going mad at the louder students. The teacher then told me that I did not have to stay back. Straight away my body language spoke louder than words as I got very hot-headed and bothered and typed on my digital organiser that I was part of this class too so I should get detention too. The teacher was puzzled but accepted that that was what I wanted. I smiled back at her with attitude. The other girls were shocked. I skipped to detention happy as Larry and sat there with a smile on my face; I was the only one smiling. From that moment on, the other girls saw me as the same and knew that all I wanted was to be treated the same as everybody else. They knew that I was mad underneath and they came up with a nickname for me Tracker or Trackerack. I loved it. I was finally unshackled from my loneliness and isolation. I loved going into school every day as I had always known deep down that these girls were nice girls. It is normal to put up a mask and pretend to be something you are not. It is more difficult however to take down that mask and reveal the real you.

I honestly enjoyed every subject that I was studying; I found home economics and art just as enjoyable as science. In fifth and sixth year, I had dropped music and I missed it, but the new subjects I was taking part in were all equally brilliant. I had a full involvement in PE. In the previous years, I would not have had a sufficient amount of confidence to participate in PE. I also took up horticulture, which was great and very interesting. I was happy with the fact that the science teacher was helping me out with the one-to-one science classes. I honestly can say that fifth and sixth year were my best years by far. During my two final years in the school, they had got me my own table, which had plenty of space on it. It was height-adjustable with a special tailored chair to assist me with my posture. The final two years in school were a unique experience for me as I developed a bond with every single girl in my class. They all loved me for the crazy yet down-to-earth kind of person I was. I was finally fully included in everything. All the girls were a bit crazy but I loved that about them because I was, and still am, similar. I love to be able to unleash my crazy side. I love to let my sense of humour out even though at times it is still difficult and at times I do feel trapped inside my body. These girls may have been mad but they would get down to work when work needed to be done. One day before the start of a class a few of the girls wanted to get up to some mischief. There was a wheelie bin in the class for recycling paper and they wanted someone to get into it so that they could wheel them around the class. A few of them took it in turn to jump in, and then they suggested giving me a go. I was laughing my head off while slightly reluctant to participate in this childish activity but they insisted. My main obvious concern was that I was aware of the fact that at any moment the teacher would come into the classroom; this fact did not seem to concern the other girls though as they lifted me into the bin. I literally roared laughing like a hyena. I must admit that when I was placed into that wheelie bin I was having the best fun in a long time. In that moment it appeared to me that I was just one of the gang. I was laughing so much that I feared I would wet myself. The girls all thought that my reaction was hilarious. Then the inevitable happened. The teacher arrived into the class and was outranged to see me in a wheelie bin. As expected loyalty goes out the window in the presence of a superior and as such the girls scattered back to their desks leaving me stuck in the bin, trying to hold back my laughter at how stupid it must have been perceived. Immediately and without hesitation, the teacher let out a roar to get me out of the bin. Two of the girls stood up and lifted me out. I then had a walk of shame back down to my desk, I was mortified. I was struggling to try and contain my laughter during that class. Some of the girls began noticing my attempts at containing this laughter and whispered among themselves, "Tracker's going to explode". That group of girls were the same ones who at the beginning of my secondary school experience gave me a hard time. How times had changed though. Throughout the initial three years in secondary school, I was extremely shy and quiet, and I hung around similar types of girls. As I was beginning fifth year I was feeling more comfortable in my own skin and I felt that I did not want to be a quiet girl anymore. I wanted to remove this stereotype that followed me around that just because I was unable to verbally communicate must mean that I am a naturally quiet person. The real Tracey that was initially caged inside wanted eagerly to be set free. Those girls who I'd thought were 'trouble', were in actual fact the complete opposite; they were loyal and considerate and they made me feel alive during those years. They were also aware that I had great hearing and would say that I had super-sonic hearing. I became close friends with one girl in particular who sat across from me. I use to make these meowing sounds at her, which sounded more like a cat being stood on and I gave her the nickname "cat". On a number of occasions, I would even say the word cat to her across the table. She would laugh and then meow back at me. The childish things we did to keep ourselves entertained. The two of us became inseparable and we would go shopping in town together. She had a great fashion sense and I was happy to go shopping with her. I finally had a friend to show me what would look nice on me. After school had ended and she began driving, she would collect me from Mam's house and bring me to her estate where I met all her family and her boyfriend's family. They were all lovely and so welcoming towards me. She became a great friend who really looked out for me. I felt truly blessed that someone like her had made time for me. She never saw me as a burden; she just wanted the best for me. She wanted me to have normal life experiences; she was brilliant to, and for, me. My social life began to expand during my final two years in school. I was invited to plenty of nights out; we would even go to a friend's house and all get ready together. The girls would all help me to get ready and I was thankful to them for that. They were very responsible young women compared to some others. They would always look out for me and would never leave me on my own. They were very protective of me and we always had great laughs together. I felt delighted to have reached that stage in my life. I remembered myself sitting in the hospital getting poked, probed, and drugged up to the eyeballs not knowing if I would ever have the normal life that I was dreaming about. I finally had that life and was finally accepted.

One day, as it was nearing the end of my school experience, I was in science class and the whole classroom was involved in a friendly discussion when, all of a sudden, the teacher encouraged me to say a few words as she knew that I could and that I had a lot more self-confidence. She also knew that I would probably end up regretting not speaking while I had the opportunity to do so and had the full, undivided attention of the class. I was extremely nervous in that moment and began laughing as the teacher encouraged me. Everybody waited anxiously presumably wondering if I would really speak. I took a deep breath and said my name, "Tracey". I said it twice because my first attempt was not great. As soon as I did that broke the ice for me and I felt amazing, I did not want to stop. I then proceeded in saying a number of the girls' names as clear as day, and they were all shocked, as was I. They were asking me if it hurts me to talk and I said that it does not but that it takes time loosening my muscles and building myself up to do it. They were literally shouting from the roof tops, "Tracey can talk!" The encouragement I got that day was unbelievable and amazing. I was over the moon. As I was leaving school that day I had a spring in my step and felt like leaping home. It was my best school day by far.

The Leaving Certificate

When my leaving certificate came around, the school once again supported me greatly by providing me with my own room so I could concentrate on the exam in peace. The room was also required because Sandra was with me to provide me the needed assistance. I remember on the day of one exam, in particular, I was running late as Mam and I were stuck in traffic. I remember being in such a panic. I told Mam that I thought it best for me to run to the school. She agreed and wished me the best of luck. I ran as though my life depended on it. As I arrived at the school the principal and guidance teacher were waiting anxiously in the corridor for me. Sandra came out of the office and took me straight into the exam room and I knew by her demeanour that she was not impressed with me. These thoughts were confirmed when she gave out to me saying that I was ten minutes late for an important exam. I immediately broke down into tears and started breathing in a panicked manner. As I had got myself into a state of panic, Sandra gave me water and attempted to console me as she calmly said we had lots of time. In the end, I did calm down and managed to get my head together. I concentrated and finished before my allocated time. Sandra congratulated me saying that she had been shocked to see me cry. She admired how I had kept going, saying that she would not have been as strong. She knew that I was under pressure that day. The principal popped his head in to check if I was ok but by then I was relieved and proud of myself that I had made it through.

Saying goodbye to secondary school

Because of me being the first disabled student to attend that school it opened the doors for far more disabled students to attend in the following years. This was due in large part to how much the school wanted to assist me and other disabled children to attend mainstream secondary school. While I had attended the school they had shown their commitment by assisting me greatly along the way and also bringing the building up to standards sufficiently to cater for any and all disabilities. They had done this by putting in place wheelchair ramps and toilets for wheelchair users. They had done them and me proud and made me feel safe and welcome during my school years. When it was time for my graduation, which took a many months to prepare for, I could not believe that I had finally reached the end of my school journey. Mam and Stepdad attended my Graduation Mass, which was a really lovely event. When the principal stood up to give his speech he made a special mention of me and how at first they did not know what to do but over time they had learnt as well as teaching. He said that "Because of Tracey, we are all aware of the need for having the facilities in place to accept many more disabled students. Tracey turned the hardest of girls into caring girls who love her for being the inspiring, kind, funny, and outgoing person that is she. She will go far and inspire and help others. Thank you for coming here, Tracey." Everyone had tears in their eyes including my stepdad, which was surprising because it generally takes a lot to set him off. All the other girls hugged me saying that they would miss Tracker!

My years spent in primary and secondary school became the best years for me. They made me realise that, even at the hardest and most difficult moments of our lives, we are never alone if we keep faith in ourselves and in others. Sandra had always said that I loved school and that I was always truly motivated to do well; a hard worker who never wanted a day off because I had so much drive in me. I would not change one single day that I spent in school.

Bearing my Cross, but not alone

When discussing my struggling transition from the hospital having been diagnosed with dystonia and the steps that I had to take to reintegrate myself back into the real world, I believe that the expression, "We all have our crosses to bear" explains to a certain extent the difficult experiences that I endured. During my transition, I not only had to readjust to life with my new disability but I also had to raise people's awareness to the fact that the new Tracey was no different to the old Tracey. Understandably, when you take that expression at face value it can leave you with quite an isolated feeling. However, even though we do all have our own crosses to bear that does not mean that we must bear them alone. From my experience of living with this disability for over twenty years and meeting truly encouraging people along the way, I now have the knowledge and maturity to recognise that simple fact. I wish to take this opportunity to thank every single individual who pushed me on.

My message to everybody is this: we are all here to help each other along our different life paths and, while we do all have our own individual struggles, if we offered support and assistance to one another our own 'cross' would become lighter and easier to carry.

"When watching after yourself, you watch after others.
When watching after others, you watch after yourself."
- The Buddha

Chapter 5
Frustrations

"To conquer frustration, one must remain intensely focused on the outcome, not the obstacles" – T.F. Hodge

Many of the drastic changes that took effect from the time I got dystonia have had equally drastic effects on my mentality over the years: the limitations of my hand functions, feeling like I have to be constantly supervised while eating due to fears of choking because of the limitation on my ability to swallow correctly and safely among numerous other things. None of these, however, compare to the distress I have experienced time and time again for over twenty years due to the simple fact that I cannot speak. Such a simple thing that people who can do take for granted. Because I cannot do this simple thing as easily as others I have felt...for the longest time...like an involuntary social recluse, which is quite frustrating indeed. I have, however, found ways of adapting over the years by using other ways of communication. It is now just about the people around me adapting along with me.

When I can't communicate

Do you know that the total number of muscles that are involved in speaking is eleven? This means that if you have a muscular disability like dystonia it takes a lot of concentration to relax these muscles. The muscles in my throat are affected by the dystonia and the concentration involved in relaxing my tongue enough to get my words out is immense. Not been able to communicate properly is one of my hardest and most frustrating challenges. The ability to verbally communicate is such an important part of you as a person. It suggests the type of person you are and it holds a very personal and important role for you. When you are unable to verbally communicate, you can be perceived by some people as stupid. "Is there a brain in there?" Because I have dystonia a lot of people do not have the patience or the time to get to know me and they can be very awkward around me which is both frustrating and saddening.

Prior to my disability kicking in, I was a chatter box just like Mam, so not being able to speak from the age of eight has been extremely difficult for me. It has left me feeling socially isolated for the majority of my teens and early twenties at a time when socialising is vitally important in the development of a person. As a knock-on effect to this isolation, I have developed extremely low self-confidence. Even though I am aware of all the amazing things I have achieved in my life and the accomplishments I have made I am still very self-conscious, which I attribute to the social isolation I have experienced for most of my life. It is not that I was purposefully isolating myself as I felt I was no good, quite the opposite, in fact. I would take part in so many different things in the community such as drama just to try to make friends. I did make a few friends but people had an awful habit of coming into my life one minute then dropping me the next and this obviously made my self-confidence issues worse. I have always battled with myself over this because there have been times where I felt so isolated; there would not be a sinner around to call my friend. I started from a young age convincing myself that it was my fault and that I was not good enough or worth anyone's time. These temporary moments of self-pity, as rare as they were, were my lowest points because I generally have a very optimistic outlook on life, even taking into consideration the fact that I have a disability that makes social interaction extremely challenging.

A lot of people who know me do not realise this but I can actually talk! Now, when I say that, do not assume that I have been lying this entire time! When I say I can talk I do not mean in the same way as a 'normal' person with full control over their vocal cords. I just mean I have my own way of talking, which only a few people (mainly Patrick and Mam) can understand. The reason I do not go around talking to everyone the way I do to my family and Patrick is mainly due to my low self-confidence mixed with the fact that I do not like the way I sound in the least. If you can imagine not having use of your tongue to make words when you talk that is how I sound. It actually is quite difficult at times to understand me and it is made more difficult if

I am stressed, emotional or tired because obviously, these things affect my muscles. A lot of the sounds I make are 'muffled' as it is very seldom that I can get my tongue to hit the top of my palate which means I cannot pronounce my words correctly. Due to the difficulty, people would have in understanding me plus the lack of confidence I would have in actually talking to someone I find it easier to just carry on accepting peoples' automatic assumptions that I cannot speak. It is easier for everyone while understandably very frustrating for me. I am aiming to work on these issues, however, as I am determined that one day I will talk normally again.

What it feels like

I can feel so isolated from the world at times like I am trapped inside my head and the world is just flying by. I can participate in other people's lives at times but mostly I am just observing, from the sidelines. I can be in a crowded room and I can still feel on my own, listening to the different conversations going on around me, a lot of it is just small talk. People sometimes talk for the sake of talking. It really is a powerful tool to be given as by just saying something nice about someone you can boost their confidence. Or you can do the opposite and say something to make the person feel bad and temporarily destroy their self-confidence. That is how powerful the spoken word is.

What I want to say

Personally, if I could communicate properly, I would want the world to know how amazing my mam and stepdad are as they have given and still give so much love and support to each of their children. They are always there to help anyone and everyone who asks, leaving themselves last. That act of complete selflessness is not the right way to be, I know. You have to put yourself first; then and only then do you tend to the needs of others. But they are learning to start doing just that though. They have both had very tough and difficult lives; not least the stress and shock of what happened to me. Mam and Stepdad have such unbelievable unwavering strength to soldier on and to try to see the good in their lives. Their willingness to carry on is amazing. Even after everything that has gone, they have managed to hold on to their sense of humour along the tough road too and they are brilliant craic to be around. A night out is such a laugh with them, so I certainly love to talk highly about Mam and Stephen. I suppose putting them in my book like this, is a good way to show how much I appreciate them.

Mam is very honest and she would describe every detail of her day. She literally does not care and it is funny because she is so open, just saying it how it is. Fair play to her, I say, as there are so many people who forcefully choose their words so carefully. I admire Mam. You should be able to say what you want to say if you are an adult and have experienced so many bad things, and if you are still able to have a laugh and a joke at the same time, then great. It is perfectly innocent, in my opinion. Why keep following the imaginary rule book? Trying to abide by what is perceived by some people as socially acceptable? When it comes to speaking, I would give anything to be able to verbalise in any way at all, socially acceptable or otherwise.

Mix up in communication

It can prove difficult for me to communicate in my own way outside in the 'real' world. However, as I get older, I may find that I am able to overcome my fears of letting my voice out and actually speak to someone aside from Patrick and Mam. At times I can make a sound when people are engaging in conversation with me so instead of me just nodding along. Sometimes when I make a sound and I can hear myself I do think, "That was louder than I expected". I actually get a fright. In that moment I am seeing how the person reacts to me and nine out of ten times usually there is no judgement, "Oh my God, did you just make a sound? I thought you were a mute," they might say.

Trust me, I am far from mute. There are times I want to let out my real voice and not give a damn, but when I do I try and nothing comes out. It is like when I did some one-on-one fitness training and I went running on the treadmill. My trainer kept turning the speed up, my legs were flying, my heart was racing, and sweat was pumping from my body. The trainer would have me fairly close to the top speed on the machine and then they would knock it up to the next level. The trainer believed in me and they knew I was well capable for that speed. At times I really want to scream, not because I want to quit, but because screaming allows me to release power and gives me the resilience to keep going. I find it hard to focus on my voice when my body is moving. I would be killing myself on the treadmill and out comes the tiniest sound I can make. It is more a sound of panic, to be honest, afraid I would fall flat on my face. When I am out walking with Patrick and Mam and we are chatting, I want to add my part to the conversation but I have to stop and say it. Trying to move while trying to talk clearly is a technique that is quite hard as speaking requires so much energy; I need to relax my muscles as much as possible. If I am tired, stressed or sick it is harder for me to be understood. The environment can also affect me, for example, if it is windy, raining, cold, hot, or calm. It is weird, I know, but so much of what goes on both inside my body and outside in the world can affect my ability to be understood clearly.

Over the years, I have been to many speech and language therapy clinics who try to assist in any way they can with my inability to talk. Aside from a 'touch talker' device, they provided me with exercises to do from an early age to try and help improve the muscles in my throat and my tongue. I found that while I know now they were only trying to help, at the time it seemed to me that they were torturing me. At times it also felt that they were screaming at me to get me to do stuff that was then extremely difficult for me. Again, I now fully acknowledge that, although at the time this was a truly horrendous experience for me as I was so young, it was all for my benefit in the long run.

There are times when people can assume that I am saying the opposite to what I am actually saying because it takes me time to relax my muscles before I am finished with what I am trying to say. People can guess and put words in my mouth, which they do. I am not criticising Mam but I find her guilty of this. Mam is a busy woman. When I try to speak with my voice, I will admit there are times when I can catch her at a bad time when I know she has a hundred other things going on in her head. Mam can give off these vibes to me at times that she is rushing me to say what I want to say, which in turn makes it harder for me to be understood because I am getting myself anxious. I know it is not a piece of cake trying to understand me. Sometimes Mam can think I am saying something that is so stupid when in fact she is not really listening closely to what I am actually saying. I am able to show my frustrations at the mix up in communicating more with Patrick. If he cannot understand me, he keeps getting me to keep trying or else I resort to having to spell each word out. If I'm doing something like charades, which apparently I am bad at, and people do not understand me, I just have to take a deep breath in and try to come up with another way to get my point across. Sometimes, if I have walked out without my phone and I find myself in a situation where I need to say something, I would need to find a way I can communicate. One recent example of this was when I was going to an appointment and got the bus into town. I realised I was going to be late and I had run out of credit. I needed to ask someone to ring the clinic and inform the receptionist that I was going to be a bit late. I went into a shop, a fairly upmarket one. I approached a member of staff and signalled for her to read the message I had just typed up, which outlined my current dilemma and asked if she could ring the clinic for me. She said that she was not allowed to use a phone on the sales floor and that the phones behind the desk were for business use only so she could not help me. To say I found this annoying is an understatement; not only was she extremely rude in her answer but she also made me feel very self-conscious because she looked at me as if I were a chancer. By this stage, I was definitely going to be late because my appointment was for 12.00 and I had got on the bus at 12.00. I looked around desperately for someone on the bus who could help me but the bus had mainly elderly people on it and I am not criticising the elderly but some of them are very quick at pre-judging and can be very stand-offish, which is understandable given their age and frailty. I noticed, however, a girl down the back who was probably a bit younger than me so I proceeded to make my way down to her and sat next to her. It took me ages to get the confidence to show her the message on my phone asking her to ring the clinic and inform them I was running late but when I did I felt a great sense of relief as she obliged without hesitation. At moments like that, I really appreciate the unquestionable helpfulness of some people in the world. Nowadays everyone is so preoccupied with their own life that they barely pay heed to other people's needs. This, however, was not one of those times, thankfully.

Situations like that are common enough in my day-to-day life but I have always had the resilience to not let it get in the way of living a full life to the best of my ability. I always find ways to overcome challenges and I always make sure that even if initially there is a mix up in communication I will always find a way to get my true message across.

How people treat me

Over the years, since developing dystonia, I have attended many counsellors to try and help me deal with the trauma I endured all those years ago. However, none of them were ever able to fully understand my situation until recently. I have been attending a local counsellor for the past few months and she has made me fully understand what happened that day at Playzone and all the days thereafter. She has told me that, given how young I was, and not fully aware of what was happening to me, or how to deal with it, that at times, even as an adult,

I can become emotionally shutdown in response to that trauma. This happens when feelings are too intense or overwhelming to process and get shut out as a way of coping. This, to me, combined with the social isolation I endured, makes perfect sense. At times, I am unable to handle social situations or large-scale dramatic events. I just shut down. This can lead to one of my biggest frustrations, a frustration that I should have control over, a frustration with myself. Because of this form of emotional scarring, it can take me a while to relax in an environment even if I am around people who know me. I can still feel insecure in myself. I forget how to be the person I want to be. It is a lack of self-confidence as I am afraid that I will mess up. I can get Patrick to do things for me like get me a drink or napkins, etc. I find that I am worried about putting myself out there and if I let something fall that I could draw attention to myself. I would then feel like a spare tool. It is frustrating because I really want to interact more and show people that I am interested in whatever is going on. It is only towards the end of the night, or event, or whatever that I start to feel more relaxed and realise that people are not there to judge me, I just need to get over my own insecurities. Afterwards, I play the day over in my mind and start regretting what I have done or said. I am hard on myself. Why didn't I make more of an effort? Show my fun side? Show I do care what others say? I then get knots in my stomach and stress myself out even more. I begin to wonder what people must be thinking of me. Is she a shy, stand-offish person who is distracted by other things going on around her and can only communicate through her phone? However, I do not want that, so, please, if you ever see me in what appears to be that type of situation then I give you permission to tick me off because I do not want to be 'that' person. There is an expression about trying to help someone get over a situation and it is "Build a bridge and get over it". This is great in theory but what if the foundations of the bridge have been badly damaged at such an early stage into its construction that it could cause great difficulty in the construction of the rest of that bridge? I am an optimist, however, and even though I said "great difficulty" I did not say impossible.

Even though I have day-to-day struggles and frustrations, I still count myself extremely lucky. Compared to some other people's struggles, mine are nothing. I used to be consumed by self-pity and anger and quickly realised that those feelings were getting me nowhere. I would never be able to achieve all I have done today if had not fought those negative self-destructive thoughts.

I have always found it vital to continue having a great life by my standards, despite my physical limitations and the way people treat me. I have learnt to get on with it as best I can while keeping my wits about me as I do not wish to be taken advantage of. It is being able to tell the difference between someone who is offering genuine support and someone who is trying to take advantage of your weaknesses that you learn from experience as you go along in life. I have learnt from numerous mistakes of trusting the wrong people over the years. If you ever find yourself in a situation where help is required then do not be ashamed to look around you and ask for it; just make sure that it is genuine support from a trusted individual.

Keep doing what you can do; your disadvantages give you your own unique limitations. What you must do is be unique enough to surpass those limitations in whatever way you can.

The 'Spotlight' is on me

Out of the many different ways I have been treated over the years the one that still upsets me and makes me extremely self-conscious is when people stare at me. I understand that at times I can stand out in a crowded room, especially if I am stressed or paranoid because my face muscles go tense. However, it is still not nice to be stared at when you are trying to go about your daily life. An extreme example of this was when I was coming back from one of my appointments; I got off the bus in town and made my way to get the second bus to bring me home. Town was packed that day and as I was walking through I was getting extremely stressed and my muscles were getting tenser as this went on. By the time I got on my second bus and took my seat I was extremely stressed by the crowds I had just waded through. I was sitting there trying to calm myself when, out of the corner of my eye, I caught a boy in the row in front staring at me. Again I tried to remain calm and relax myself as best I could. I actively avoided looking at him as I knew that would only make the situation worse for me. His mother who was sitting beside him asked him what he was looking at and then proceeded to look at me. She then looked at him again and then me. She got up out of her seat and took her son with her and moved to the other side of the bus. She then said to me, in front of everyone on the bus, "I moved because you're scaring my son". That was not only a shock to me, that someone would be as ignorant as to make a statement like that, but it was distressing that she said it loud enough so everyone could hear her. When I got home, Mam could see that I was obviously shaken and upset. I told her what had happened. She wanted to go out and kill the woman for being that ignorant because she obviously hates anyone putting me down. My stepdad said that it was not me, nothing I can do can make people any less ignorant or rude and that the problems with society lies in each individual that actively partakes in society. Every individual brings their own piece of input to the table, be it bad or good. Some people have no consideration as to how hurtful their words can really be. Again, words are so powerful.

Despite constantly feeling like I stick out like a sore thumb, I recently read something very interesting as to why people feel that they are constantly being stared at like I do. It is a psychological term coined in 1999 called the spotlight effect. What this term means is that people tend to believe they are noticed more than they really are. Given that one is constantly in the centre of one's own world, an accurate evaluation of how much one is noticed by others has shown to be uncommon. This sounds good in theory, however, in reality, it still takes away so much self-confidence from anyone disabled or not who is temporarily subjected to this fairly common and socially unethical human behaviour, particularly when you know with certainty that you are being stared at. However, even though I used to take offence to being scrutinised I now understand fully that people are only staring at me because of my uniqueness. They see a woman with a disability and probably automatically feel sorry for me when in fact it is I who feels sorry for them because their lives must be pretty uneventful. They clearly have not travelled much and witnessed the vastness of this planet if they are surprised to see a disabled woman on a bus, on her own, in Dublin. Small-minded people living in their small "safe" bubbles.

False Hopes and Disappointments

Disappointments and knocks in life are hard to take especially the ones you had your heart set on being life changing in a positive way; where you could actually see yourself doing the things that have been promised or expected. When that vision does not happen exactly the way you imagined or not at all, then it does kick you in the teeth. You find yourself disappointed for yourself firstly but also you are so worried what others will think of you. I hate to think that everyone looks at me as if I have failed and that I am not capable of fulfilling my aspirations. I know it sounds like I am being paranoid, but that is the impression some people give me. I can sense it immediately.

Deep Brain Stimulation (DBS)

DBS or Deep Brain Stimulation is a medical device that is primarily used to treat people with Parkinson's. The device is surgically 'installed' into the patient's brain and controls the electric flow created within the brain. Many people who suffer with Parkinson's have seen great benefits in both relaxing and controlling their muscles after the device is in place. Doctors have recently seen many benefits from this procedure being used in treating people with dystonia. However, as there are many different types of dystonia and, as I have stated before, my particular form is rare, they have not seen anyone with my form reap any benefits yet. I was one of the first guinea pigs to see if it could help in any way, shape, or form.

There were a lot of high hopes that this new procedure would benefit me. The doctors were all very excited about it, encouraging my family and me into believing that it would improve my mobility. They gave a description as to how it would work and the amount of work I would have to endure in the build-up to the procedure, which did sound tough. Up until that point I had never had a major operation before, just a few teeth taken out when I was a child but which was done via local anaesthetic. The one awkward thing was that the operation had to take place in Oxford because it had not yet been brought to Ireland. The doctors kept hyping up the procedure talking about the successful cases from people who were extremely restricted prior to the DBS and then after it they were back doing their normal hobbies again such as horse riding. It all sounded very positive and I believed it would work for me because the doctors and my family believed it would. Of course, I was not going to have an internal debate with myself and weigh up the benefits with the risks and what ifs. I was ready for my life to change. I was twenty-one at the time and was at the stage where all my friends, which I had made such an effort to make, had disappeared; nobody was there to assist me in my decision making.

Every night without fail I would put on music and I would stand in my room on my own visualising myself fully mobile and relaxed. I would see my posture straight, my hands were relaxed enough to allow me to open and close them effortlessly. I would be getting ready to walk onto the stage to sing. I would visualise every detail of what I was wearing; my hair style, my make-up and my facial expressions. I was so beautiful it gave me butterflies. I felt the nervousness as I was about to walk on stage. I could hear the crowd chanting. I did not know what they were saying but through the chants, I could hear my name several times. I walked up each step to get the top as I began to make my grand entrance onto the stage. People started to clap and repeat their chants of "Tracey! Tracey! Tracey!". Trying to remain calm, my right leg began to shake, and I laughed. The nerves were getting stronger and I was saying to myself, "Oh finally this is happening." I made my entrance onto the stage. Everyone stopped and stared. This time, I wanted people to stare and not take their eyes off of me for even one second. I was stunning. I stood there for a moment and took it all in. I could see Mam, Stepdad, my two brothers, my nanny, and granddad all smiling at me, with John Carty and Brian sitting right behind them also looking so happy. Brian had tears in his eyes. I looked around the audience and took in a big deep breath. I was given my microphone as the music started playing. I told myself once again, "I am powerful. I have got this". I began to sing. During the song, the music stopped and it was just me belting it out on my own. When I finished, everyone was so quiet you could hear a pin drop, and everyone had tears in their eyes. Everyone then stood up and clapped intensely, roared, and whistled. This vision was magical to me. Tears rolled down my face as I unwillingly recessed back towards my reality. I knew however that this time I would be getting closer towards achieving aspects of that fantasy with the assistance of the DBS so I went for it. I made my way to Oxford to get a procedure done that I assumed would change my life for the better.

When I made my way to Oxford for the operation I was put up in a B&B with Mam, my aunt, and brother Dean. The night before the procedure, Mam washed my hair as I did not want to go into an operating room with dirty hair, which is normal, I assume. The next day while I was awaiting the procedure the doctors were running their routine checks on me. This involved an MRI scan. After the scan, the doctors came out looking confused and informed us that something was interfering with the scan as they could not get a correct image of my head. They asked Mam had we done anything out of the ordinary last night to which Mam replied, "No, we just washed her hair". That was followed by an instant disapproving realisation from the surgeons who said we should not have done that. Apparently, whatever the shampoo or conditioner contains interferes with the ability of the MRI providing an accurate image of the head. How were we to know? The surgeons attempted to wash my hair to try and remove any excess shampoo/conditioner and see if they could have better luck from the MRI. They did not succeed however and we were told that the procedure had to be cancelled. We had to stay in Oxford until the following week for a repeat performance.

After the procedure, I awoke in recovery and it took me a long time to readjust. I felt very vulnerable. All I wanted was to see Mam, Dean, and my Aunt Helen, all of who had travelled over to Oxford with me. When I was brought into the ward I could feel myself emotionally welling up. "Where is Mam?" I thought to myself. Then the three members of my family walked into the ward all looking a bit apprehensive at how I would look. Mam came over to me and almost immediately proceeded in carrying out the "mother's inspection" of the wounds left on my head after the operation. "You look fine." My head felt very heavy and I went into emotional hysterics. I was crying and I could not stop; I was overwhelmed by the fact that it had finally happened. Mam was trying to calm me down. My nanny rang and attempted to make me laugh and my aunty was rubbing my feet. Eventually, I calmed down. I was exhausted and sweating. Dean came over and dampened my forehead with a cloth.

Post operation

The doctor's first attempt at DBS proved to be unsuccessful and I had to make the journey over to Oxford, four years later, to move the DBS to another part of my body as the doctors hoped that by them moving it this may make a difference. After the second operation, Mam, Dean, and I went on some day trips in Oxford, to make it feel like more of a holiday for Dean, as he was quite young at the time and did not fully understand what was going on. We went on boat trips, got pictures with monuments, and played lots of ping pong. Given that I was still in recovery from the operation, I was like a zombie. It was difficult to move around and I did not know how I was going to survive the day. It was all worth it, however, when I saw how happy it had made Dean.

I grew this barrier up after the operation and felt a comfort from being in Oxford. When it was time to go back home, I was suddenly afraid as I did not see or feel any noticeable difference. The doctor said it would take time and that it would be better to be around my own surroundings. I did not want my family and friends to see that there had not been any drastic difference yet, as to me it would feel that I had let them down. I did not want to feel that the procedure had failed.

Needless to say, The DBS did not work as much as everyone had hoped. It had, in fact, made me worse. It made all my muscles tighter regardless of what setting it was put on. There were numerous settings and they were all tried over a number of years. I even went back to Oxford to get the position of the device moved; this did not make any difference, however. People made me feel that it was my fault it did not work because I could not adapt to the different settings and because I was used to being the way I was that I was indirectly interfering with the DBS preventing it from working by not relaxing enough and not allowing it to do what it had to.

I felt very claustrophobic when the realisation hit me that the DBS had been a failure. It had been a false hope that I had hyped up in my head as being the answer to my many struggles and frustrations over the previous years. In a very melodramatic manner, I desperately sought for the ground to swallow me up. Throughout the whole time after the operation, I was trying not to make any noticeable references to the fact that I felt worse. Everyone came up to see; to see if I had been miraculously healed. I felt like I was in a circus. I felt no good changes and I was more stressed out about whether or not I was being judged. I began to develop agoraphobia shortly after returning from the disappointments endured in Oxford. I knew, however, that I needed to focus on getting myself back out into the real world again as I was not willing to become a victim of anxiety due to the failed and false hope that I, and everyone I knew, had invested so much of my life on. I began taking baby steps in achieving this. I did this, first, by walking to the end of my road and back. I have never been as afraid in my entire life, as I was extremely self-conscious. I felt eyes were piercing at my every move. All these negative comments started swarming around my head. "Look at that poor girl. My God, she looks really tense and fatigued. Obviously, the surgery didn't work."

If I saw people approaching ahead of me, I would get myself worked up and would think to myself, "I have to stop and calm myself down." My heart would be pumping in my chest and I would feel lightheaded and my body would keep trying to go into a spasms. I would attempt to get myself together before the person passed. That was a really difficult and frustrating time on my body. I would also experience this anytime cars passed by. Whenever I would go up to the local park, I would rush to the entrance gate from my mam's house and walk around it as far away as possible from the busy road that was triggering and intensifying these nerve-wracking anxiety attacks.

During those times, I felt the need to be accompanied by someone if I wanted to go further than the local park. I would get my brother Dean to cycle down to Charlestown Shopping Centre in Finglas with me. The walk down to Charlestown was a straight enough journey and took about fifteen to twenty minutes. I felt at the time that it was essential for me to walk further than the local park and I missed the random strolls to the shops. Even though at that time, Dean was only a young kid, he was all too aware of my fears. He also saw my determination to overcome those fears and he wanted to help me get back on track. Dean would cycle up ahead of me and if he went too far he would always turn back. I would try to ignore the cars and passers-by telling myself that I had to keep going. It was extremely hard but, my God, when I reached the shops I'd be so relieved! Dean saw how happy I was at making these achievements.

Mam got me to go to the shops with her a few times to assist me in my recovery. Eventually, I began to feel comfortable again. It then reached the stage that I felt that maybe I could look around myself. After making that decision, anytime I went to the shops with Mam, I always made sure that I could see her. One time, in particular, I lost her and began to panic. I stood in the main part of the shop to better her chances of spotting me. At that moment I wanted desperately to be invisible. I was trying not to draw attention to myself. I felt that people kept staring at me as they walked by. I tried to relax my breathing to remain calm; not crying at that moment was such a challenge. Eventually, I saw Mam, which was an extraordinary relief for me. I wanted to run to her and hug her tightly. In that moment, I'd had enough of the shops for one day.

One time while I was at home and was having a bad panic attack, all these emotions began rushing through my head, which in turn greatly intensified my physical disability. I could not stop crying and struggled desperately to catch my breath. Mam began to panic and asked one of her neighbours to come up as soon as possible. She was a good friend to us and had a good understanding of my struggles at that time. When she came up I was in the sitting room still in a state. She sat beside me and put her hand on my shoulder and started breathing loudly but calmly in an obvious effort to calm me down. Eventually, I did and she told me "You are so strong. If I went through what you did, I'd be hiding up the chimney!" she said and pointed to the fireplace. "The fact that you go out trying to get past those barriers is amazing. You really should admire yourself because I do."

It really helped me to hear those words. I realised in that moment that I needed to get out and about again.

The physical aftermath of DBS

I was ten times tenser with the DBS. My two arms kept trying to pull back; my head was up and pulled forward like a tortoise. My jaw was tightly clamped closed, which was deliberate as to prevent me from dribbling because I was so tense I could not swallow correctly. A pool of saliva would gather in my mouth. I would be so stressed about dribbling in front of people, and I would not be able to wipe it quickly enough as my arms were locked tensely behind my back.

I could not even grip my cup because my hands would not hold things correctly. I was so frustrated, I got myself in such panics, screaming and crying, "I'm worse! I can't even grip my cup!"

Even if I did manage, the problems still occurred with my neck. I was not able to bend my head down because my neck muscles were tensely rigid. It was torture. There were no explanations for these symptoms, which was also frustrating. I had to wait for my next appointment in Oxford before I could get any answers to these frustrating symptoms from the supposed 'cure' to my condition. I was left waiting a good few months. I remember hearing the doctor clearly repeating again and again, "it will either improve your mobility or do nothing but it doesn't make you worse". I thought to myself from hearing those words that I had nothing to lose. I am a big believer in trying anything once if it does not make my situation worse. However, I was disappointed after putting myself through all of that only for it to in fact intensify the dystonia. I honestly felt so dejected after getting myself so far from the initial blow that I was dealt at the age of eight and the success made with the Endorphin Release only to be kicked back a few steps by the DBS. As I write this, the DBS has been successfully removed and I have got myself back to the physical standard at which I was prior to DBS being even mentioned all those years ago.

DBS took up a massive chunk of my life for so long. Eight years to be exact. I would spend those years with this uncertainty in my life, afraid to make any plans, all in the expectation of being summoned over to Oxford.

Personally, I feel that the DBS did not work for me because of the pressure I was under given the hype from the doctors and subsequently my family. Everyone, including me, expected a miracle to happen. However, despite me having to go over to Oxford back and forth over a five-year period and getting two separate operations done within this time, my miracle never occurred. I was one of the first with my form of dystonia to undergo this procedure. My chances were always going to be 50/50.

NRH

The NRH or National Rehabilitation Hospital has done and is doing, amazing work on people who suffer many different types of brain trauma in Ireland. A number of years after the DBS proved to be unsuccessful it was thought that it may be good for me to attend this hospital to see if they could assist me in anyway and also for me to get intense daily training specifically tailored to my needs. When this was proposed to me, I immediately thought that might benefit me because I knew the physical results I got when I constantly worked out. My going into the NRH all seemed to happen very quickly. I was expecting to go in on the October of 2015. That was when I was told a bed would be made available. I was due to start my evening college course in psychology at the end of that September, the classes for which were meant to be on every Monday evening. It was agreed, however, that I could go into the NRH every Tuesday morning and stay for three days a week.

That evening following the agreement, Mam got a call from the NRH saying that a bed had become available and I was to go in that night to make sure it was not taken. Mam subsequently rang Patrick and told us. I was not ready and had nothing prepared. I was in a panic and felt as if it were a life or death situation.

When I eventually got into the hospital I was placed in an open ward. There were many other patients in the ward all suffering from a variety of different illnesses. Lying in a bed opposite me was an elderly man who appeared to be very ill. I was very confused because all the nurses in the ward were referring to him as a woman and constantly called him by a lady's name. I plucked up the courage to ask one of the security personnel whether that patient was male. He laughed as if to say "Don't ask". It turned out that the elderly man thought he was a woman trapped in a man's body. I have nothing against that. In fact, I instantly felt sad as this was an elderly man who had been looked upon as a male all his life convinced he was a female, trapped inside his own body. What I could not grasp, however, was that he did not act in a feminine way.

He made me laugh the way he went on; he was so demanding of the nurses, he would shout every few minutes, "Nurse, Nurse, Nurse". Always in the same mundane tone. It was funny if I am being truthful and it kept me going. I saw the funny side initially and then it got a bit annoying after the first few days of listening to the same thing being repeated over and over, being woken up every morning to, "Nurse, Nurse, Nurse,"

The first morning when I awoke I got liquidised mush for breakfast, having ordered something solid. I was not impressed and questioned it immediately. I was told that was my prescribed diet, I went ballistic and told them that I could have solid food. I was informed that they prefer me to eat soft foods while there so as to avoid the risk of choking. To say this was very upsetting to me is an obvious understatement because I am more than capable of eating normal food once it is cut up for me. I do not require it being blended into mush. My family and I had spent years previous to that contesting that "recommendation" by the doctors because I know what I can and cannot do. Besides, the fact remained that if I was to choke I was surrounded by medically trained people who could assist me if need be. When Mam arrived she could tell I was annoyed and I gestured for her to look at the food I was given and expected to eat. Mam took me to the hospital café to get me a sandwich. She told the nurse where we were going. The nurse objected but Mam replied that she would be with me. I even got Patrick to bring me up Subway food later that day and every subsequent visit thereafter. It was great to be able to eat normal food that I knew I could handle.

The therapy sessions I had while in the hospital were brilliant. I had speech therapy, occupational therapy, and physiotherapy. This was amazing and of great benefit. The staff were all lovely and really helpful, but they started to acknowledge the fact that the place was not for me and that I had done a lot of work on myself already. They could also see that I was getting fed there, which was not helping them to assist me. I have always trained really hard, however, I find that this is pointless when my mind is being weakened by people telling me what I should or should not do. After just a few weeks attending the NRH, I knew that it had reached the stage that I had to leave. I wrote a letter explaining this and gave it to one of the therapists. A meeting was arranged to discuss my issues where they listened to me and fully understood my problems. They said that they admired my strength and courage. I left feeling dejected, feeling that the time I had spent in there had been a waste and I was disappointed at getting my hopes up only to be shot back down again. I found myself questioning, "Why does everything get talked up like it will really add benefit when really it does the complete opposite?"

After these big knock-backs and false hopes, I am supposed to act like it does not affect me when in actual fact it does to a certain extent. However, I have realised along the way that I can choose the extent to which these false hopes affect my morale and self-confidence. Sure, I have my moments of despair pondering over the 'what ifs'.

These are only brief, however, as it is and always has been vital for me to move forward. I feel that I have the right attitude now. Nothing is impossible.

Acting as an Extra

I used to love acting and it helped me grow as a person. As soon as my stage experience ended, because of my age and the fact the theatre group I was a part of had moved on to a bigger theatre, I tried for many years searching for a drama group I could join and get the same level of support and encouragement I'd had from the youth drama. Nobody would even entertain me, however. I believe they just saw my disability and that the time they would have to put into me put them off. It was very disappointing. Drama was such an important social activity that I had been a part of. I did many writing classes, which were great too, but I really missed being out there. As soon as drama ended reality hit me again; there was no drama I could get into.

A few years ago, I tried registering as an extra with Mam, because Mam is very dramatic and she would be great at it. Mam got called a few times, but I never did, so I wrote a letter to the company asking them why. They said it was due to me having a physical disability and that for insurance reasons they find it difficult finding me work. I was raging. I explained everything that I had been involved in prior to that and that I believed that to make programmes more realistic, the disabled should not only be able to take part but should feature in any programme that is supposed to be based on real life. What harm is it having a person with a physical disability being given a part of walking up the street? I told them if I am not getting called I want my money back. Within a few days, I was to take part in Fair City with Mam. We were in a scene that was shot in the recreation centre. It did feel good but after that, I was not called again. I kind of felt they were thinking "We'll give her a try, just to shut her up". There are constant disappointments I have experienced due to my disability, which have been very frustrating for me and difficult to just let blow over. On the outside, my physical demeanour conveyed that I was too disabled to partake in more or less anything. Inside, however, was the person people hardly saw. I was not disabled; there was nothing I could not do once I believed in myself.

Every day "normal" things

Things that frustrate me on a daily basis range from dressing myself to doing my own hair. Over the years, I have learnt to find ways of managing to do things in my own way so that I can be as independent as possible. Some days, however, if I am tired, it can be really frustrating to work my muscles. My muscles are constantly having a work out. The challenge I have in dressing myself is huge. Over the years, I have worked out ways so that I can dress myself to an extent;

however, I still require help in fixing certain pieces of clothing. My hair is my biggest challenge. Living in my own apartment, since I was twenty-four, has taken me out of my comfort zone immensely.

My thumbs are often stuck in a spasm meaning I cannot really move them: when I get my thumb around a cup or pen, it can require a great amount of force to release it. At times, I wear different types of hairstyles over the weekends. I do not want to get into the habit of going up to Mam's house to get her to assist me because I do that on weekdays. However, at times I do need to because I require her help in fixing up my hair. I can usually find someone else willing to help fix my hair on weekends or holidays if I am not around Mam, which sets me up. I am happy then. The challenges I face when Patrick and I go away either abroad or somewhere in Ireland are also difficult. Firstly, neither Patrick nor I can tie up my hair so when we go away, we are hoping that there are nice people to help. Usually, there are. However, when we go abroad we sometimes struggle to be understood.

The sense of achievement I get when I do even the simplest of things like pouring myself a drink is wonderful. This boost in self-confidence leads onto bigger achievements like cooking dinner by myself, putting a wash on by myself, getting showered and washed by myself and even going to places without Mam or anyone else all have a sense of achievement and help me feel very independent.

Locking the door on a cubicle in a public toilet can prove extremely challenging for me. At times I can use my hands pretty well, however, there are times when I am so stressed or anxious that my hands go into a spasm. Locks on public bathrooms can be a nightmare especially during these times of spasms. Why they cannot be straightforward to open and lock I do not know. At times I am sure people wonder what I am doing in there for so long. Little do they know the reason why I am in there for so long is all to solve the great enigma that is the lock. If I know the lock is far too awkward, I will take a chance and just leave the door unlocked holding it closed with my outstretched hand. Obviously, I do have to make sure the coast is clear for me to go without someone walking in. Who wants to spend any longer in a cubicle than you should? They are not the nicest places on earth to get locked into and I have plenty of experiences of that same misfortune. I remember a time when I was in Heathrow Airport heading to Paris with my uncle Andrew and his girlfriend (now his wife) Kristy. I needed to go to the toilet so Kristy and I went to the ladies together. I got into the cubicle, locked the door, and did what I needed to do. When I was finished, however, I quickly realised that I was unable to unlock the door and was beginning to panic a bit about my current dilemma. Kristy, who had been waiting for me outside the cubicle for a few minutes, asked if I was ok. I responded "no" in a distressed tone so she proceeded to go into the cubicle next to me and stand on the toilet to look over into my cubicle. She quickly realised the problem I was facing in opening the door and went to get a member of staff to unlock the cubicle. She got an on-duty cleaner who had keys to the cubicles to unlock the door. I was relieved twice in the space of five minutes! In those types of situations it is hard not to panic; thankfully, however, I'd had Kristy with me. If I had gone into that toilet on my own I would probably be still in it now!

Feeling like I am not part of society

I have always wanted to work and contribute my part to society; I hate to see people not working because they get more entitlement being on the social welfare. In my eyes, that is not the way to live. I believe that if you can work and are not then you should be actively out looking for work on a daily basis rather than living off the welfare state. This problem in society is deeply rooted in the way in which governments provide assistance to the unemployed. It has imbedded into some people's psyche that as long as their government provides them with "free money" and free health care then that leaves the individuals questioning as to why they should work at all. In my view, this is a backwards way of governing as I feel that having full-time or part-time employment is a strong self-empowering tool and should be promoted and encouraged more. It has always been difficult for me to get a job, not through lack of trying; I just feel that employers are not willing to take a chance on me. I believe that employment would not only allow me to be a contributor towards society but it also would contribute on a small scale to me obtaining that one thing that most people in the world seek out...a life purpose.

Getting on with life

As I have stated previously, I have attended plenty of counselling and healing sessions throughout my life in order to help me move on from the difficult times I faced growing up with a physically and socially limiting disability. I would strongly advise anyone who finds themselves in a similar situation to speak to a professional and remember that, even though it may feel like the opposite, you are never alone. If something dramatic or negative in any way or form happens to you and you feel that it is holding you back, you may need to do the work on yourself. This could potentially mean facing your fears and frustrations head on. That is how I dealt with it.

Another piece of advice I wish to give is this: do not keep lingering on past events, remembering all the hard, sad and frustrating times asking, "Why did this happen to me?" Replaying those memories in your mind only achieves one thing: it lends power to the original feelings from the event itself, which can, in turn, make you sick, stress you out, upset you, and decrease your confidence.

Life passes us by so quickly. You cannot change your past but you can learn and take strength from it. You can show people that you are powerful and strong by being your confident, amazing self.

"You have power over your mind – not outside events.
Realise this, and you will find strength."
— Marcus Aurelius, Meditations

Chapter 6
Taking back my power

"I am not what happened to me...I am who I choose to become"

- Carl Jung

From my early childhood until late adolescence, I had felt that my good nature and vulnerability were preyed on by people whom I regarded as friends. I also felt that I was being taken advantage of. At times, I was treated like a piece of dirt; it took a long period of time for me to develop a sense of trust with anyone due to this mistreatment. I would now say to the people who treated me wrongly in the past that, due to my strength and determination, I have moved on. It is due to the strength of those values that I am the person I am today. I feel no anger or resentment towards those people now; at the time, however, I was extremely bitter and quite upset. I did not like the person I was becoming. However, in order to move on, I needed to forgive them because those self-centred people had no idea the hurt they were causing me. In my mind, I let go of all the bitterness. All I can do now is to wish them well; I do not wish them any ill-will. In order for me to create a happy life and to allow all the good to flow into it, I needed to let go of all the negativity that had built up in me. It took me a long time to release this as it was such a huge part of my mindset for so long, but I did it and I felt AMAZING. Try it yourself, the simple warmth of just letting go of all your hatred and resentment. You will feel so content and free, and you will realise what life is really all about, trust me.

"Who can't relate to the idea of leaving one chapter behind and moving on to the next?"
- Mike Shinoda

There were times in my life, particularly when I was younger, that were just long periods of me doing nothing at all with my days; times that I felt nothing was happening for me. When I was in my late teens, it felt as though my life was pointless and that I had no purpose. I was not doing anything with myself during the day – just floating around; I felt like a lost soul. There was only so much self-worthlessness I could take, however. I needed to take back control of my life and destiny I needed to get my power back, and I needed to do something worthwhile. I had no idea what direction I was going in and I had nobody in my life to assist me in achieving what I wanted. I knew I had to go out and take part in something and that no one would come knocking on my door and transfigure my life for me. I believed in myself and told myself that something would turn up for me and that it was meant to happen. I also believed that I would experience amazing opportunities if I kept being motivated and worked towards achieving my goals and making my dreams a reality.

It is very common for people who have challenges (like I do) to become victims of circumstance, feeling that they are not a part of society...however, I chose to take back my power. Society usually labels people according to their circumstances but I am more than a circumstance…

I am not 'disabled'... I am Tracey!

Endorphin Release Clinic

The doctors did not hold out much hope of improvement for me. They actually said there was a strong possibility I would get worse as time went on. Their prognosis was that the dystonia would affect my muscles so badly that I would eventually be bedridden, due to my muscles becoming progressively tighter, to the extent that my whole body would be in a constant spasm. My family were understandably very disturbed by this as they did not know what was going to happen to me. Even though I was so young, I knew by the way my family was acting around me after their chat with the doctors, that something was not right. I sensed fear from all of them, which in turn brought on the fear in me too. However, I knew deep down that something would come along and be of benefit to me and it would aid in my recovery. How right I was!

One night while in my aunt's house, Mam was pacing up and down the living room having a justified dramatic meltdown over her concerns for me, my present situation, and the uncertain future I faced. She was obstructing the TV while my nan was watching it and my nan had to keep waving at her to move out of the way because she had just noticed something potentially beneficial on *The Late Late Show*. A man called John Carty who was an endorphin releaser was being interviewed. There were a number of people in the audience who attended John's clinic due to the pain they were experiencing. In certain cases, the pain was excruciating and as of then, nothing had been working for them. When asked by the interviewer to summarise what it was he did, he said that he releases chemicals that are naturally made within the human body called endorphins. Using a gentle massage technique he takes away any restrictions i.e. tension or pain by releasing these natural chemicals in the location of discomfort. There was a woman in the audience who had suffered with sciatic pain. She explained that she could not walk for two months and had been bedridden. She had tried everything to help ease her suffering and felt no benefit in anything that she had tried. One of her friend's had recommended that she go to the Endorphin Clinic. She went twice a week at first and then gradually decreased her visits. She said that she had felt such a release and that "John took the pain away". She said that she fully believed that it would work for her because, from her first meeting, John was very confident he could be of benefit to her. She told the interviewer that she has never looked back and that she now has a new lease of life and could not be more grateful to the Endorphin Clinic. John said in his interview that he had helped a lot of people affected by car accidents who suffered with muscular pain and tension. He also said that he helps people who suffer from sciatica, frozen shoulder, back pain, stiff joints, arthritis, hip pain, whiplash, and neck pain.

My nan was engrossed in this and immediately said to my mam, "He can help Tracey." My mam was very sceptical at the time. She felt nothing was going right even though the doctors had backed off with their assumptions regarding her being the cause of my illness. I still was not allowed home at this time as the doctors thought it would be best to stay in hospital but when all the shit happened about putting me into residential care to keep me under observation, Mam felt that I could not stay in the hospital for the rest of my life. She had gone through a lot of fighting, constantly having to keep proving she was a good mother. Even after it was discovered that it was a genetic condition, the treatment of Mam by the doctors and 'specialists' did not finish completely. My nan took down John's number and the following day, she rang the Endorphin Release Clinic, explained my situation to John and that she had seen him on *The Late Late Show*. She explained to him that Mam was getting an awful time from the doctors even though it had been discovered that my condition was a genetic muscular disorder known as dystonia. My nan believed that John could help. Anything was worth a try. John did not hesitate at all. He got Mam's number and called her to arrange a meeting with her to talk about what he does and how he has helped a number of people with different muscular problems. He understood Mam's scepticism at the time. However, he wanted to help. He arranged to meet Mam in the hospital canteen. Mam gave John the background information and told him that she felt so helpless. She just wanted her daughter to live a happy, normal life and for this horrible journey we were on to stop. "It's really not fair." John comforted Mam with positive words saying. "You'll get through it". He then asked, "Can I meet your little one?" Mam agreed.

At this stage, my mam was still feeling dejected and weak. She was uncertain about whether John could really help. She knew that she needed something to come about though.

Mam and John came into my room in the hospital. Mam said, "Someone wants to meet you, Tracey." I stood in the room leaning against my bed and I immediately felt this unspoken connection with him. He was a lovely, bearded man, very warm and kind. My little face lit up. I knew from that moment that he would help me. Now, remember, I was just a little girl and John could have been anyone but my instincts told me that my prayers had just been answered. I was fed up being probed and prodded by the doctors with no end in sight. It was wearing me out.

John did a quick analysis to try and determine how extensively my muscles had been affected. He was shocked to see me that first time as he described me as being in the foetal position because of how contorted I was. He also said that he had never come across anyone like me before, which did not surprise me as my condition is very rare.

He said that he was willing to put his time into getting me right again because he believed we were good people from that brief moment he spent with us. My mam smiled and I assume thought to herself, "Ok maybe this man can help".

When my mam told the doctors about John doing the endorphin release the doctors were very wary of it being used as a treatment because it was a different approach to medicine than the modern medicine that they had been taught. The doctors were still a bit overcautious of me trying things unsupervised, even though they knew my getting sick was not due to anything my mam had or had not done. The whole team of doctors and nurses was ganging up on her, accusing her again of being a bad mother because she was trying to aid me in my recovery. John did not know my mam too well at this stage but as soon as he found out about the doctors accusations toward my mam he soon corrected their perception. He found out this through the doctors themselves who pulled him to one side during one of his visits to me and asked for a reference from him declaring that, in his view, my mam was a good mother. He, in turn, told them out straight, "You couldn't get a better mother to look after that little girl."

One thing was certain, my mam did not want the doctors to be correct in their prognosis that I would get extremely and irreversibly worse. At that time the doctors wanted to have me tube fed but there was no way that would happen now with John. He was a good support for both Mam and I. We felt protected by John, for which we were and still are very grateful to him. I needed to learn to eat by myself, which was a challenge, a challenge though that I could not overcome without self-determination and the amazing assistance I received from John. I became stronger each day. John worked on my throat and neck muscles to get them to open and expand when they were supposed to and worked on their reaction times. I needed to be fed at that time as I was still in the process of retraining the control in my hands. It felt very degrading for me to have Mam or Stepdad feeding me. My food had to be liquid or I could choke. I was very underweight, weighing in at only five stone and my bones protruded outward. Mam would make my food at home, blend it up and bring it into me in the hospital. It was bad enough that my food had to be blended, however, if I had to have the blended hospital food I think I would have cried never endingly as it was pure muck. Mam knew how stubborn I was. She did not want to see me falling through the cracks so she took it upon herself to make proper home-cooked meals that were more nourishing and that she knew I would enjoy.

The tube feeding never occurred, thank God, due to Mam, Stepdad and John who collectively kept me strong and focused. They knew if the tube feeding had happened then it would have been harder to retrain myself because I would have got too used to it. I would become reliant on it and my brain would find it harder to begin re-adjusting to the old ways of eating again. It would have been twenty steps backwards instead of forwards. They knew what was right for me.

When I got out of hospital, Mam made it her business to bring me over to John's clinic, which was behind Our Lady's Hospital, in Drimnagh. Mam had fears of driving to the Southside on the M50 especially on the Red Cow Roundabout, which was always a nightmare if you were not used to it. She would definitely be too nervous driving through town; she was used to the M50 when she drove to the Spawell in Tallaght for her line dancing. She quickly overcame the fear because she knew this was of more importance. All the staff in the Endorphin Release Clinic were so welcoming and friendly to us when we arrived. It had not been long open. The place never felt like an actual clinic to us. Mam and I were made to feel at home. The Endorphin Clinic staff took me under their wings. John was able to work on me better now. He put a lot of time and energy into me. For the first couple of sessions, the pain was bad as John had to press into each nerve to try to release the tension that had built up. There were times I would cry my eyes out.

I still wanted to go back to see John after that though. I could have said "No, it's too painful," however, my gut told me that it would be of great benefit to me in the long run. As I began to see John more and more, he really worked tirelessly on keeping my legs going. My legs were the very first thing to go on me that day in Playzone and every so often after that my legs would sporadically cease working. It was as though they'd lost all their power and my brain had forgotten how to control them. I would sit on the edge of the bed not knowing if I would be able to keep myself up if I took the first step off of the bed.

There were times when I would stand but would feel very unstable as my legs would shake. I could not stand flat on my feet, they just wanted me to go up on my tippy toes. My feet were so tight, my toes would be blue and I would get a lot of ingrown toenails because my toes were curled up most of the time which meant that the blood supply was being cut off. It also affected my balance making me extremely unsteady because my feet would want to turn in. I would feel very uneasy as I could not keep myself up any longer; my energy would be draining very quickly. I would have to throw myself sideways onto a bed to protect myself falling face first onto the hard floor causing me more harm. My arms were locked into one position always, so I would not have been able to prevent myself from falling onto the floor. Mam and Stepdad would have to basically pull me around to put one foot in front of the other when walking. It was really hard and it became so frustrating as I remembered clearly how to walk and run whenever I wanted. It seemed more of an impossible challenge during those earlier times with dystonia though. There were times that I could walk easily but it was always a big concern in my mind. It felt as though I was being pulled back. Gradually I would lose my ability to walk altogether; I did not like it at all. I remember the nurses put me in a wheelchair while I was in hospital; this was so a nurse could take me out to the garden. If Nurse Helen was taking me, I would wait until we got to the end of the corridor and I would indicate to her that I wanted to get out and walk. Helen knew that I did not want to be in a wheelchair. I did not want to concede. Even if it took me longer, it required more effort for me, to walk or I was holding onto someone for support I would still prefer it to getting into a wheelchair. My fear with the wheelchair was that if I got into one even just for a bit, I would become used to it and then become completely dependent on it and forget how to walk altogether. What a scary thought.

At the start of the endorphin release treatment with John, many people commented that they did not see any difference in me. They kept questioning Mam as to why was she still bringing me. "It's not doing anything for Tracey," they'd say. Mam would reply, "But Tracey likes going. It makes her feel good afterwards." What people fail to realise is that change is not instantaneous, at least not to that degree. I will accept the argument that can be made that the dystonia changed my body overnight so the reversing of the effects of my dystonia should be just as quick to accomplish. However, it is often easier and quicker to make a huge mess than it is to clean one up. This treatment had a lot of people expecting miracles, a quick fix. "Bang! It's Tracey again". I knew, however, that I was on a long, tough journey. What John was doing was working on me inside through to the outside, I felt that. I knew it would be a very slow process.

I had a slight shake in my hands because my condition has a mixture of Parkinsonism in it. John took away the shakes. People started to notice the tiniest of changes in me and corrected themselves by saying, "Oh, maybe it is doing something." I strongly believe that John got my legs working the way they are now. We both worked strenuously on that. I kept in my mindset that, "I can walk." The changes did not happen overnight. However, with that extra support from John, I was flying again. I believe I was caught right on time as if it were left any later for me to see John then I do not think I would have recovered as well as I have. He also took away the nauseating pain I had in my whole body. I saw him as a magic man. I was thrilled. However, I had very little feeling in my feet. If my feet were being worked on I would not react at all, which was unusual. I could feel something slightly in the far distance but that was all. John worked on correcting my nerves in my feet to fix this problem for me. Why would I not want to keep going to the Endorphin Clinic? To me, I felt that I was getting so much out of it. The staff at the clinic were always good to us. They never took a penny from Mam because John always made it clear.

"I do not want a penny, honestly. We do not charge for a treatment that may or may not work."

I began attending the clinic weekly when it became apparent that I was starting to improve. Every time I went into clinic John would measure my height against the wall. It was very exciting to see how much I had grown while I was attending there. Another guy who worked in the clinic had developed a very close bond with us. Brian was his name. He was a lovely, caring man, who was such a funny character. He always made me laugh so much. He had this naturally funny personality and he could make anybody within his vicinity laugh. He had this witty sense of humour. If I ever felt grumpy he would do amusing things to get me to smile like pretend he'd got lost in the curtain or pretending he'd fallen asleep, and then started talking in his sleep. He could pull it off and keep it going for ages. He would sometimes pretend that he was a dog; he would be on his hands and knees making barking noises and hiding under the bed. He would pretend to try and bite me, John would keep going to slap him saying, "Go away, doggie." This would have my mam and me in stitches. Then he would appear from the curtains as Brian and act like nothing had happened. Mam would call him a 'Wally' to which Brian would reply "Why? I was upstairs for ages doing nothing out of sorts". This would then prompt him to burst into laughter. He would also tell funny jokes. He always managed to keep my mind off of what was happening and the pain I was going through with my condition, both physically and mentally.

My arms were no longer wrapped around my neck as John had got them down by then, although they were still badly twisted and I had little control over them. I could talk wonders with my eyes. I was still very scared but I always had a glimmer of hope that I would get through it. I knew I was in the right place. I would get to where I wanted to be eventually, with hard work and determination. I had a frozen tongue that just lay in my mouth. It affected my eating as I had no control over it; that was why my food had to be blended. I still had very little muscle movement in my throat; it took a lot of my energy to eat. John worked intensely on getting my muscles working as they should so that I could eat easier and safer. He also kept working on my hands to loosen them up; it was like my brain had forgetting completely how I should use them. John got me to do simple exercises like point to my nose to work on my coordination; I attempted this a few times but each time I would always point somewhere that was miles off and nowhere near my nose. I had lost most of my coordination, which was very frustrating. He even got Mam to do this exercise with me during the week. Daily she would get me to take my hands, keep bringing them up to my face and to say that is my nose, mouth, ears, eyes, and keep bringing my hands up and down. My right hand did not want to respond to the instructions sent down by my brain. My left hand had more flexibility but this was still challenging. Mam kept on repeating the exercises; my right arm would want to do its own thing each time. Mam had to keep telling me to relax until it began to register in my brain. These exercises were very exhausting. My mam kept encouraging me though, "You can do it, Tracey."

She would show me by example. She'd take my hand and bring it up to my nose. "Now you try." I would put all my effort into trying this by myself. I'd start bringing my arm up. "Go on, you're doing it. Keep going."

Then I would begin to laugh thinking, "Yes! I'm going to touch my nose," and then I would point to my face. It would feel to me as though I was touching my nose. My mam would say, "No, Tracey, you're not near your nose."

I was so frustrated. "Why can I not do the simplest of things? I had no problems before. I was a nose picker when I was younger and now I can't even touch my nose. I can hardly feel it when I am." Mam then recommended holding a mirror in order for me to see what I was doing. John did this as well with me. Eventually, my coordination improved greatly and the feeling began to come back. It really was a great achievement when I was able to do this simple thing without the same level of effort as when my treatment had begun.

In between appointments with John, I would have to go back to the head neurologist in Temple Street Hospital for reviews. While at these, I would have to walk up and down the room with my arms out, open my hands, open my mouth, stick out my tongue. They would see how my writing was coming along. All of this would be done while one of the staff videoed me. During one particular appointment, the doctor asked my name and then said, "Are you still taking her to that man?" My mam replied, "You mean John Carty? Yes, I am. Tracey likes going." To which the doctor replied, "Yes, but he's not making much difference, she hasn't improved". My mam replied, "Yes, but it's a slow process."

The doctors started talking about prescribing me medication to relax my muscles but I did not want to go on medication as I had been on it before and I'd looked as if I might as well be somewhere else. I was out of it. I looked drugged up to the eyeballs and that was only a tiny tablet. I did not want to go back there. It was truly horrifying and disturbing for a young girl to look spaced out and I said to my mam, "No, I'll take my chances with John".

I knew he could help and so did Mam. Over time I went back and there were improvements. I felt them and I know I looked as if I was improving. Everyone from the neurology department was commenting to Mam about my improvements.

"She looks really well."

My mam just smiled and said quietly, "Let's hope the neurologist sees that".

When we walked in and sat down the doctor looked very surprised and said, "Tracey looks different, what have you been doing?" Mam replied, "Nothing much, still bringing her to see John Carty regularly but haven't tried anything else in the meantime. We feel we are getting results with John. It's slow but it is something that is working."

The doctor replied, "Well, she does look like she has definitely improved."

The doctor then got me to repeat the same usual exercises. The only one that I found really difficult was sticking out my tongue. That was always the hardest to do especially if I felt pressurised. The doctor seemed very impressed, even with regards my smile, it looked genuine. Her exact words were, "Well, whatever you're doing, keep doing it because it is working".

She would not acknowledge John or endorphin release as being the reason behind my greatly healed body. That comment from her was as good as we could hope to get in terms of any recognition of John and the effectiveness of his work on me. She did, however, say, "Well done, Tracey's Mam, for being so headstrong because God knows how Tracey's life would be now if it wasn't for your drive".

My mam was delighted to hear those words being spoken by a medical professional and thanked her saying, "Only for Tracey being so strong too, I don't think we would have got here. We worked together," to which the doctor replied, "Yes, you're both great. You should be proud of yourselves. Keep up the good work and see you in another couple of months. Well done again to you both".

Mam felt overwhelmed by those comments. She never thought she would get any nice words said to her by a doctor. We both were delighted. Mam phoned all her family... "You'll never guess what?" I felt very proud in that moment and I was delighted at seeing how happy Mam was. It alleviated the difficulties experienced during this journey and gave us all determination to keep on the path we had chosen. The following week we went to see John and Mam told him the good news. He was delighted.

"I told you not to worry from the start. From the moment I met you both, I knew that the darkness around you would lift. The best thing you did was getting Tracey out of the hospital. Look how much she has come on. She is a credit to you."

Mam and I could not have been more thankful to John, for everything he had done. He has the biggest heart.

John started to work intensely on my face, mouth and tongue as I got older. He knew from my eyes that it would mean more to me, to be able to loosen up my tongue and get words out. My tongue would not work at all; it was extremely tough to get it to relax. Whenever John attempted to release my tongue he found it very slithery until one day Mam came up with this idea that she assumed would work which involved a suction cup from a radiator being used to grip my tongue. Mam tried it on herself and her idea ultimately failed due to the suction cup not being able to grip her tongue because of the moisture, I think it was more a funny thought Mam had, one of many she has had over the years to try and lessen the seriousness of the situation. It made us all laugh even though it did not work. John managed to get my tongue out with a suction pump syringe device which his assistant Denise came up with.

At times while my tongue was out, John would get behind me and work on it with his arm stretched around the back of my head. He would keep pushing and pulling my tongue in and out. Then I would try by myself, which was difficult for me but with a lot of concentration I could eventually move my tongue in and out of my mouth. John would be full of praise.

"Wonderful! You're a great girl, Tracey!" or "I'm delighted! I really am!"

Every time he would work on my tongue Brian and my mam would help. Brian would slag me saying, "I have a vice grips in the office, I'll get it and pull your tongue out for you."

We would all laugh. Eventually, I could manage to get my tongue out by myself; it was the best thing ever. Everyone in the clinic congratulated me. John would show me how it looked in the mirror:

"Look at your beautiful tongue that had been hiding away."

I would smile with delight. My tongue would not always come out but eventually, given time when it did John would say, "Well done, Tracey, wonderful!"

John's reaction made the entire struggle we had been through so worth it. Now somebody get me an ice cream so I can enjoy licking it to death!

My laugh was very weak at first. It required a great deal of focus to let it out. Even then it sounded very faint and distant like something was obstructing it. Laughing more, combined with the treatment, strengthened my laugh and made it louder. In all the years I have been going to see John I honestly cannot remember a day when I did not laugh. Laughter is the best medicine, as they say. The more I would laugh the more floppy my hands would become. Brian could shake them all around up and down, and around in a circle. Brian and my mam would laugh when this would happen and Brian would say;

"That's it, Tracey, you've no choice now but to keep laughing for the rest of your life and that should not bother you seeing as you never stop laughing."

At the Endorphin Clinic, I was always made to feel comfortable in being myself and to laugh while I was there. I really would laugh my head off.

John also used to get me to make sounds and then eventually to try saying a few words, "Say 'Hello, John.' Keep practising it." He would also get me to count aloud to ten and sometimes twenty if he noticed my voice becoming stronger. My voice at this time was so soft and low it was like a little mouse and it was very hard to hear and comprehend. Eventually, over time, it got louder and I'd manage to say a few words depending on how relaxed my facial muscles and tongue were. Without thinking too much about it, I could say a word clearly and that word was "Ok." It was not exactly perfect but every so often I would roar out a clearly understandable word. This would leave John and Mam gobsmacked. "Wow! That was wonderful!"

"You are a little treasure. You are some girl, I tell you. You are a credit to us all. We all love you to bits in here. It's people like you that make this world a better place. People who don't give up on the first hurdle. People who keep pushing through the hard times with a smile on their face."

I was delighted with those uplifting complimentary words from John.

I Have Come a Long Way

As I grew older, I felt more independent and safe enough to go to the clinic on my own on the bus. I needed to get two buses to get to the clinic from Mam's house, which I did not mind. I knew in order for me to improve, I needed to face the real world as often as I could in order to become more confident. I knew this would aid in my independence and contribute largely to me feeling a part of society. Mam came with me the first time as I knew it would be a very daunting experience for me and also to make sure I knew the way. I will openly admit that it was difficult at first for me to take that step. However, with practice, it honestly became much easier. I felt very proud and had an overwhelming sense of achievement, which I am sure was clear to everyone around me. John and the other staff were very impressed at how much I had come on from the little, scared, frail girl they'd first met to the young woman standing in front of them. A woman who was ready to spread her wings and grow into the Tracey who knew nothing would hold her back.

A few days after my twenty-first birthday, I went over to the clinic. John was working on me as usual. Towards the end of my session, he pointed behind me and said, "Oh, what is that behind you?" I looked and saw Brian and all the staff gathered behind me. Brian was holding a birthday cake that had lit candles on it and they all started singing *Happy Birthday* to me. Brian then gave me a card. I was shocked as I never expected it. It was such a lovely thought.

In the early years of me attending my appointments by myself, John and the nurse Denise would work on me, and Brian would always pop in when he was finished seeing to his own patients to check up on me and find out how I was getting on. If he was busy while I was there and did not get a chance to see me then he would pop his head around the curtain to say goodbye to me or even shout, "Bye, Tracey" as I was leaving. On the very rare occasions if Brian was out of the clinic while I was at an appointment then I would miss seeing him, and have this empty feeling walking to the bus stop to make my way home. I would be livid because I would miss him that much. I always looked forward to seeing him. He would make my day shine brighter.

Brian – My Mood Raiser, Endorphin Releaser and Friend

After John got me to the stage where I could live my life freer and with fewer physical restrictions, Brian took over my treatment sessions. I loved going over to see everyone at the clinic and Brian especially. There were times when I thought to myself, "Should I keep going? Twenty years is a long time. I don't want to seem like I'm taking the p***! I'm moulded into the furniture at this stage!" However, I was getting absolute wonders from the treatment both physically and socially so I wanted to continue keeping my muscles relaxed. Brian always made it very clear and would say to me, "The door is always open to you". I knew it was good to keep working on my muscles via this treatment as I did not want to relapse back into my original state prior to meeting John all those years ago. To this day, my muscles still have a tendency to go into spasms and cause me great discomfort. I know that is natural, though, as I will always have this muscular condition. I have come to terms with that. Brian and John have always told me that I am like family to everyone there and if I feel that I must go there for the rest of my life then so be it.

Brian has such a big heart; he puts his all into his work with his clients. At times he would even work through his lunch-break to make sure everyone was seen to. He would not turn them away or treat anyone half-heartedly because he would miss part of his lunch-break. While at my sessions with Brian, I would communicate with him via my phone and he is great to talk to. I honestly feel that I can talk to him about anything. I do not see my sessions as just treatment sessions anymore as we have gone through a lot together. Brian and I have a great bond; well, I would hope so after all those years. He is inspired to hear about all the adventures that I partake in and that I face everything head on with such doggedness. I believe even though he is older than me that to some extent he looks up to me. I honestly feel connected to all the staff in the clinic and feel that I can be myself around them. They deserve the best for being fully there for me always.

I get such a laugh from Brian and laughing definitely does what everyone knows it does; I release a lot of endorphins due to this laughter as does every single person when they laugh. Brian always says to me, "I think you just come over for the laugh".

He loves to see me laugh. He says he could be having a really horrible day and then when I walk in he feels a lift, I brighten his day. I just smile, laugh, and slag him off. He cannot help but laugh to himself and ask me, "Can I not enjoy my bad day? Then you ruin it by wanting me to laugh."

He is slagging when saying this, as usual.

Throughout the years I have had so many good, hard laughs thanks to Brian. I think other people must think he is tickling me with a feather behind the curtain instead of treating me because all I do is laugh. Here are different moments that stand out in my mind from when Brian did something funny. Separately, they are just stupid little funny moments but when I replay them all in my mind, however, I believe he has earned the name I have adopted for him, my mood raiser.

There are times I would walk in for my appointment and it would be windy outside, which would ruin my hair. Nobody else notices that my hair is a bit messy. One time, however, after my treatment, Brian was helping me get organised to head home when he noticed my hair and he said, "What's the story with your hair, Tracey? Is there a hurricane outside?" He then tried fixing the bits back in place. "Ah, do you have any clips? Your hair is all over the place. I can't let you go home like that to your mother".

As he was trying to fix it up he was saying, "I'm making it worse"

Everyone else in the clinic had gone for lunch already but Brian would not leave until he'd fixed my hair. He went looking for clips. "Tracey, I'll be back"

He left for a few minutes and returned with a hairdresser from next door, "Now look, Tracey, I brought you your very own hairdresser, so don't ask for anything too fancy as we don't have all day."

Another time when my hair was messy and the hairdresser from next door was on her break, Brian decided he would do my hair for me so he went to the shop and got hairclips. When he came back he got himself into character as a Geordie Shores male hairdresser.

"Now, Tracey, what can I do for you today? I was thinking shaved along the side, some pink and blue tips, nicely layered hmm… that'd be gorgeous."

Then while putting the clips in my hair he said, "Oh stop moving, you'll ruin it. Now look".

He then got the mirror and showed me different angles, throwing all these funny shapes while talking and giving it loads of over the top gestures.

"Don't you look gorgeous?"

He had me in stitches. He then suddenly jumped out of character and back to normal Brian.

"I've no idea how to do hair. That probably isn't the way, but at least you won't be eating your hair all the way home."

John and the other staff usually leave for lunch before Brian and me and they would lock the door behind them. They always left spare keys for Brian. One day he was just finishing up with me.

"Right, Tracey, all done."

He wrote down the next date for my appointment in the book, and then as he went to let me out he could not find the keys and was searching everywhere for them.

"I can't find the keys."

I thought any minute he would find them and that John was playing hide and seek with them. No joy, though, as he literally looked everywhere. John always left them in an easy place where Brian could find them. I could tell Brian was starting to get anxious as he was pacing up and down looking distressed. He figured that John had left with the keys. Brian could have rung John to tell him we were locked in. By then John and the rest would probably have sat down and ordered their meals so there would have been no point in everyone missing out on lunch. I was thinking, "Can we not scream for help?"

Brian stood on a table in the far cubicle and started banging on the wall at irregular intervals and then placed his ear against the wall to hear if any of the neighbouring shops took notice. I was thinking to myself, "What is he playing at?" It was like he was trying to open a secret passage. Every now and again, I would attempt to say something to him and he would tell me to be quiet as he was too busy listening intently for any hint of noise coming from the neighbours. I began to think "Is this getting anywhere?" and that Brian and I would have to starve until someone came back, which would probably mean I would have killed Brian because I do not cope well with hunger. Gone would be Little Miss Laughter to be replaced by Little Miss Hungry.

After a few minutes of Brian knocking energetically on the wall, I heard a sudden knock on the clinic door which scared the life out of me as I did not expect it. It was the hairdresser from next door asking if we were ok. She was signing this out as she did not want to be shouting and making a scene. Brian indicated to her that we were locked in. Thankfully, she had a spare set of keys as otherwise, Brian's attempt at a distress signal would have been a complete waste time. We were saved, though, so it worked. The hairdresser said she and another girl were in the back listening to the strange noise coming from next door and thinking, "That's no ordinary banging noise". It was funny and the good news was Brian had enough time to go off for his lunch. More than likely he would not get away with this now as the hairdresser's has been closed down for a while and in its place is a funeral home.

One time I had been away in Panama and when I got back I made an appointment to attend the clinic. Brian knew that I had been away on holiday somewhere exotic and when I went into the cubicle to begin my treatment he asked, "How did you get on in Panama? Did you actually go away? Where's your tan? You're whiter now than before you went".

He is such a teaser. I would look good walking into the clinic in my holiday clothes in January. You still would not notice if I had got a tan, though, as my body would have been full of goose-bumps from the lovely Irish, January weather.

I really appreciate how Brain has come to understand me better over the past few years. He always makes that extra bit of effort, which is nice. I also get some lovely healthy tips regarding what foods to eat from his wife Paula.

Recognition at last

One day a number of years ago, my neurologist from the Mater, whom I had been seeing since I turned eighteen, informed me that there was an event being held in the Convention Centre in Dublin that he would like me to attend. Doctors from all over the world would be there and a number of other volunteer patients were to attend also. We were asked to go onto the stage and display our disabilities to them. The doctors in attendance had to write down what medical difficulty they thought each volunteer had. I was asked by my neurologist to attend given the rarity of my disorder and the fact that I had recovered greatly as opposed to others with a similar condition. It was a great opportunity for me to showcase how far I had come. Mam and I could bring a guest along with us so Mam asked John as we felt that he should be there among the doctors as he deserved to be recognised as the primary reason for my obvious recovery. John was delighted when we asked if he would like to attend.

On the day John met Mam and I there, we all dressed up nicely as we knew this was an important day for us all. When we went in, we made our way to the green room and then John left to take his place in the audience. Mam stayed with me. When my turn came to go on stage Mam had to wait with the other parents and volunteers in the green room. We were each designated a number to determine the order we went on stage. We were called three at a time and while one was on stage the other two would wait to the side. This was done so that there would be no long gaps between the viewing of one volunteer to the next. In the group that I was in, there was a girl in a wheelchair and she went first. I had a quick glance at the audience and thought,

"Oh my God, it is packed." I took a deep breath. "I'll be grand. It'll be over in no time so I might as well make the most of this opportunity."

When it came to my turn to go on stage I felt this wave come over me. I saw the presenter on the other end of the stage smiling and waving for me to come on. When I started to walk out I could not really see as the lights were on me full focus.

Oh my God, I'm being blinded.

Then the event presenter stood in front of me and asked me to do some things like walk up and down, put my arms up, and do different movements. I looked to my left and noticed John as clear as anything. We shared a smile. I did what was asked of me and after each task that I had to perform, I would look at John for a comforting glance from a friendly face surrounded by a sea of strangers.

Afterwards, we all went into the green room where we were treated to some fancy sandwiches, cakes, and lots of tea. The doctors came in their numbers, one of whom in particular was my neurologist from Temple Street. She was the doctor who had given my mam that compliment a number of years before. She could not get over to us quickly enough.

"Hello Tracey and Mam, do you remember me? I saw you on stage. I couldn't believe that was you. You look absolutely amazing."

My mam smiled graciously. "She does, doesn't she? By the way, this is John Carty, the endorphin releaser, you know, the man who's helped Tracey."

The doctor shook John's hand firmly and said, "Yes, of course, I know who you are. She looks great, doesn't she?" John replied very proudly, "She certainly does." The doctor looked at Mam and said, "She's a credit to you."

My mam replied, "I know, yeah, look where we got. It was a battle but we got through it with all the support". The doctor replied, "Oh yes, it's marvellous!"

As I write this, it is the eve of my twenty-ninth birthday. I wish to take this opportunity to acknowledge with thanks my current, unmistakably positive situation that was made possible by John and all the staff from the Endorphin Clinic. My family and I have always seen John as our knight in shining armour who continually rescued me from the doctors' "medically experienced" grasps. He healed me and assisted me through the great difficulties I was experiencing initially with dystonia. He guided us all through the darkness that at the time seemed would never shift. It is easy to see how everything changed for the better for all of us once John Carty came into our lives. They say there is never anything good on television. Well, that night, all those years ago, John was on and I, along with my family, are so thankful of that.

When I look at the person I have become in comparison to the person I was with my disorder and how it affected me physically and mentally, I am very grateful to my nan who took heed that night over twenty years ago and believed that John Carty could help me in a big way. It is an extremely scary thought for me to think how I would be now if I did not have, and persisted at having the treatment. What would my life be like? I know that because my muscles were deteriorating so rapidly that the outcome would not be good. I needed that extra bit of help and as they say, extra help goes a long way. I would like to take this opportunity to thank John Carty, Brian, Denise and all the staff who contributed to my recovery. I believe you all collectively contributed to my physical and mental health becoming stronger than I would have ever thought when I first got struck with this disorder.

For anybody who is currently attending the Endorphin Release Clinic I implore you to stick with it; do not give up on the first few sessions. If the pain gets too much you must build up resilience and realise that this pain is just temporary and it will become easier in time. If you have any muscular disorder that hinders your movement then bear in mind that it can take a bit longer for this to be rectified. There are no instant or painless methods to heal a muscular disorder. The Endorphin Release treatment can do wonders for you but remember also that it is a two-way treatment. You must put the work in too. Do not just hope that the endorphin treatment alone will get you right. Personally, I have never looked back.

Extracurricular activities

Drama

When I was nineteen years old, I was attending a local job centre on a regular basis to assist me in getting employment; something that suited my capabilities and needs, something I would enjoy. One day, I was contacted by the job centre informing me of a youth drama group that was based in the Reco centre in Ballymun, which was just down the road from my house. I was advised to go check it out that Tuesday evening. They said the lady running the drama was brilliant and would be extremely supportive. I felt excited so I arranged to meet with the lady first. Her name was Louise Lowe. She had a good chat with me asking me lots of questions as she was interested in my story. I was going on holidays with my family for a week around this time so she told me to come back the week after I returned. She said that when I joined I was to make an effort to get involved; that it would be better for me to just dive right in instead of looking on from the sidelines, questioning if I could do it or not. I was so excited to be joining. I remember thinking, "I hope the other people will be nice to me". I am sure it can be strange at first seeing a person who has a physical disability combined with the inability to speak properly. It can take a while for people to figure out who I am. At first, I probably seem like an alien from a different planet. I was afraid as to how they would react and also how they would treat me as people generally fear what they do not understand.

When I arrived at the drama club the other members started streaming into the building. Every single one of them was very welcoming and I was thrilled with how they treated me. It was like I had always been there. Louise Lowe was amazing with me. She knew my strengths and weaknesses from day one. I developed tremendously over the months. I had never felt so happy in all my life, and the feeling of belonging was incredible. I could not get over how each individual made no judgement about me at all, or get annoyed if I was put in a group with them. Their understanding and patience blew me away. I partook in workshops, which developed my self-confidence in such a positive way. We started performing shows in the Dublin Theatre Festival and my first show was called *The Bus Project*, which was staged on an actual bus that stopped off at different locations letting the actors on and off. The bus left from Parnell Street in town and headed toward Ballymun. The audience was on the bus too. I was up first. My piece was with a red-haired young lad and in the show, we were planning on running away. We were already on the bus before the audience got on board. As soon as they came on and settled down our piece began. In the show, we had a bag of stuff to tide us over for the duration of our 'get away'. We were going through it making sure we had everything we needed. I was communicating through gestures using body language. I was to fall asleep on his shoulder after we checked we had everything and, while I was supposed to be asleep, he would have had second thoughts. He'd stuff his jacket behind my neck to make a pillow and then leave me. I was to wake up looking all around and get off at the next stop with his jacket. It was my spotlight moment, being on the bus on my own; all eyes were on me in those moments. We performed that show twice a night for two weeks straight. It was great to be part of it, and I was absolutely delighted. I was involved in great shows that got even greater reviews. I was involved in a number of shows for the Dublin Fringe Festival as time went on. It was an incredible moment in my life.

My social life exploded better than I had ever dreamt. I was never left out. I was invited to nights out that were amazing. I even had a few cocktail nights at a friend's house, which made me realise what I had been missing out on in the previous years. I was never afraid to be myself. I could communicate in my own way. I could laugh my head off if I wanted. We would constantly slag each other off, in a humorous way, though, as friends do. One night a few of us ended up doing an all-nighter. We had rehearsals the next day at 10am. I got a bit drunk...just a bit though. My friend's sister had gone to bed at a reasonable hour because she had work the next day and as soon as she left for work my friend put me in his sister's bed for an hour, to see if I could sleep the drink off. I had a sleep but after the hour I woke up hearing the gang downstairs still laughing. I thought, "Why am I here in bed?" I jumped out of the bed still feeling a bit tipsy and skipped down the stairs, did a move into the kitchen and proceeded to lean against the counter throwing shapes around then burst out laughing, twirling around like a fool. When the time came for us to go to rehearsals, we all felt better. We were so smelly from staying in the same clothes all night – the smell of stale drink and dried in sweat. I can easily say it was the dirtiest I have ever felt in my whole life. Moments like this were a rare occasion so, to me, it really was worth it.

As time went on we were obviously starting to age beyond the point that we could be considered youth anymore, which was such a pity. We could not stay the same age forever. Eventually, things change. That is life, I suppose. Louise got offered a great job in the Abbey Theatre. Drama really made me feel so good. It improved me in so many ways so I was sad to see it end. I found it so difficult to find other drama groups to get involved in that mirrored the experience I had felt with that first group. The years I spent searching and feeling that I was back to doing nothing again were brought to a halt when Louise contacted me out of the blue a few years later and asked me to be a part of a massive show for the Dublin Theatre Festival. It was two weeks of extremely intense work, from 10am – 6pm everyday excluding Sundays. The show was on a repetitive loop during these times. It was about the Magdalene laundries. The play was actually performed in the exact location of a former laundry based in Sean McDermott Street. It was very draining. I would fall in the door when I got home and then I had to repeat it all over again the following day. I loved every moment of it and during that time while participating in it, I did not feel I was disabled. The show was awarded for best stage production. The awards' night was amazing and will always stand out in my memory. I felt like a real celebrity. I even got the pleasure of being introduced to Cillian Murphy. Rubbing shoulders with the likes of these people was such an amazing experience. I just felt no one was more famous than me during that time. I brought so much to the table with the feeling of self-pride I had, especially when my mam and other family members saw my shows. They were shocked at seeing how much I had grown and had become so popular. For the first time, in a very long time, as strange as this may sound I felt like a real person; a real person doing ordinary things. Well, maybe it was a tiny bit extraordinary, after all, it is not every day you get to mingle with celebrities.

Sadly, I lost contact with my drama friends over time. I understand that people can come in and out of our lives and this is a natural part of life. No matter how brief the time was with my drama friends or how hard it was seeing them leave my life, I am very grateful for the wonderful friendships that I formed during my time there. There were plenty of laughs and great memories that I will always treasure. I feel blessed that I was a part of it and that I was welcomed into it.

When drama ended I could have taken a massive step backwards in valuing my self-worth as I had done previous to drama. "Ah, nothing else for me to do now. Drama was good while it lasted but it is boredom and no growth from now on." Instead, I chose to continue soldiering on and began thinking of something new that would give me a different experience and the confidence to develop myself more. I was determined not to give up.

Boot camp

One day I was coming back from town and I saw a lady putting leaflets through the doors. I just thought it was junk to be honest, as nine out of ten of those leaflets usually are. But we Irish tend to automatically prejudge leaflets before even reading them properly when some of the stuff that is posted out could be actually interesting. Seeing this lady with the leaflets, I thought by the time I get to the gate that she will hand me one. Usually, I try to avoid these situations if I can because my hands do not always grip the paper right and then I get myself in a panic and draw more attention to myself. I wasn't avoiding this situation. I would draw more attention to myself if I just stopped and stood there like an ass waiting on her to finish at Mam's house, so we met at the gate and she handed me the leaflet. She copped on I had a disability but she did not treat me like I had one. She was able to tell me what the leaflet was about. A new boot camp starting up in the local park and that it was going to be great. Straight away I felt this rush of excitement. I ran into my house where I read the leaflet numerous times. I thought that this would be great for me. The contact name on the leaflet was a man named Clive who would also be running the boot camp. I contacted him via email, and I explained my situation to him. That I have a muscular disability and how it affects my movement. He had no problem at all with it and he was very happy for me to join. He also said that he would support me anyway he could. I was so excited.

It was that following Tuesday at 7pm that I went to start my first ever boot camp. The local park was literally just five minutes (if even) away from my mam's house. It was a nice day in April and I walked with a skip in my step towards the park. When I arrived I was greeted by Amanda who was the girl from whom I got the leaflet a few days earlier. I registered with her and paid my fee. She was very friendly and helpful. Then I was greeted by Clive who as it turned out was Amanda's husband. He was a really nice guy and he was more than happy that I had decided to come along. He told me that he was willing to assist me in any way possible so that I would get the most out of it. While I was waiting to begin my intense training session, more people started to arrive. There was such a good atmosphere in the boot camp. This was very new to me and I really enjoyed it and got amazing benefit from it in both physical and mental boosts. It also helped that it was in such a lovely location too, Poppintree Park, which really is a lovely park. We made good use of our nice surroundings and began our session. For me, this was to be the first of many training sessions to come. We started by running around a patch, about a square metre in size. Mind you, it was on a little slope and as such really tested my fitness levels. I was so bad that anytime I tried I had to stop. I felt like my granddad Tommy (my stepdad's father who is a heavy smoker) huffing and puffing out of me. I was thinking, "How the f**** can I do this?" I got through the class just about, feeling totally drained. I thought to myself, "Yes, it was tough, but I have accomplished something". Everyone who joined the boot camp was pretty much in the same boat. I was a little bit fitter than some though. We did things like lunges, sit-ups, press-ups and so on. I did my best and made an attempt at everything. If there was something that I could not manage like catching and throwing a ball, I would just do something else. I was not made to feel left out. I continued to attend the boot camps and started to notice my confidence was coming up again and that I was feeling fitter and healthier. It reached a stage where running around that little patch seemed too easy. A few weeks into it I started to notice another guy who was kind of taking part but mainly just watching. His name was Scott. The following week, he taught the class with Clive. The boot camp was turning out to be such a success that they had decided to add an extra evening. They added Thursday to the boot camp roster, which I was thrilled about. They worked the schedule out so that Clive instructed the Tuesday class and Scott would instruct the Thursday class.

When the six-week boot camp had finished, immediately and without hesitation, I signed up again for another six weeks. Some of the same people who attended the previous one also signed up with me. Some did not, and some new people joined too. At the beginning of the next six-week boot camp we all noticed that the warm up was not around that same patch, instead, we had to jog right over the field, and it was a much bigger area. Scott was mad into his running. He had done and still does to this day, lots of marathons, all over the world. Scott always pushed us to our physical limits; he would make sure that we were not slacking off. Some of the new comers would have to cut corners at times. In fairness, I probably would too as I remembered when I first started and we were running around that little patch, it seemed impossible at times. I could run better as I got fitter because my endurance had greatly improved. I felt great when I completed the run. When I was younger and before I got dystonia my nickname was Forest Gump. For those who have not seen the movie, it is a story about a man who has mild learning difficulties and loves, among other things, to run. Running to me felt like such a freedom. To clear my head, I would run so fast and so hard that it would feel as though my legs would fall off.

They added a Saturday morning class, which started at 10am and mainly focused on running. It was great. I was so committed; rain, hail, sun, or snow I was always there. They were always shocked on bad rainy days; they would be thinking, "Nobody will show up", but then I would arrive. They were very impressed at my commitment. Most people stayed at home wrapped up in their blankets with a cup of cocoa. I was getting so many benefits from it. I felt so positive and my positivity was rubbing off on everyone I knew, and it was a much nicer feeling. I could never do much with my right hand as I had very little control. As time went on though both Clive and Scott made me use my right hand and made sure that I did not ignore it as they knew it needed just as much of a workout as my left hand. I would hold weights and really try to work the power. It was quite difficult for me to even open my right hand let alone put my arms up and bring them back down keeping them even but I always tried. As time went on I noticed that I could place my right hand nicely on the counter without any strain. It was so relaxed. I even tried gripping a cup and lifting it up to my mouth, which was a bit wobbly at first, but eventually, I did it without spilling the contents all over me. I even fed myself with my right hand, which felt strange, but I managed. I had not used my right hand since developing dystonia, so being able to do those little things showed me how much boot camp had improved me. Words cannot describe how happy I was or the sense of self-achievement that I felt. Finally, I believed I was a winner. I felt that I had the power to improve myself. Every day the boot camp was on I was getting more enjoyment and benefit from it. I was praying to God, "Please, don't let this end".

I got major enjoyment from playing different activity games that worked on our physicality while in boot camp, and I was always included in every activity in the different teams. These fun exercises brought me back to my early childhood before the dystonia when all the kids played games outside, like racing, What time is it Mr Wolf?, Queenie Eye Oh!, kick the can, and rounders. These games we played in our youth were a great example of social inclusion, teamwork and being physically active. I feel sorry for the younger children in the last few years due to the absence of such games. Now they all have computers and mobiles to keep them busy. Some children today have little or no interest in playing outdoors games; they label it as being only for babies. I find it very upsetting that the current youth have lost the true meaning of what it means to be young and, in my opinion, that includes playing games with other children on your street. I admire teenagers who keep active and do it because they want to, not because they are peer pressured into it due to being mocked by their peers.

Being a part of that boot camp was a great experience for me personally because the games we played and the laugh we had was truly uplifting for me. When you are a child you can be very competitive. I never saw it like that, however. I just loved being involved and laughing with my friends. If I was in the team that won, well, then fair play to us and if we lost then well done to the opposing team.

In the boot camp, we were always encouraged to aim for the win though. We got into our teams and our friendly 'conflict' would commence. We would compete at different things like running through cones, hitting the boxing pads ten times, then jump through hoops, and run back down to tag your team mates for them to do the same. A great laugh was had by all. Another thing we would do would be to break into two teams with both teams standing up with their legs wide open. You would stand in a straight line behind one another and the person in front of the queue would crawl under their teammate's legs. When they got to the end they would stand in the same position as their team mates and then the next person who was top of the queue would do the same. This would go on until all the team mates had gone under and the winning team was the team that did it fastest.

Gradually, as the months went by, fewer people were attending the Saturday classes, I think some of them felt we were being worked too hard and they were not able to keep up the pace. In fairness to them, the Saturday mornings were a lot tougher. My face would be like a tomato, bright red, ready to burst, but I loved it. I was always knocked out after it, feeling lifeless. I would always revive myself and would feel on top of the world. I needed a full day to recover though.
It got to the stage that I was the only one that would show up on the Saturday mornings, I would do a one-on-one with Scott, which was not what he had signed up for. As I have said Scott's main passion was running. He took full advantage of the fact that it was just the two of us and we would go on long runs through the park. My legs were exhausted as we ran that much; he, on the other hand, never stopped running. In fairness, I did not want to stop. I wanted to look good. There was plenty of self-talk from me. I would have to say to myself, "Right, when I reach the tree I have to stop." Then I would run past the tree and think, "No, I can keep going to the bench" and when I passed the bench I would be in bits, just about conscious, dragging myself around at a snail's pace. Even though I would start slowing down, **I never gave in**. This would make the classes go on for longer and with the sun belting down this was harder. However, when something is hard and I get through it, this makes me very happy. **It is in times of physical or mental difficulty that enables us to see the nature of our true strengths.**

Community work

While I was in the boot camp, a man called Proinsias – who was high up in the Reco centre – got in touch with me as he had this idea of setting up a monthly disco for the children with special needs who had mental disabilities such as Down's syndrome and other intellectual disabilities. The children, he proposed facilitating these discos for, attended Saint Michael's House on the Ballymun Road and another special needs organisations close by. There was already a group called the Rainbows Group. However, they mainly kicked off in the summer in the Reco. That was like a summer project to keep the children active throughout the summer. There was nothing like the monthly disco that Proinsias was proposing for them, to give them something to look forward to, a chance to express themselves and socialise with their friends. Proinsias asked if I would like to get involved with the planning of this and come up with different ideas. He felt very inspired by me coming in and doing drama. He saw some of the shows we had put on and he was amazed at how I presented myself with great confidence, letting nothing hold me back. I believe that he felt I would be a great role model for these children. I felt honoured to be asked and got involved straight away. I felt very positive in myself in that moment; another door was opening for me. Through this volunteer work, I met some other volunteers; they were lovely people who wanted to make a difference in people's lives. They were all caring, good-natured people. The disco took place in the hall, which was a nice size. They had someone to do DJ and had the coloured lights. There was also an area outside the hall that had a sofa. If it got too loud for the children then they could find a space to sit and chat. On the nights of the discos, I would be sitting at the desk welcoming the children and their carers and taking their names. The children would be smiling as they were so looking forward to the disco. This made volunteering at the discos worthwhile as I became a lot more grateful for the small things I had, and that made me smile. As I got to know everyone well they were all shocked that I did the boot camp three nights a week. They all said that I put them to shame. As time went on we were talking about me joining boot camp again, Proinsias was there and mentioned that a man had just started a thing called boxercise that previous week. He was not really sure what it was though. He was trying to describe it. "He started boxing into the air. It is something to that effect. Come down Saturday morning and have a look." I thought "Yes, why not?" I arrived that Saturday morning earlier than I should as I was keen and curious at the same time. The boxercise man arrived a few minutes after me to set up. His name was Frank, a tall, pleasant man. My first impression of him was that he was a very kind-hearted, understanding man. The funny thing was that in that moment I recognised him. I had met him before at a course I had thrown myself into a few months before. It was in the Sports and Leisure in Finglas Community Centre. The course mainly involved playing team games in the hall. I had never had a proper conversation with anyone while there though because there was not enough time for me to get my phone and text plus it was only a few days. I did not know what to say, to be honest. They were just beginning to get the idea that I could not verbally communicate. I was only there a few days and I just wanted to enjoy the experience and not to be stressing out about "How do I communicate?". I had fun regardless.

I think when Frank met me in the Reco first he did recognise me a bit. Proinsias was there and introduced me, explaining a little about me. He told Frank that I was doing boot camp three nights a week that I am very fit and active. Proinsias said that I was "well able for anything. Can she check out your class?" At first Frank was a bit taken aback as he had never come across anyone like me wanting to do his class before. I believe he then thought that it would be something new for him and he was open to new challenges. He asked me to follow him down to the hall and he would explain what the class was about. I went down smiling ear to ear. My heart was racing a bit and I had butterflies, not knowing what to expect. To be honest, though, I had a good feeling about this.

Boxercise

When we got to the hall, Frank began showing me different exercises that he does during the class: sit-ups, different stretches including standing stretches and working with the boxercise pads. He told me, "Just do what you can, no pressure. The main thing you can get from it is enjoyment."

He said that it was a pleasure for him to meet me even though he was pretty sure he'd met me before. He was just trying to pinpoint where. I was laughing during this mental block he was having. He knew I remembered him and, all of a sudden, he remembered me.

"Ah yes, now I remember!" He began to laugh and said, "it would have driven me mad during the class. It is great to have you here and I hope you have fun because that is what life is all about, enjoying each moment." I could tell from that comment that Frank was a very positive man who appreciated the simple things in life.

People started to arrive and soon the class began. I threw myself into everything and giving it my all. I really enjoyed it, especially having Frank as my trainer. He made the class more enjoyable with his attitude towards life. He pushed everyone and complimented them on their efforts with everything they had done in the class. He told me to come again if I wanted to, that I was more than welcome, and it would be great to have me there. He said that the classes would start on Mondays at 9.00 am, Wednesday 9.00 am, and Friday 8.30 am.

After I joined, I quickly got into the swing of it. I loved getting up early on those days. I was so energetic and enthusiastic. I would run or power walk down to the centre every morning. I got to know everyone well. There was a couple called Mark and Angie with whom I got on particularly well. Mark was very funny with a very witty sense of humour. They lived across the road from Mam. I used to time myself before I would see their car pass by. A lot of times I made it in the door before them, or I would be two minutes away and they would pass me in their car. Eventually, they copped on it was me and would stop at a safe place to give me a lift. I would be thinking, "The next day I will get further". I used them to help motivate myself, and I was so driven and felt unbelievably fit. Frank really helped me with my motivation. My participation in boxercise enabled me to transmit my desire to stay on top of my 'disability'. It also gave me the benefit of participation in a fun activity and encouraged me to put myself out there socially too. I was always shown respect and made to feel that I had every right to be there. Frank would keep bringing me to the front of the class. We would stand in front of mirrors and learn stances for boxing moves. My confidence grew greatly with this because I found it difficult looking in a mirror especially in a group exercise while I was trying to copy everyone. It forced me out of my comfort zone, which I feel is always a good thing. I believe Frank felt very proud and inspired by my efforts and the fact that I did not complain. He could see I worked that extra bit harder and we developed a great friendship.

One time, I asked Mam to give it a try; I wanted her to see what I was involved in and to meet Frank. Mam said, "Ah no, boxercise. I couldn't do that". I replied, "I'm saying just come down and see. You have to meet Frank too. He's such a really nice man. You'd like him". Mam eventually conceded and came down for "a nose" and she was amazed at what was involved. She decided not to go back though as she found it too hard. She would stick with just her line dancing. She was very impressed by me, however, and said that she thought Frank was a decent, nice man.

I was still attending the boot camp. However, it had faded out as people just lost interest. There were still two other girls and myself who decided to meet up every Thursday morning in Poppintree Park and do our own boot camp. This was a great laugh and we encouraged each other the whole time. That boot camp lasted a good few months. After that finished, the only thing I still had was boxercise. This meant at least I was not losing out on the physical exercise I believed I required. Frank had also decided to start up an evening class, which was held in St. Joseph's school hall. It was mainly men that attended that class though. He kept on telling me about the evening class and saying, "You're more than welcome to come down". I think he wanted to show me off. Frank never charged me for his classes. He only charges very little as it is but he told me not worry about it. He said that seeing me coming down every time, and getting something from each class, means more to him. He loves to see me eager to start the class, and that my motivation keeps him inspired.

The mornings were becoming a bit of a struggle for Frank as he would have to drive out early; he lived just outside of Dublin. Then, after the morning class, he would be left hanging around for hours not knowing if he was coming or going waiting for the evening class to begin. He did not want to be driving back and forth. The evening classes were gathering more of a crowd than the morning classes. They were increased to twice a week due to this. I eventually conceded and decided to take the plunge and attend an evening class to check it out. I walked down on my own not knowing what to expect. I got to the door of the hall and immediately noticed the sounds coming from inside. It sounded like a boxing class. When I walked into the hall there was a cloud of steam and I could not see a thing, then it lifted. I saw a lot of hard men with big biceps ripping, most, if not all, of them covered in tattoos. Then Frank appeared, "Ah, Tracey, you came." Finally, a face I recognised. I wanted to cling on to Frank for the entire class, I was so embarrassed. I was the only girl in the whole class and I had a physical disability. Talk about drawing attention to myself. Frank had told me beforehand, "Now this class is a bit different to the Reco class but you'll get into the swing of it. You show these lads how it's done." I was a bag of nerves though. All the men were looking at me. Talk about feeling like a square peg in a round hole. I could have said, "I can't do this" and left, feeling dispirited. I was there to take part though, so I just got on with it and finished the class.

After that class, I walked home and I thought to myself, "I can't believe I just did that". I was in shock that I had taken part in that class. Even though I felt a sense of achievement at the action I had just taken and felt very good in myself I also thought I'd just stick to the morning classes. I felt more comfortable in them. That was too much out of my comfort zone. What must those guys have thought of me? What must I have looked like trying to copy them all? In that moment I felt like a spanner. Looking back on it now I know that what I was thinking was laughable. It should not have mattered to me what other people's perceptions of me were as the mere fact I was participating, even with my noticeable disadvantages, was shocking. The fact remains that people stood up and paid attention to the action that I took to get on with my life even through my so called 'disadvantages'. I continued attending the morning class and getting as much out of it as I could. Frank saw me as a good runner and would give me advice on good practises for my running, which is something that will stand with me forever. Frank would arrange to meet me in Santry Park and he would encourage me to do a lap around it to increase my fitness. He bought me a bottle of water that I could hold while I was running to keep myself hydrated.

Evening boxercise classes

It got to the stage Frank felt he wanted to focus more on the evening classes as opposed to the morning ones. I assume he felt that as there were more attending the evening class and there was more of an atmosphere so, it was better use of his time. It was also something that was really needed within the community. I know that Frank felt bad towards the people who were attending the morning classes when he ultimately decided to abandon them. Frank had told me before the class how he was feeling and I could see in him that he was not himself. He looked like a man who had the weight of the world on his shoulders. In that moment I honestly thought that it would pass and that he was just having a bad day "He won't go. I'll be lost without these classes," I thought. Later on, the reality of the situation hit me.

He could not just stay there in order to please the few people who attended. At times only two would show up and this was a huge waste of his precious time. It would be selfish of us to try and convince him to stay when his heart was not in it. I texted him and said, "Do what's right for you, don't worry about anybody else. Do what makes you happy". Frank was glad to hear those words and he soon took my advice. He thanked me and said, "Remember you are always welcome down. I would love to see you at the evening classes." I took in what he was saying but felt that it was not for me. A number of weeks passed and I had not been doing any fitness. It was getting to a stage that I felt I was going out of my mind. I was so upset and I did not like how I was feeling. One evening I'd had enough and thought to myself, "I am gonna grab the bull by the horns and go to boxercise. I've already broken the ice with the guy." I took the leap of faith and headed to the centre. I felt a tiny bit confident because I knew exactly what it was that I was about to face. I still felt very nervous and thought, "What are you doing, Tracey? Round two of looking and feeling like a fish out of water." I arrived at the door and heard the lads roaring from inside the hall. I took a deep breath. "Here it goes." I entered to the same thing as the first time, a puff of steam which then lifted to reveal the sight of the tattooed muscle men. This time they nodded at me as if to say, "Alright." I decided in that moment that I was just going to give it my all. Yeah, it felt weird that I was the only girl and that I had a physical disability but I had to be confident. "Own the feeling." I smiled at everyone there and immediately joined in on the conversation to show the lads that I was a real person who is a little different but can interact and have a laugh the same as everybody else. Even though I cannot respond back like most people they could tell instantly that I was listening and fully tuned into the conversation. It made me happy that I was instantly included.

It felt great to have Frank back as my coach again. Everyone knew me through Frank. I enjoyed the class more; I assumed that they were all very impressed that I had decided to come back. After that class, I decided that I would go back and keep at it, which is exactly what I did and I am still in it to this day.

For the first number of weeks, I was the only girl in that evening boxercise class until one day I arrived there to see another girl. “Am I seeing things?” I could tell she had experience of boxercise as she had brought her own gloves. She was very friendly and did not bat an eyelid at the fact I had a disability. She had no issues and was understanding, which was extremely comforting to me. We had a laugh together. At times when she had her car, she would drop me home; she was a really genuinely nice girl. Then, one day, when I entered the hall she was not there; she had moved on. I was back to being the only girl again. At this stage, all the lads knew me and they were all sound. One of them in particular, Billy was extremely friendly. He started chatting and agreeing with Frank about everything positive that he said about me. I did not know what way to take him initially as he was covered in tattoos and looked a bit dodgy. Prejudgements should never be made, however, as looks can be deceiving. He is a real sound guy who would always shout out this random word, "Whoosa!" when he was working out. He still makes that sound to this day and it is still hilarious. The class is not all really intensely serious so we have a laugh.

As time went on, different girls started, stuck with it for a while and then inevitably moved on. Frank's class was a workout that anyone could get involved in for the first half an hour then some of the class would do sparring. I would feel like a spare tool as the men enjoyed sparring each other. I could not spar good enough to enable my sparring partner to get a good workout. In all the time I went to boxercise I have never had to worry about who would help me with my jacket because Frank was always there and did this instinctively. He was always happy to help. He is a real gentleman who does not want to see me struggle even though I can manage to some extent. I got to know the other lads well too who were all genuinely nice guys. They all looked out for me and encouraged me along, and they would mess fight with me. I was so proud of myself that I decided to stick with the classes as at any moment I could have quit. However, if I was to quit on the first go and made my prejudgements then I would never have reached as far as I have and got to know these really good people. It is all about facing your fears and putting yourself out there.

A number of years ago, Frank and I made plans to do an organised 5k run. I got the ball rolling and put it out there to him. It was something I really wanted to do and I wanted to do it with Frank by my side. It was in the Docklands near the 3arena. We had got our T-shirts that we required to participate in the run; it was very exciting and real when they arrived at my house.

On the day of the run, Frank met me at the Reco; he was telling everyone what we were doing. When we arrived we were all ready to begin, we had our green T-shirts on and looking ready. Frank was getting everyone to take pictures and he was saying to them, "Isn't she some girl. I'm so impressed". He would then look at me so proudly before I had even done the run. When the run began we paced ourselves and I felt grateful that Frank was there with me every step. During the run, he was telling everyone about me and taking lots of pictures. I found it difficult towards the end. Frank ran a bit ahead towards the end and just before the finish line he stopped and took lots of pictures of me passing. "Go on, Tracey. You're brilliant!" When I crossed the finish line, Frank patted me on the back. "Fair play to you Tracey, you're a real trooper". He could not have been more proud and neither could I though, in fairness. The fact was that I was living my life the way I wanted, always making the effort to overcome new challenges. After the race, while we were heading home in Frank's car I felt my head getting bigger by the second and I was laughing to myself while thinking, "You are going to have to chop the roof off the car. My head is getting bigger the more you talk. Thank you! I know I am just great." He drove me home and told Mam all about the race and went through the pictures. That was a very proud and happy moment for me. Frank kept on bringing up at the class how inspirational I was. I was thinking, "I only did a 5k. It wasn't a Forest Gump moment, running across America unable to stop." Ah, but it is right for me to give myself credit and feel glad that I have a good person who really supported me every step of the way during that race and many other times since I first met him.

There are times when other things come up that mean I cannot attend boxercise in the evenings. However, no matter what goes on in my life or how many classes I have missed I would always go back when my evenings freed up again. Frank is so committed to the classes; for as long as I have been attending the classes he has hardly missed one. Fair play to him, is all I can say. He is committed.

A number of years ago I returned to boxercise after not attending for a while. I instantly noticed that there were a group of women older than me and fewer men this time. I was thinking, "Am I in the right class?" Frank was talking to me in front of everyone as though they all knew me. He was telling them all little snippets about me. "Me and Tracey go well back. We did a 5k run and all. She is such an inspiration" When the class started he said to me, "Go on, Tracey, you take the lead. Show them how it's done". At that moment I was thinking, "I haven't been here in ages!" Our warm ups usually require running round in a circle, swinging our arms, touching the floor, out for three then in for three, walking while punching and then stretches. As the weeks went on, I got to know all the women well. They were really nice and chatty. I felt these women connected more with me, which helped me get more out of the class. They each wanted to know me and made me feel involved, which I was delighted about.

I started to get to know Billy more. He has his own inspiring story and that makes me happy that I can be around like-minded people who want to get the best out of their lives. Billy's life path took a wrong turn and at one stage he was in the gutter feeling like he had nothing and was nothing. He openly talks about this to everyone as he is proud of his accomplishments and wants to teach others how to do the same. He has overcome obstacles and taken ownership of his life. He is inspiring to me and everyone who is lucky to know him. People now look up to him as a role model, instead of looking down on him and regarding him as a waste of space. Despite the harsh knocks he received over the years, he rose beyond it and took action in creating a better life for himself. He now teaches boxercise and helps a lot of people who have a similar life to what he had, feeling that there is no end in sight or light at the end of that distant and sometimes never-ending tunnel. He has gone on to study in order to equip himself with the knowledge required in offering support to people. He also volunteers mainly with the homeless. He is very committed and the time he gives to this volunteer work is incredible. He is such a good-hearted guy.

The women who have joined the boxercise in recent years are more committed than any of the other girls had been. I think when you leave anything physical for too long it becomes harder to get back into the swing of it. The women are so friendly and helpful and they always make me feel included. The class now catered more for women – in the last few years – and, as a consequence, the sparring is now on for an hour before the class. The women, Billy, and Frank give me a hand taking my jacket off and putting the gloves on. The women got to know my physical capabilities and they make sure I grip the weights correctly by helping my thumb get a proper grip on them as they know my thumbs have tendency to get stuck. Billy is always slagging me saying, "Tracey hasn't even broken a sweat." I still manage to inspire Frank and he would say, "You're keeping the classes going, Tracey". Billy would agree saying they needed me as much as I needed them. According to Frank, I am a 'legend'. Every now and again we go out for social nights, and these too are great fun.

My message to you is this: If you enjoy doing something and it is beneficial to either your physical health, mental health or both, then stick with it. Turn off that part of your brain that starts making excuses for you and reasons why you cannot do this because those self-limiting beliefs are preventing you from bettering yourself. Take the leap of faith and you will reap the rewards, believe me.

One-on-one training

After the morning boxercise classes had been cancelled, I felt that my motivation and energy levels had dropped dramatically. I needed to find some other form of outlet for my excess energy before the decline spiralled out of control. I needed to find something where I would be offered good support and encouragement along the way, which was just as important to me as the potentially beneficial activity itself. I spent a number of weeks looking into different activities that I could throw myself into. However, the pivotal moment came when I asked Patrick to contact the Poppintree Community Centre, which is a sports and fitness centre near my home and is run by Dublin City Council. Patrick made some general queries on my behalf and arranged a meeting with the manager of the centre and myself. I arrived at the centre a little bit anxious but eager to see what they could offer me. The manager was very friendly and welcoming towards me. He told me that there were a number of different fitness classes that I could get involved in, which I excitedly and enthusiastically got involved in for a number of weeks.

One day, I received an email from the manager offering me my own private one-to-one sessions that would be tailored to my needs, which I was very excited about. For a brief time when I started my one-to-one training it was with a man who worked in the centre. Shortly after those few classes a woman took over; she was amazing because she pushed me to the limits, which was what I wanted and needed. She was around the same age as me, which I found easier. She was a lovely person and we worked on a vast amount of intense regimes. My hands have a tendency to close most of the time and due to this my thumbs get locked inside this "unbreakable" grip that my hands create. During my one-to-one sessions this would be one of the main areas that she would work on by getting me to release my hands enough to roll or catch a ball. I am going to assume that this may sound easy to you but it was an extremely difficult challenge for me. She would also get me to stretch out my arms and hands to take a ball from her, she would not allow me to take the ball if my hands were clenched closed. This required an enormous amount of concentration from me. However, when I relaxed my mind enough, my muscles would then also relax and through a determined and relaxed mind I would always achieve this apparent simplistic task. I loved doing the TRX suspension training as it really is an amazing workout. At times, however, I would not grip the handles correctly and they would slip out of my hands. She would get me to work excessively on my grip and on relaxing my thumbs enough to enable me to have a good grip. To train myself to achieve, this she would get me to grip a long stick and lift it over my head while imagining that there were buckets of water attached to either side and to avoid spilling any water from the buckets while lifting the stick over my head. This visualisation technique greatly improved my coordination and grip at the same time. She would then get me to do a few laps of the hall where the training was based. This hall is a standard-size basketball hall and I would do around twelve laps of it; she never allowed me to slack off, which I found great. If I wanted to stop I could but never did. She was always amazed at my tenacity to not concede. I was of the mindset that I was there to train and that I was not going to moan about being "too tired" or that it was "too difficult". You would be surprised what you can achieve once you put your mind to it. The last thing I would always do during my one-to-one training classes was the rowing machine. She would always make sure I had a proper grip while using this and that I was not cheating in any way, shape, or form. Every week, she would get me to reach new distance and resistance targets on this machine; I would do three kilometres most of the time. This was always a difficult feat, however, I would always feel this overwhelming sense of achievement afterwards. I would attend these sessions twice a week and understandably be sweating after each class. On the finer days we would go to the park for a run or a power walk. She would always tell me to make sure I drank lots and not just a dribble. That woman moved on after a period of time. There were other instructors who put me through my paces too. I am so grateful to all of them as they collectively contributed toward me bettering myself both physically and mentally.

Running club

I have always been of the determined and defiant mindset; determined in doing what I feel would be beneficial to my well-being and defiant in not allowing people's perceptions of my capabilities dictate my achieving these potential benefits. I do not, however, sit around and wait for somebody to offer me the opportunity of involvement as I know all too well that may never happen. If there is something I want to participate in, I know I must throw myself into it, and I always do just that.

A while back I decided that I would join a running club that was held in the Clonliffe Harriers Athletics Club in Santry Woods Park. It was on every Thursday. Patrick and I met up with the lady who ran the running club. She was a very nice lady and was delighted that I had shown an interest in joining. She decided to take me under her wing the first few nights, running beside me around the park and encouraging me the whole time. She said that she felt truly inspired that I decided to join regardless of my 'disability'. She also admired Patrick for bringing me down each week and staying there from the beginning till the end. I would jog what felt like the entire park for an hour each week and then go back to the club where Patrick was waiting. In the darker evenings, we would jog along the road for an hour up through Northwood in Santry. There were a number of other runners there also, all kitted out in their running gear. I would get back into the car after the hour, absolutely sweating and so tired. My feet would be on fire. My legs were aching. I didn't know whether to laugh or cry, realising I was too exhausted to do anything as breathing is all I could manage. It was so worth it though. I always felt brilliant the next day, a lot more positive, and content in myself. It goes without saying the importance of physical exercise in aiding your mental and physical state. It is vital in my eyes. The truth is I like a bit of pain!

Other things fitness related

Every so often, different programmes are announced from within the surrounding area. I am always watching and listening out for these as I love to involve myself in physical or social activities. As I write this book there is a new programme that is starting soon in the Poppintree Sports Centre called "Change Your Life". In this programme there will be boot camps, group runs/walks and even Tai Chi, which I have done in the past. A number of years ago, I took part in a ten-week fitness course that included Tai Chi and yoga. Tai Chi is so beneficial to me because it primarily focuses on relaxing the muscles and balance improvement.

If you are ever feeling low on physical energy and/or that you are not doing enough work on yourself physically then maybe all you need is to get involved in a physical activity. If you are sitting there wondering where you would find such activity then bear in mind that the closest activity to you may be in your local community centre. Keep your eyes open and your ear to the ground and you will find something. It is not that difficult nowadays anyway, as we are all becoming more health conscious. If you feel like you need to do something to keep yourself physically fit but are debating with yourself whether to or not, then I implore you to just take the leap and go for it because in most cases the potential benefits far outweigh the possible negatives.

A number of years ago, I took part in a few spinning classes. When I got to know the lads in boot camp I found out that one of them did a spinning class in a community centre near Croke Park, on a Tuesday morning for one hour. I thought I'd like to give that a go. I had to get a bus from home to Dorset Street. I would get off near Quinn's pub and walk for a good fifteen minutes. The classes themselves were very tough on my legs, which felt like jelly towards the end of the first few classes. However, the more classes, I attended the easier it became, as my leg muscles were getting stronger. It was a great workout. Then, of course, I would have boot camp that evening. Everyone was amazed at me for managing to do all of these things, in some cases, one literally after another. They wondered how I had the energy for boot camp after that workout. I always felt great after them though. To me, the end justified the means.

I even tried my hand at line dancing. Mam brought me to classes as a young teenager. It helped a lot with my coordination, balance, confidence, and fitness. It was a great social scene as I started back. I go every so often and enjoy the fast dances. It involves good concentration. I know I do not do the steps exactly how the dance is taught but I know the flow of it. It is great to have that time with Mam too.

I love to set physical challenges for myself e.g. seeing how I far I get up the road before a bus that I could have waited for passes by. I find great pleasure in making it to my final destination on foot before a bus that I could have potentially waited an hour for at a bus stop. This gives me a small feeling of self-achievement. I am happy that I have made it to my destination and have got exercise at the same time. That being said, however, there are times when I do need to wait on a bus because otherwise, I would not make my appointments, etc. On my way up to Mam's house some mornings, I do the same. A number of times I have actually arrived at Mam's front door only to see the bus that I could have got on pass by. I feel delighted with myself. If it is lashing rain then obviously that makes the situation a little different and a bus is the best option unless I am wrapped up in some rainproof clothing. On the rainy days when I unwillingly decide to get a bus, both I and the other people at the bus stop are like sardines all hugged under the bus shelter trying to stay dry. On days when it is not raining, I am free to exercise to my heart's content and beat the bus at the race that goes on in my head.

At times if I am going down to Mam's house and I am being collected I will generally walk in the direction of the house as fast as I can so that whoever is collecting me does not have to drive all the way up to get me. I push myself to the physical limit to try and get a little closer, each time I do this.

The family dog, Sam, also keeps us all on our toes. He is a Border Collie and like myself loves being physically active and running around the park feeling the freedom of his muscles getting their workout. I can relate to that. Sam is very clever as he has mastered the art of opening doors with his paws. Whenever I am in the kitchen he will open the door at times and cry out until I come out and play football with him.

I hate becoming ill, the same as everyone else. However, the reason I hate getting sick is because it significantly affects my disability i.e. my muscles feel more tense, which in turn makes it difficult for me to participate in my physical exercises. I can just about manage one day feeling like that. I cannot handle been laid up because of the lack of exercise I get during this time.

Other than the rare times when I am too ill to do anything, I still persevere and get on with a physical exercise to some degree. I feel that a lot of people wrap themselves up in cotton wool when they get even the sniffles, sore tooth, or mild cramps. In my opinion, they are not doing themselves any favours in the long run unless they are really ill or have other medical issues. I feel certain people indulge in self-pity. I personally find it holds me back from doing all the things I feel essential to me. Do not get me wrong though, I acknowledge 'time outs' and relaxing moments in life are important in order to let my body heal properly, and to give my body time to heal, step by step. I always build myself back up and get back to what is important to me, my physical health, and fitness.

I cannot sit around the house all day in my pyjamas because I need to be constantly moving my muscles. It is always on my mind to move and to get the blood flowing, even if it just my toes. This is not due to my disability; this is and always has been due to my state of mind.

A Vocal Workout

I have always wanted to use my vocals again but I found speech therapy too stressful and always felt judged and pressured by the therapists. Sitting in a room, trying to work on my vocal muscles, it would feel good if I said a clear word or even managed to get my tongue out, even to just belt out a few sounds or words. I did not really get any praise if I really tried my hardest. All I got was a "That was not hard to do, was it?" They would say this in a patronising tone and I would be thinking, "It was hard actually, yes, but I did it regardless." I thought singing classes would be cool to do and would be equally therapeutic for my vocal muscles. To be able to practise using my voice in a fun way without that strain I felt in the more clinical therapies was what I craved. I started researching into different ways I could strengthen my voice and singing seemed the best option. I went to a singing teacher for a few lessons. I felt it was not suitable for me though as the way he was teaching me was not very beneficial to my needs. I needed someone who understood these needs and would push me. A few weeks later I was sitting at home and reading a brochure that I'd happened to pick up from the Axis centre in Ballymun. I saw they had different classes on and, lo and behold, singing was one of them. I took the leap and texted the mobile number that was on the brochure and explained my condition. I asked if the instructor would be willing to give me lessons. Michelle was the instructor's name. She immediately responded to my text and was very interested. I asked Mam to ring Michelle to explain my condition in more detail. Michelle was very nice and professional. She was more than happy to take me on and she wanted to research into my condition to give herself a clearer understanding as to what I had been through and what dystonia entailed.

It was January 2012 when I first met Michelle and I was twenty-four. Mam came with me just to introduce me then she left me to it. When I saw Michelle for the first time I could tell straight away that she was a really nice person with a lot of understanding and patience. I felt that I could dive right into it as she made me feel very comfortable around her. She chatted first to break the ice, a very bubbly and witty woman who I knew I would get on with. She then guided me through the exercises. She was using a keyboard to keep me in sync with the keys she wanted me to try to hit. I felt safe around her, safe and comfortable enough to open my mouth and let my voice out. At first, I admit that I was nervous naturally enough. When I sang my first few words, Michelle knew that it was difficult for me to do so. She complimented me on doing it. These compliments made me smile and feel good about myself and I got a massive sense of achievement. It felt as though I had accomplished something huge in that moment and knew that this would work for me. Maybe not for my vocal cords to the extent I had imagined previously but definitely it would add to my confidence. Patrick had always told me that if I improved my confidence in communicating around others that would relax my muscles enough to be understood more easily. Self-confidence and the ability to relax my muscles go hand in hand. After the first class with Michelle, I wanted to go back because I knew it was what I needed. I set up a ten-week course with her. Every Tuesday at 4.15pm, I would go to her and use my vocals. I would stand in front of a mirror and see what I was doing. I found I would always look beyond the mirror, however. Michelle kept on getting me to look at myself directly saying it would help. When I got into the habit of doing this I found it great and my confidence expanded dramatically. I felt very impressed with myself and decided to sign up to do another ten-week course. I knew I was much better in that one. I knew the system and I was getting used to it. After the second ten-week course I wanted to sign up again. However, during the time between the end of the second course and deciding to go for a third course I received a text from Michelle informing me that she was leaving the Axis. This message was not sent just to me directly. I could tell it was sent to all her other clients too. She informed everyone that she would be doing Saturday classes in Temple Bar and that we are all more than welcome to have our classes with her there. I did feel a bit disappointed as the Axis was near me and I could not always commit to Saturdays. These things happen though and we cannot expect anyone to stay in the same place forever just to suit our needs. Besides, it was not like she had stopped running the entire course so all was not lost.

The new course was a four-week programme. I could just attend one class but I found it was better to pay for the full course, as a 'thank-you' gesture to her for her assistance over the past few months. Every so often I would organise with Michelle that even if I could not make one of the Saturdays I could put it forward to another week.

Michelle and I became good friends; we would meet up for a coffee, a chat or go to the cinema. I never would have expected a friendship would occur from these lessons; it truly is amazing where you find friends who serve as such positive influences in your life. She really is a great person to talk to. She allows me to talk, giving me the time required for me to communicate. She always wants to know how I am and she does not just fob me off with a nod. She has a great understanding; she always makes me think about my situation and what I can do to improve it. It is not just her telling me what I should do, she is a good listener. We do have a good laugh. Whenever I have been around her and I am leaving her I always feel good and positive. That is how true friends are supposed to make you feel.

College life

Anyone can hide. Now, facing your challenges and working through them…**that is what makes you stand out!**

Through my life, I have done plenty of FETAC courses, which, in fact, I did not thoroughly enjoy as none of them were in fields that truly interested me. I feel that I just partook in these courses for the sake of keeping busy. They were not something I felt at any stage as being worthwhile to me and because of this, I got bored fairly quickly in them. I knew I was capable of more and strongly believed that I had a larger purpose in life. I felt that my story had to be told to demonstrate to people that sheer determination, focus and motivation can aid **anyone** to achieve their goals and or dreams.

In 2015, I took part in a diploma course in psychology, which I found intriguing. One of the most interesting things I found during this course was the overemphasis on looking back at what happened in your life to try establish a reason as to why you feel the way you do presently. The reason I was so interested in this was because I believe that you should not spend so much time delving into past events. Yes, they shaped your current state but the only way to improve that state if it warrants an improvement is in future planning. **This is just my opinion**. From that interest, I began to focus in on one aspect in particular within that field. I am referring to personal coaching. While not as prestigious as psychology, I felt it would be more helpful for me if I took part in a course in this field. I found a course through Google, which seemed good and I enquired about it. The one 'disadvantage' to this course was that it required a great deal of communication skills. I began to doubt if I could I do it. Patrick kept at me to do something about achieving my ambition so I bit the bullet and went for it. I knew in my own heart that I was well able for this intense course. It was just taking that leap and giving it my all. Life requires a few leaps of faith every now and again.

The course itself only lasted a week. It was from 9:30am till 5:00pm and we had two assignments to complete and submit six weeks after the course. It seemed manageable; I knew it was something I needed to do in order to gain experience and knowledge to progress in the field that I wanted to develop in. I went for it and I will say now that I am glad I did and I never looked back. It was such an incredible experience. The title of the course was Performance and Personal Coaching and it was a QQI level 6; a nice level of achievement. It was meant to take place in a hotel in Blanchardstown, which would have been handy for me as it was a short distance away. The location got changed however to the Louis Fitzgerald Hotel on the Naas Road, which was on the south side of Dublin. Due to this, the inevitable self-doubt began to creep in and I started thinking of obstacles. The traffic will be mental, the thoughts of been stuck in traffic, not getting home till all hours, having to leave really early. Patrick kept telling me I could do it so I got past that obstacle. Patrick was off work the first day of the course. He took the effort to bring me over the first day and help me to break the ice and to make sure everyone would see my capabilities. I quickly realised throughout the week that this particular course will stand me for the future, in my personal life and would assist me in achieving the next part of my life dream, to help others. On the first day, Patrick and I were the first to arrive, which was great as it meant that I was able to settle in and find the seat I wanted. I could tell straight away it would be a very small class, which I was very pleased about; we would all get equal time given to us by the teacher. Everyone arrived and we introduced ourselves. I had my introduction pre-typed out on an app I use to speak for me. My stomach was turning more with excitement though than nerves. That said, I was feeling nervous too. People listened to what I was saying via the app and I was delighted with that.

At first, the teacher along with the other students did not fully know how I would get through the course as it was intense and nobody had met anyone like me before. As time went on, however, they quickly realised I was very determined and had my own way of communicating. It was this determination that got me through in the end. It helped also that it was a small enough class with only around eight people involved all together. I tell you, this particular course really did put me miles outside of my comfort zone. I am used to sitting back and allowing someone else to talk to me and for them to control the flow of the conversation. Every day in this course I was involved in a one-to-one conversation with a mock client and I was supposed to control the conversation in a structured way. My confidence increased as the week progressed. I inspired everyone. They all said I taught them what determination truly means and that I would make a great coach and that I have no self-limiting beliefs from what they can see. I will try my hand at anything even though I have a challenging disability. I do not let it hold me back. That is why I did that course. I had to find a way to communicate with my disability greatly limiting my communication ability in a course that involved a substantial amount of verbal communication. I have this inner strength that yes, I could do that. Deep down, we all do. I was delighted that I took part in that course and faced it head on. It was quite intense, to be honest. I felt exhausted, which was not surprising considering I was just back from Panama two days prior to the first day on the course, but it was so worth it. I finished my final assessment for the course, which involved another mock session, which was recorded and I felt it went very well. The teacher even told me that she thought I was amazing and that I can do one-to-ones with people because I have great listening skills and knew how to ask the correct, probing questions. I felt proud that I completed that course. To have made that leap and achieved what I temporarily had assumed, a number of weeks beforehand, to be unachievable. I feel now that I am definitely on the right track. I also have this book, which I feel is an important stepping stone for me to achieve what I want to achieve in life. I feel I would make a great inspirational motivational speaker as there are not many of them in Ireland with my type of experience. The course itself was a fresh learning experience for me as it required a great deal of verbal communication from me. I got through it in the end though. This was a steep learning curve. It was essential for me to put myself out there and learn a new skill in the process.

Networking

Since leaving secondary school, I have always sought that big thing that helps people make the transition from the learning aspect of their daily routine to the next step into adulthood. I have always wanted a job. While I have held some temporary jobs over the years these were more work-experience type jobs and nothing that really made me feel that I was contributing to society in anyway. It did not give me the feeling of purpose that I would associate with an actual job. One day in early 2016, while on Facebook, I stumbled across a business. I came across this on a friend's page. Her name is Jenny and I knew her from the drama I had done years before. She had taken part in "the Madeline Laundries" too. I was very interested in this business venture as it allowed me to effectively run my own business under the umbrella of the Company itself. I was intrigued at the concept of having a ready-made business, which did not require much of an investment from me so I jumped on this opportunity.

The company has opened up a lot of positive self-motivating belief in me that I never even imagined or knew was there. It has given me the encouragement and self-confidence to make videos on social media promoting my business. From the reaction that I received, I knew people were more interested in me and my story than my business. I never in a million years would have had the confidence to expose myself in such a way without the unbelievable encouragement I got from people, some of whom I knew from the company, others past friends from years gone and some were complete strangers. Every aspect of my personal growth went through the roof. My 'Up line' or managers with the company, were Amanda and her husband Ian who are both such inspiring, beautiful people. They took the time to get to know me and they always listen to what I have to say because they know I have important input into whatever is being discussed. They feel that people need to take heed of me. Amanda understands my sense of humour and she can tell I have a cheeky, funny side. She is able to tell from me that, despite my life being shadowed by negative events, I am always trying my best to stay positive and upbeat. Amanda loves helping people; she gives great advice and knowledge to others due to her years of experience with the company and the product range. I have met lots of people in the positivity minded circle who look up to me and feel honoured to meet me. I have people doing everything in their power to meet me after seeing my videos. This indeed really means the world to me, not because of the ego boost I get from it but because the message I am putting across is hitting home with a lot of them.

I have also been honoured to meet an extremely nice couple who are business owners and professional coaches, Donna Kennedy and Pat Slattery. They are amazing and inspiring speakers who had their own struggles but through their positive mindset and continuous hard work, they became successes in their own right. They now teach people positive strategies in order to conquer self-doubt and how to be motivated toward reaching goals. Amanda, Donna, and Pat are always making very inspiring videos, using their knowledge and experience in these videos, which are aimed at helping people. They always help me.

I often find, however, that I can dive into workshops looking for the answers to improve myself, when I really hold all the answers I need within myself. Nobody can really react to my situation. I realised the only person who fully gets me is me. That is ok because the tools I have taught myself have worked. I am so strong.

I now feel that I have met and surrounded myself with the right people. I met a lovely fabulous woman through an event and we connected straight away. I felt very inspired by her as her passion is helping others to succeed. There is not a selfish bone in her. She treats everyone with the same level of respect and always makes time for people. Her name is Bronagh. I am now part of the company she is involved in, which is more up my street as it is primarily for people who love to travel. This is a brilliant social group for me to be part of. When I was younger, I visualised going away with a group of lovely, down to earth and good-natured people. I would see myself surrounded by positive people, loving life. I believe everything you visualise will come to you even if you have forgotten because it's been so long, but eventually, it does come in a different shape or form. It was once a thought, and thoughts can manifest themselves into an end result, once you stay focused on the end goal.

The people in my life right now know what they are talking about. They speak about how important a healthy mindset is and letting things go; seeing the good in everything. I love to hear their positive views on life as it is exactly how I see things. Surrounding myself with positive people who see the person I am and look past my disability is one of the things that I am extremely grateful for in my life. I feel comforted by that collective feeling of positivity. Through their belief in me, I now have a self-belief in my life and feel that I have more to give. They have made me see that my story and my determination to never give up should be told and for that, I am thankful to them. It is sad that not everyone follows good advice. There are lots of people who have this perception that they cannot alter their circumstances and they choose to stay in that same pessimistic frame of mind. These people are clearly fed up with their situations. However, they generally have very little self-belief and at times are afraid to make the changes that could potentially better their lives.

I have found from my own experience that we tend to spend most of our life waiting for things to change for us. We moan when things do not go our way and feel sorry for ourselves; this is human nature, I suppose. I have found, however, that in order to overcome this human flaw we need to take dogged action in reaching our life goals while realising that nothing in this life gets handed to us. Nobody is here to take full control of our lives for us and assist us in obtaining our own definitions of happiness. Ultimately, we are in control of shaping our own lives and pursuing our own happiness. We are in the driving seat. We not only control but we choose our destiny. We need to stop waiting on that out of the blue knock on our door or that phone call that will bring a huge change in our lives. Go out, take action, and make the rest of your life count. You and only you can do it.

I have always had to find ways of searching for solutions to problems that most people cannot even relate to. I now believe that I have the capability of doing just that with full self-belief in my eventual success. To me, that is the true meaning when I say that I have taken back my power. Now, go out, remain positive, and actively ***take back yours***!

"Every adversity, every failure, and every heartache carries with it the Seed of an equivalent or greater Benefit"

-- Napoleon Hill

Chapter 7

Feeling positive when I am depressed

"Unhappiness, Misery, Sorrow, Dejection, Downheartedness, or even Depression; Whatever word we use to describe those moments of helplessness and despair we must come to realise this: if we stay focused on achieving our desired goals we can create an abundance of self-worth and happiness in our lives"

– Tracey Ellen Maria

Firstly, allow me to state that I am not claiming this book or my story will inspire any change in your life. Whatever changes you need or want to make in your own life you will not get the desired answers from a website or a book. I am not a trained doctor in the field of mental health. I do, however, have twenty years of experience dealing with my own mental health issues. I am merely equipping you with some of the methods that have shown amazing results for me personally, and a lot of other people who I know. Ultimately it is down to you to implement the suggested changes in order to improve your life. With the right mentality and determination, self-help will ALWAYS benefit more than shelf help.

The day that my life changed I felt that a part of me had died. Even though I was still the same Tracey underneath, it felt as though I was trapped. It was hard to lose that part of me that I held so precious: my ability to speak freely, and clearly, and without any effort. To have that taken away in an instant, combined with my inability to use my hand functions, was quite distressing. It took a long time to adapt and learn new ways of doing everyday things. Some people can go their entire lives without getting even the flu; others cannot even remember the needles that they received when they were babies. I have often felt jealous of those people. I did not choose this life, but I believe it chose me because the 'power that be' saw in me an inner strength and the ability to push myself beyond this challenge and to inspire and encourage others to do the same. I would not change the path that was given to me, as it has shaped me into the strong, determined and brave person that I am today. I am now fully aware, through my own life experiences, that every hurdle we are faced with, we can overcome together.

The importance of physical and mental health

In this day and age, mental health awareness is more openly discussed. People are encouraged to open up and share their issues with no judgement being passed. However, this is only within the past few years because when I was growing up, mental health was not discussed. I am sure that this was the case over the previous decades and generations. During those times, if you were not feeling yourself and felt that it was different to just having a 'down day', questions would then arise. People would automatically assume that there was something wrong with you and that was that. Due to my difficulties with communication, I felt so cut off from society as a whole. There were days I felt that I needed someone to help me and give me the time to allow me back into the circle of society. I felt that people acted as if they were afraid of me and that they did not understand. More than that, however, I felt they ***did not want to understand***. I would think, "I am human, and I am here". People can talk to me like they do anyone else if they just get past the presumptions they attach to me, for example, that if I cannot talk, then I cannot understand what they are saying. I can understand, however, and, believe it or not, I pick up on a lot more than people who can talk do because I give the amount of patience and attention that I require when I am trying to communicate. I have learnt from years of people who are willing to give me the time, that communication is a two-way thing and from this life lesson I have come to the conclusion that if people just paid a little more attention to what each other says and valued each other's opinions on things, the world would be a better place. A far-fetched thought, I know. Thankfully, I do honestly value myself more now, and surrounding myself with like-minded people who appreciate my company has greatly aided me in dealing with the mental health issues that I had to experience on my own for so long. This book will be the first time I have spoken openly about my depressive moments and how I dealt with this seemingly daily struggle. A few close family members and Patrick are the only ones who know how truly unbearable it was for me. Hopefully, by my sharing my story via this book it will inspire more people who feel as I felt to speak up and, most importantly for them, to realise that even though it may feel that they are alone in their struggles, they are not.

Moments of depression

I have thrown a few tantrums in my teen years and even in adulthood. I feel this type of behaviour was justified, however, as I was struggling with the acceptance of not having the ability to do 'normal' things. These outbursts have subsided a great deal, but every now and again they can recur. These events are triggered by my life struggles becoming unbearable at times and the constant battles I am faced with. In these moments, however brief they may be, I have felt dead inside. Hollywood has, over the years, made a great deal of movies that highlight the frustration of feeling as invisible as a ghost with the main character in these movies trying desperately to be seen or heard. This is how I feel during those moments, like a ghost, desperately struggling to be noticed while people just pass by me without hesitation as they seemingly stride through their lives. I am sure some of you can relate to feeling this way occasionally. I can also experience moments where the challenges seem too unbearable to overcome and feel that I am hitting brick walls at every attempt. I would find myself wondering if there is any light at the end of this God-forsaken tunnel, or if I would be constantly given difficult tasks to overcome. However, no matter how low I feel or how often I find myself thinking, 'What is the point?' I would never give added fuel to my self-pity for too long. I allow myself a moment to feel like this, just a moment, and then I would get on with my life again. I would always drag myself out of bed, brush myself off, and paint the artificial smile on my face, even if it killed me. I want to hide my negative emotions away from the outside world. I only want them to see my positive side. Some things are not worth expressing in public, as most people would not understand.

Depression can, in itself, be a struggle to overcome. One of the most depressing things that I have had to deal with was the way I was being constantly treated. This always made me feel cut off from the world for such a long period of my youth. Nobody wanted to know me; they made it obvious that they were awkward around me, and that they had little or no patience for me. I had moments where I would struggle to figure out who I was and question if I was needed at all. As I was growing up, my development was deeply affected because the friends I was making never stayed around for too long, and I had no self-identity. I had no idea what to say to the people who would listen to me, what was fashionable to wear, what music to listen to or what the 'in' thing was. I was confused and messed up. It was an extremely frustrating and deeply depressing time in my life. One day I felt that I could not cope anymore and I lashed out in front of my family, screaming intensely at the top of my lungs. I would not stop for a breath. I was going mad, jumping up and down while trying to focus on the words I wanted to scream. I attempted to calm down. Obviously, Mam was upset and shocked at my sudden and abrupt outburst. I ended up walking out because I felt so terrible due to the way I had just behaved. I thought that my family was better off without me and that they deserved better than me. Whenever I felt myself starting to boil over with frustration I got into an awful habit of writing up a list of things I hated about myself in big black bold words. I am worthless. I am a bad person. I am not worth anyone's time, etc. I would then print this list off and read it over and over again; as I did this self-destructive act, I felt myself getting angrier and angrier.

I would be lying if I said these outbreaks were at all seldom. I would lie awake all night crying but trying all the time to be silent. I could not switch these depressive thoughts off no matter what I tried. I would be questioning, "Why am I here?". Constantly worrying about the person I was. I hated who I was becoming. I felt I did not know who I was or what I was supposed to be doing here; I felt the world was completely against me. I made myself very distant from everyone, spending hours in my bedroom alone feeling sad and full of rage. I always put on a mask and tried to hide how I felt away from the outside world. There was no hiding it from Mam and my stepdad though. They could read me like a book. My depressive rages got so bad that it seemed like I was possessed. Mam was just short of throwing holy water at me and making the sign of the cross. I was like a demon in disguise. My mam and stepdad would be horrified at my behaviour, but when you feel yourself ready to explode and you have no way of expressing it verbally it only adds to your frustration. I had no other way to express myself. I was in a dark place during those times; I wanted to escape from my reality. At times I wished my life away thinking that I could not wait until I was older and my teenage years were behind me, that things would be easier. I would lie on my bed feeling empty and worthless, looking up at the ceiling and saying in my mind, “If there is a God, please, just take me. I cannot cope on this earth any longer. I feel I don’t belong here, so, please, put me out of my misery”. I would hold out for a response from above to see if I was being heard, but nothing. Then I would take a few deep breaths, I would calm down and fill my mind with positivity by repeating to myself, “I am strong. I will overcome this”. I would then look to the ceiling again and say in my mind, “God if you are listening, I did not mean what I said. Just give me the strength to keep on going”. I would visualise a white light surrounding me like I was being protected by God and commence going about my day again.

Those situations seemed to be an on-going process with me for a number of years. I would self-talk myself around a lot, and thankfully, it always worked. Anytime I would turn to God and ask him, “Why am I suffering?” only then would I feel myself being apologetic for lashing out, and feeling sorry for hurting my family. I do not regard depression as being a part of my disability. I get moments of feeling depressed but I am not in a constant depressive state, however. When people talk to me like the rest of the population and make me feel that I am understood, I feel positive and self-confident. I actually get a bit of a fright when someone gives me these boosts in self-confidence. Communication is an important thing. One day, I stormed off out of

Mam's house because I felt that my dreams were too far away and that I was looking for too much in life. I got on a bus to a park; my head was spinning. I did twenty laps of the park, running around it like I was demented, and then I sat on a bench. Darkness was setting in but I would not budge. I was too stubborn to go home. In that moment, I felt that there was no point and that giving up was the easiest option I would never achieve my dreams.

I realised a number of years ago that I could not stay in this state of mind for much longer as I was very much aware of how unhealthy it was becoming for me. It was affecting others around me also. I did try my hardest to get on with life and stay in a positive mindset. I felt people did not realise I was trying to do this in order to ease my feelings of social isolation. I realised the people I had around me were bad influences on me and I needed to move away from them, and not focus all my energy on those particular people. However, with me being so young, they were the only people I really knew. It can be very daunting to try and make a fresh start. You can only make so many attempts at self-rejuvenation, feel you are not making any progress, and keep falling back into the same patterns thinking that it would be easier if people just accepted you. I could not go back to that way of thinking though. I was given tough challenges and I could either cry and be angry for the rest of my life, which would not get me anywhere, or I could keep striding through and take each day as it came, acknowledging the fact that I would get so many knock-backs along the way but continue in my belief that I would come out the other side as a more stronger and self-empowered Tracey. The key was to not give up; I had many days where I really felt tested and too dejected to keep going on. I needed to allow myself those days where I felt it was too hard, but then I would always quickly snap out of it and get back on my horse. As the saying goes, what do you do when you fall off a horse? You get back on it. It was fight or flight...I chose fight.

"It is never too late to start over again and be happy"
– Tracey Ellen Maria

Making myself positive

I discovered while studying psychology, that the messages we feed into our minds from the outside world can have a drastic effect on our mindset. And as such, a number of years ago, I began listening to positive YouTube videos. What I have learnt from some of these is that, even in my darkest moments, if I forced a smile on my face it sent signals to my brain to feel happy. I would force myself to stand or sit up straight to try not to look as though I had the weight of the world on my shoulders. This seemingly simple technique also had great benefits on my psyche. This form of tricking the mind is probably common knowledge; it was, however, just a temporary solution to my underlying problem that I needed to address.

I found that the most difficult thing to do was take that first step. When attempting to motivate myself to make the necessary changes, I felt like I had these invisible rocks tied to my ankles; anchors holding me down. Also, it was like I had an invisible glass wall positioned in front and blocking me, preventing me from progressing. It caused me great difficulty trying to punch through this wall and kick away my heavy shackles. However, I found that as soon as I had built up enough positive mental strength to break down this wall, I felt motivated towards making changes in my life. I would get up, get washed, get dressed, have breakfast, and then go out the door to embrace the beauty of the day. Even if my depressive bouts came on throughout the day or evening as opposed to the morning, I would do the same – keep my body and mind busy by giving myself stimulating things to do, things that would aid me in achieving my desired goals. Without sounding egotistical, that type of determination seriously deserves a pat on the back and, I hope, leaves a message with you, the reader. If you are ever 'down in the dumps' and feel like obstacles are being placed in your way everywhere you turn, then take note of the following mantra and repeat it to yourself again and again, especially in moments of seemingly never-ending despair:

'I am powerful and strong. I will get up, I will stay up, and I will NEVER give up'.

It could take reading thousands of positive quotes over and over again or even attending numerous positive talks before we ever took any true action in our lives; if that action ever occurs. I recognise that these quotes and talks are great at serving the purposes they were designed for, instilling within the receiver a motivation to make their desired change. However, this motivation is generally, and sadly, only temporary. When I decided to take action in my life it was something that I acknowledged as vital to my mental and physical survival. No amount of positive quotes pushed me to do it. They inspired me, yes, but I still needed to take the first step.

Another important thing that I realised was that I had become accustomed to many aspects of my negative existence, as terrible as that may seem. I had become reliant on Mam to do so many everyday things for me, things that I knew I was more than capable of doing independently. I realised that I needed to get out of my comfort zone in order to grow and develop into a more independent and strong person. I needed to involve myself in things that I would not normally have done. As I began pushing myself further and further away from this comforting reliance, I slowly but surely started to reap the benefits. My confidence grew and I began to feel more self-worth. This type of self-help, in my honest opinion, is the most beneficial. It helped me in many ways throughout the years because as I was becoming more positive in myself, I was attracting positive people towards me. All it took for me to achieve this was to recognise that in order to change my life, I needed to change my mindset. To change my mindset, I needed to change the information I was allowing to be fed into my mind by the outside world. All it took for me to achieve what I have achieved was for me to change the channel in my mind. For large portions of my life,

I blamed others for the fact that I was not being accepted by them or that they were treating me badly. Over the past few years, however, due to my involvement with people of the same mindset as myself, I have realised that it was not those individuals from previous years who were at fault. It was simply due to my negativity. I now would find myself considering how I treat myself before even thinking about how others treat me and how I talk to myself before questioning why others are not talking to me. I used to constantly tell myself that I was ugly, I was not good enough for anyone, and I would never amount to anything. I would ask myself why I was getting those judgemental looks. Why can I not be better looking? Who would want to be my friend? What can I contribute to society? After all those self-destructive thoughts I would then have the laughable cheek to question why I had such a negative mindset. It was not easy, and it took a number of years for me to do, but all that was needed in order for me to improve my life was changing my mindset by not allowing those thoughts to take control. Self-talk is a very important thing.

Religious therapy

I ended up turning to prayer a lot. Every Sunday without fail I went to Mass on my own. Sometimes my brother would come with me. I acknowledge it is not everyone's cup of tea, which is understandable. Some kids were forced to go, which straight away put them off, but I went willingly, however. I started to get so much comfort and internal strength from it. The parish priest, Father Terry, was a genuinely lovely man and everybody knew him for his natural kindness. He took the time to get to know each individual in the community, and he visited the local schools and homes of his parishioners. In his younger years, he had worked in the Philippines helping out within a local community. He took part in almost everything and encouraged others to do the same. He developed a special bond with everyone in our community and made no prejudgements. He was such a down-to-earth man who loved the Dublin GAA team; an avid sports fan. He made my experience at Mass more beneficial to my personal well- being. This was my first and proper time at gaining the knowledge of the importance of surrounding myself with positive people, and how doing so opened up many doors for me.

In his later years, Father Terry developed Parkinson's disease, but he still continued to serve the community throughout his ordeal. Whenever he said Mass, I sat in the middle seats and he would always see me there. During the Mass, he would stop, say my name to acknowledge my attendance, and smile. He would then continue on with the service. He visited me a few times in Mam's house to have a friendly chat as he was aware of my condition and felt she and I could relate to his new struggles. We even shared the same neurologist and at times we would often bump into each other while attending our hospital appointments. He even managed to get me some work experience as I was struggling to find something to do during the day. It was in the flats where they ran courses for women who had not got a lot and I typed up the timetables for these courses among other admin-type jobs. As time went on, Father Terry's health declined and he had to stop all his parish activities. He eventually ended up spending the remainder of his time in a home, which primarily catered for elderly priests. My family and I went to visit him a number of times. The last time we visited he did not recognise us, which was sad. He was in a daze looking out the window and had no interest in watching TV. We got the vague impression that he remembered Mam to some extent but we could see that he was struggling. Sadly, Fr. Terry passed away in March 2016. He received a beautiful send-off from all members of his parish and was surrounded by the people who he loved, and loved him dearly in return. I still think about him and feel grateful to have known such a lovely priest while growing up. He was a wonderful, supportive man, who I truly appreciated for all his kind words. He always said that he knew I would write a book one day and then jokingly would also say that he would love a mention. Although he is not with us anymore to read this book, I am sure he would be very happy to know that I did not forget him. Shine bright, Father Terry. Rest in everlasting peace.

I know a lot of people question the existence of God or think it is pathetic and laugh at others who turn to prayer for strength and comfort, but when you are desperate for help you need to believe in something in order to give yourself that extra boost that a higher being is watching over you. In my opinion, the problem with the modern world is that we fear how others will judge us based on what we do, or do not, believe. It is your own life to live, however. No one else knows exactly what you have gone through or are going through in your own life, and their opinions do not, and should not, matter. As my stepdad would always say "an opinion is like an arse-hole, everyone has one but just because you have that doesn't mean it's right". That was the road I needed to pursue in order for me to get to the next chapters in my life. Because I had engulfed myself in the church environment and surrounded myself with lovely people, I decided to go a little further. One of my friends with whom I had gone to primary school with began helping the local community through volunteering for charities, which I wanted to do also. One of the things that she was partaking in was altar service at the local church and I thought, "I could do that; be lovely to do". I attended a meeting at the priest's house with my friend. This would have been the first time I had taken the plunge into joining something without Mam being my support and my voice. I was twelve at the time. We met in a little room in the rectory; lots of other kids were staring at me as if to say "Who is she?" and "What's wrong with her?". A woman called Margaret ran the altar service. I knew of Margaret from around the area. she lived across the road from Mam's house; she was in an electric scooter. I waited for her, feeling timorous. I was so nervous. I did not know what way she would take me. When she came into the room I felt a little less apprehensive. I assumed that Margaret would judge me because I could not verbally communicate like the rest. However, when I saw that she could barely walk I wondered why I had put up barriers before we'd even properly met.

Before Margaret arrived, the other kids and I heard something outside. "Here's Margaret," one of the kids said. I stared into my friend's face and made a panicky sound. I kept rubbing my palms on my knees because they were extremely sweaty. When Margaret came into the room I was the first person she noticed. She made her way over to my seat and leaned over, looking right into my face, and asked who I was. My friend introduced me and told Margaret that I wanted to join the altar service. Margaret kept eye contact with me and did not realise I was not able to talk, she just thought I was shy. I had a big red face and felt that the spotlight was on me. She asked me to go outside with her. I was panicking as I did not know why she was taking me aside. While we were outside she asked me to talk saying it was just me and her now. I did and I showed her my voice. She got it. She knew I had difficulties talking and brought me back into the room. I was glad that happened as she made me feel good and like she wanted to hear from me, not anybody else, about my 'disability'.

Ever since then, Margaret had nothing but love for me. I joined the altar service and I gave it my very best. I loved it and got a lot of self-confidence from it. I felt calmer and had a great sense of giving back to the community, which indeed made me very happy. I did the Stations of the Cross around Ballymun too, which Margaret also ran. Every time I would see her outside she would make sure that I gave her a hug. Margaret was a caring woman who did not just see her blood family but welcomed everyone into her life and treated them all like her family, and if she had a problem she would let you know. I am so happy that I had a lot of positive influences in my life which outweighed the negative ones. I would regard Margaret as making one of the first, everlasting, positive impacts on my life. I did the altar service for a while and then I moved on to other things. Over the past few years, I did not see Margaret much; I had heard that she was very sick. My heart went out to her knowing that she was suffering. I also felt for her family as it must have been tough seeing a woman who had so much "go" in her and did so much for the community, go through all of that suffering. By the end of October 2016, she had passed away. Even though I had not seen her in years, I made it my business to go and pay my respects at her funeral.

I really appreciate the good-natured people that I have had throughout the different stages of my life. Margaret was definitely one of them. Shine bright, Margaret.

There is also another local woman who I have grown very fond of. She is from the parish community too. When I was growing up I would occasionally see her around attending the church events. She has told me recently that she always had an interest in getting to know me. I remember a number of years ago that I had signed up to take part in an evening course, which took place down the road from Mam's house, and this same woman was also taking part. This course allowed me to communicate with her face to face, and for her to see my capabilities first-hand. The woman's name is Dolores. She said to me that I had always amazed and inspired her. Every so often I see her on the bus and she always attempts to have a conversation with me. She asks how I am doing and how my family are. I want to keep her updated as to how I am doing and also ask how she is doing. Among many others from the local parish, she was a great support. One day, while on the bus with her, I managed to quickly get out my phone and inform her that I am in the process of writing a book. She was blown away by this and ever since has asked how it was going. She is always delighted with the tiniest updates regarding the progress of this project that I have undertaken. The next time I saw her, I managed to get her mobile number so that I could 'keep her in the loop'. I am delighted that I can mention her in my book as she is a genuinely lovely friend who I truly respect. I know that anytime I see her, she somehow always manages to brighten my day. She honestly is a lovely, kind, caring, and very funny little woman, and one who I am grateful to have met.

I have mentioned Madeline previously in this book, who lives down the road from Mam's house. We all have a great bond with Madeline and her family and she has been such a great support to us all. She has always been there as a great family friend who listens to our problems and offers her advice. There are not many people like Madeline around. My family and I have always been grateful to Madeline for all her wonderful support throughout the years as it has been amazing. She has been a great friend to Mam and me along with another family friend, Jacinta, who we also got great support from. Jacinta has her own struggles but, she got a great deal of inspiration from me and vice versa. We both refused to give up and expect the world to pick us up. We both had the strength to make our lives as great as we wanted. We are positive influences for one another. I am so grateful to Jacinta for lending her ears and her shoulder. She has been a great support to us all.

I am a firm believer in our abilities to heal ourselves both physically and mentally via positive mental attitude. While, to some, this seems a bit 'out there', it honestly does work; I am living and walking proof of that fact. Another thing that I hold a firm belief in is human cooperation in the assistance of overcoming any or all obstacles. I owe a great deal of my current life to not only my ability to readapt physically and mentally but, also to, the undeniable assistance of others. Aside from my family, who have been a great support to me, I have also mentioned a few others throughout this book. Again, I am grateful to them all.

Flying solo for the first time

During my late teenage years, I desperately wanted to go on trips and explore the world without Mam and my stepdad by my side. I was at the age where I wanted to go and roam the amazing planet I lived on. What was stopping me, however, was the small fact that I had nobody to travel with. I needed someone to go on these adventures with, someone to look out for me because as much as I denied it at the time…I needed assistance with a number of things. Instead of living in the moment like I wanted, I needed to look for a solution because I was determined to travel and knew I could not do it alone. One day I got chatting through social media to a girl who had been my PA while I was at Killester College. This was a few years after the course and we were chatting about holidays and trips away. I am a very stubborn woman so if I am not happy with a situation I always try to do anything within my power to make the necessary changes. At the time of me attending Killester, I did not like the fact I had a PA with me most of time. I like my own space and at times I felt smothered. I felt it was not benefiting me in gaining independence. At times during the course, I would go to the pub for my lunch along with my classmates without confirming with her. She would be looking for me and this would understandably make her very sad and anxious for my well-being. At one stage during the course, I decided to switch to photography. I was in a business and computer course before that. However, I could not grasp it and was not enjoying it. When I started in photography I noticed it was more of a "doss" course than anything else; the teacher would be doing his own thing. It was during this course I began to see my PA as a person and we became friends. Her name was Vivanna; she was originally from Argentina and had a little girl. We would occasionally go for coffee in town and collect her daughter who was in a crèche at the time. She was wired to the moon but was an extremely kind, considerate woman. When I finished up in that college I was relieved because, although I had found a new friend, I had also found the course itself was not as interesting as I had hoped. When we reconnected via social networking and started chatting I was telling her how I would love to go on a holiday. She asked me if I wanted to visit her as she was living in Madrid at that time. This was a light bulb moment for me and I instantly said, "Yes! Good idea." I started asking myself the obvious questions as to whether I would be ok and would it put me out of my comfort zone. I ultimately decided to go for it. It was time for me to take that step.

I booked a four-day trip to see her in Madrid that April. As it got closer to my departure date, self-doubt started to creep in. I had not even told Mam about my planned trip yet because I could hardly get my own head around it and I did not know how she would react. I told her five days before I was due to go. I started telling her in the most awkward way possible asking if she knew where my leggings were as I'd need them in a few days. Mam looked at me curiously wondering what I was about to do. "I am going to Madrid," I said. Mam was actually speechless for a second. I now know that was not the best way in which I could have told her; I was very self-centred and made it all about me. At the time I did not realise but Mam dedicated her life to protecting me and felt that I had gone behind her back. Everyone got involved, my grandparents, the neighbours, and some other family members all gathered in the house to discuss the predicament that I had put Mam in. They spoke in the kitchen telling me that I could not do this trip on my own. This started to make me feel full of rage as I knew I could do it. I had that strong sense of self-belief. In retrospect, what I failed to realise at the time was that while I had given myself time to get my head around it and adjust to the idea that I could do it and be safe, I had not prepared my family. They were understandably fearful for my safety. I ran out the door the moment they started all the negative talk about how dangerous it was for me. The neighbour next door greeted me as I passed. The look I gave her said, "Leave me alone!" I was in the height of it. My stepdad ran after me trying to call me back. I ignored him at first and then turned at him and screamed, "Go away!" I was fuming at the idea that I was an adult and could not even travel on my own. My stepdad caught up with me and told me that I was going. It was such a shock. "It'll do you good getting away by yourself," he said. I walked back to Mam's house feeling so embarrassed and having to walk past the neighbours again. I apologised to Mam and she accepted. We moved on from that drama and I ended up going to Madrid on my own to meet up with my friend. It was a great holiday and an even greater achievement.

A place to call my own

When I was in my early twenties, I began wanting my own place. it was getting to the stage that I felt I needed to get out of my comfort zone and to grow and develop into my own person. I was at that age where I wanted to progress into young adulthood and 'learn the ropes' of life and to have my own space to figure out things for myself.

The Irish Wheelchair Association (IWA) has independent housing primarily aimed at the disabled so that they can get the feeling of what it is like to have a place of their own for a few weeks. Sometimes you can share the house with someone else that also has a disability. It is a good idea for those with disabilities to use this service as it helps give a sense of independence.

However, I personally wanted my own place, a place that I could do up, and create my own home. I wanted to get my own furniture and bits and bobs in order to give it my personal touch. Ultimately, I wanted somewhere that I could settle into and know that I did not have to leave. It took a great number of years and a lot of battling by my stepdad who was determined for me to achieve my desire to live an independent life. Eventually, despite many obstacles being placed in my way, and thanks to the unquestionable, dedicated support of my stepdad, who was with me every single step of the way, I got my own apartment.

As much as I have come on independently, I still need help with small things that able-bodied people take for granted, e.g. brushing and tying my hair up, zipping up my coat, putting on my clothes, and making certain foods. I enjoy wraps with healthy stuff in them such as cucumber, scallions, avocados, and beetroot. Not all at once, mind you! As a lot of these foods need chopping up so that I can eat them safely without the risk of choking, that is where my dependence on the assistance of others comes in.

Forming a bond with someone is important for our happiness

When we were babies, we all craved love and attention from the person or people who gave us our primary care; it is a part of our survival and is known as forming an emotional attachment. We did little things such as burp, sneeze, and make a big mess, or just go "goo goo, gaga". Most adults who were in our vicinity would laugh at us and think we were adorable. As we got older, however, we started to lose that adorableness and slowly began to realise we needed to do other things be it bad or good to get the attention we craved. In essence, the rules changed as we got older and we had to adapt to those changes to keep the spotlight on us. At times we would try being something that we were not. All we ultimately wanted was to be loved and praised though without feeling that we'd let anyone down; that we'd failed them. How many of you can relate to this scenario in your daily lives now that you are adults? How many of you "act out" or do something that would generally be regarded as uncharacteristic of you just to get the attention of another? I bet if you sit back and think hard you will remember a moment when you did exactly that. Maybe it was years ago or maybe it was as recent as yesterday or today. This is human nature, it is what we have done not only when we were babies but even into adulthood. We act differently from normal, just to get the love and attention we crave from another person. In my view, there is nothing wrong with this as long as no one gets hurt. We all seek approval from a certain group of people that we feel the need to belong to.

Also, most of us are desperately searching for that 'special' person, our potential other half with whom to create an 'unbreakable bond of happiness'.

When I was growing up, I always wanted a sister in order to have that female bond with; that sisterly love. Mam wanted more kids and would have loved to have had another girl, but she learnt to be grateful for the children she had, as she realised that she was blessed. There are mostly boys in my family, and I do not feel that I have any strong connection to most of the girls. I did with my cousin Jenny who sadly and suddenly passed away a number of years ago though. We did not just have dystonia in common but we both wanted to get the most out of our lives – to help others – and we both had a good positive mindset. I am part of a big family to which, as I was growing up, I felt a strong connection to. As most families do, however, we grew apart and I became separated from some of them. I feel, to some degree, that this was because I can seem somewhat different to some of them. I believe that this is not because of my disability, but because of my ability to continuously strive to remain positive, despite having every justification to being the opposite. My cousins now understandably have their own lives, responsibilities and completely different life goals to myself, which I respect and admire. I still have a lot of love for each of them as we shared a lot of happy memories together growing up, which I am grateful for. I occasionally meet with them for a casual chat, a catch up, and a laugh together.

I am grateful for all the people I have in my life right now. I find that I want to meet with them more as I find that I feed off their positive mindset; we support one another like a family. We praise each other at our highs and are a shoulder to cry on at our lows. That, in my opinion, is the very definition of a true family bond.

Therapy comes in many forms

Over the past twenty years, I have experienced different types of therapy. These have ranged from medical, holistic, alternative, religious, and even astrological. Some of these therapies are scoffed at as voodoo ritualistic nonsense. However, the benefits of these should not be overlooked by the closed-minded as each therapy has benefited me at some stage or another in many different ways, be it physically or mentally. Let us take the alternative therapies as an example, one which has benefited me the most, even more than the medical therapies that have been prescribed to me over the years. What I am referring to is the Endorphin Release Therapy. It worked for me along with many other individuals who have vouched for it, so, please, resist the urge to laugh when reading the following passage and keep an open mind.

Like I have said, I can feel people's energy, be it negative or positive. I am very open to these different forms of energies. They can have an effect on me. Also, when there is a full moon I find that I am mentally all over the place. During these times I do not know what is going on with my moods. There is a form of astrological therapy that alleges that the moon can affect you psychologically. This, from my own experience, I agree with, to a certain extent. When I was growing up with dystonia, as I have previously stated, I was heavily reliant on religion to assist me through my struggles and I noticed that my world came together with people who cared and offered me more spiritual assurances. God works in mysterious ways as the saying goes, and I found that the way in which I was meeting all of those kind, considerate people was an act of God; I felt God was watching out for me.

When John Carty came into my life all those years ago, I felt at that tough time he was sent as my guardian angel. One time a lady visited me in the hospital, for extra support. She had the ability to see and talk to angels. I knew that I was going to be looked after and was protected, and I had a very strong feeling that I was completely right about the therapy that John had to offer.

Making yourself positive.

When I was a teenager and even into my early twenties, I suffered from hyperventilation combined with excessive sweating, weakness in my body, uncontrollable shaking, shortness of breath and feeling that I would pass out. Over the years, however, I have learnt how to calm my mind through remaining as positive, mindful, and motivated as possible. Once I learnt to distract my mind by keeping myself constantly busy, I would successfully avoid such panic attacks. I did not want my disability to affect my life or my mental health as it had done over the previous years. A panic attack is at times brought on by the fear of the unknown. I would excessively fear about how my life would turn out. Sometimes it would just come on me spontaneously; however, things in my day-to-day life generally triggered these episodes. If I saw someone I knew that caused me hurt at some stage in my life that would be one thing that would trigger attacks. Also if I overheard a comment about me made in my general direction on a bus or out in a shop. There was always something that would trigger these episodes. I believed that as well as the dystonia, this mental problem was now part of me and would follow me around throughout the remainder of my life. I wanted to deal with this on my own as I felt nobody would truly understand. I was telling myself that that was is all in my head. I did not want to hear that though. I even started blaming myself for my mental state at the time feeling that I had brought it all on myself. I knew at that time I was not only physically but mentally unhealthy and knew I had to do something about it. I attended numerous positive talks and quickly came to realise that, while I could only do a limited amount to improve my physical state, I could do a lot of self-healing on my mental state.

Learning to control the mind is **vital.** By 'controlling the mind' what I mean is being aware of the types of information we are filling our minds with in our daily lives. Is it positive or negative information? Do you know how important it is to use positive language in your life?

- Are you the type of person that constantly has the news on loop every hour?
- Do you constantly read into the negativity going on in our world?
- Are you constantly criticising yourself?
- Do you listen and actively participate when people around you start bitching about others?

If you answered yes to any or all of the last four questions then stop immediately and pay attention to what I am about to tell you. Firstly, the news is MOSTLY going to be negative. The only time it is not is generally toward the end when they do what is called a 'fluff piece'. Do not give your full attention to the negative bulletins that populate our daily lives.

Secondly, the world is not a negative place; it is, however, full of negative people who force their opinions, etc. on others through violence thus causing wars in some instances. The reality, however, is that the world is AMAZING; it is such an educational and breath-taking life experience to be able to travel the world. I have been to over eighteen countries covering four continents and have loved every minute of my travelling experience and by no means have I ever dreamt of stopping. There are certain parts of the world, however, that would be deemed unsafe to visit but you cannot pigeonhole an entire part of the world as being the same as that country or city.

Thirdly, there is a high probability that I have never met you before, even still, I will tell you this, I think you are AMAZING! Take it from experience; no one deserves to be subjecting themselves to being self-deprecating. If you need someone to talk to then I am here for you, my contact details are at the back of this book.

Lastly, there is a common saying that goes 'People in glass houses shouldn't throw stones'. We all know what this means YET some pay little heed to its message. Every single person on this earth has a problem of some kind. As fellow human beings, we should be helping each other through life, not adding to somebody's issues or laughing behind their back. If you cannot offer a solution to another person's problem or problems then certainly do not add to them by talking about it behind their back because while it feels like you are saying to yourself "at least I don't have those problems, my life is much better", what you are actually doing is inviting similar problems into your life by mentally and or verbally projecting them.

Remember, by you discussing another person's negative situation that is you effectively inviting in, with open arms, negativity to influence your own mentality.

If you suffer from anxiety attacks then the following tips may help you. When you feel an anxiety attack come on, do you think negative thoughts such as, "I am never going to get through this. It is back"? These thoughts actually give power to your anxiety so you need to change your thinking to, "I am a very positive and strong person. I will get through this if I remain calm". Repeat it over and over until it registers. Along with these positive thoughts, it is very important to control your breathing, concentrate on making sure that you take a deep breath through your nose, and exhale slowly through your mouth. This slow breathing technique will relax your body and mind. Another great tip I can give you to prevent the occurrence of these attacks is to make it your daily routine to say affirmations to yourself. An affirmation is something positive you tell yourself, e.g. "I am strong and in control of my life". These affirmations, if done correctly, will promote a more positive mindset. Remember, you control most aspects in your life so do not let one negative thing define the person you are. We are all born fearless and happy; as we grow up we become conditioned not to be. This type of negative conditioning is influenced by many factors that are out of our control be it the environment we are in or people who we are surrounded by. However, even though we may have been conditioned to feel the way we do we can change it and we can recondition our minds through positive mental thought.

One hugely important thing is to give yourself credit for even the little things you do. Do not compare yourself to anyone; we are all on this earth dealing with our own separate 'disabilities'. No one is perfect. Do not put yourself under any unnecessary stress so if you can avoid a stressful situation then do. If you cannot then make sure you face the situation with as calm a mindset as possible. We all go through bad days even if at times we pretend that we do not; it is only human to have up-and-down days, and life is not all plain sailing for anyone. No matter how terrible we feel, we all must continue to get up, show up, and never give up. You are doing great, life is amazing, and it is under ALL of our control.

Another big tip I will share with you as regards to getting positive is to realise and appreciate what you already have, and not to want what you do not have. Do not be petty and jealous of people who have found success, but instead come to realise that if it is something you want to achieve also, then you must be prepared to work for it. There is far too much begrudgery going on in this world for you to join in. Do not envy someone's accomplishments. With this in mind, it would be easy for me to be constantly envious of a person who can communicate without difficulty and has proper control of their hands. However, if I kept focusing on just that envy and self-pity then that could lead me to even more negative self-talk. I would find myself questioning why I should get up in the mornings to face my day; I may as well throw in the towel and give up. But I feel that I need to allow myself these feelings every so often. However, I need to persevere. In order to keep going, we all need to keep moving forward. Keep looking forward and work day in and day out at achieving our dreams, focusing on what we have and being grateful for it, even the small things. This is such a powerful tool. Remember, also, to take nothing for granted. You can find yourself basking in the sunshine in one moment, and then suddenly be fighting the toughest enemy you have and will ever face…your own mind.

Here is a little exercise for you to do. I would like you to write down everything you have to be grateful for in your life right now. I will get you started via the below example.

I am grateful for the following:

- I am alive
- My amazing family
- My health
- How far I have come in my life
- My wonderful partner Patrick
- My fabulous apartment
- My positive mindset
- My ability to get around on public transport
- The food I eat

When we write down our list of things that we are grateful for we effortlessly extract happiness from within our minds. We all have things that we are individually grateful for. In today's busy society, however, we tend to forget these things or take most of them for granted. The above tool is a great way to jog our memories. Here is something that I personally have got great benefit from. Every morning when I am having a shower I imagine all my negativity being washed away. I watch the water as it makes its way down the drain and picture that it is clearing any negativity I hold within me away with it. I then proceed in saying positive affirmations to myself.

I have another exercise for you to do, which is similar to the previous one. I want you to get a blank piece of paper, or alternatively use the notes section at the back of this book and write ten things that you love about YOURSELF e.g. I am a strong-minded person, I am loved etc. Put on the top of it a header, 'My top ten'. When you have finished that, I want you to take another piece of paper and write twenty things you hate about YOURSELF e.g. nobody wants to know me, etc. Call this, 'My worst twenty'. When you have your two lists completed I want you to think about the following question. Which list took you the shortest amount of time to write? My top ten or my worst twenty? I can almost guarantee you I know that the answer in most cases will be the second list. This is for two reasons: firstly, it is because a large number of people are too humble to speak positively about themselves, and do not recognise their own self-worth. Lastly, as sad as this sounds, a high percentage of people on the planet are pessimistic and as such, find the negative in everything, even within themselves. This is because, to some degree, for generations, it was viewed as 'wrong' to 'speak yourself up' and you were automatically accused of being 'cocky'. However, believe me when I say this, there is absolutely nothing wrong with having self-confidence as it is essential to all of our mental well-being. Personally, and I do not know about you, but I would rather be deemed egotistical and cocky, than meek and self-annihilating.

Remaining positive

Once you apply all the suggested changes that have been mentioned above and throughout this book, you should, if done in the correct manner, notice two things. Firstly, you should notice the changes that I have described, and secondly, you will notice that these changes, while seeming amazing, are only temporary. This is due in a large part to the persistent level at which these changes must be continuously adhered to. There is no quick-fix solution to having a negativity-dominant mindset as it can take a great length of time to abolish and then keep out this unwanted trail of thought. To overcome this, we ALL need to continuously strive towards an optimistic mindset by applying all of the suggested changes. Here are some tips to assist you in achieving this.

- Continue to set life goals for yourself and constantly work towards achieving those goals.
- Continue doing daily affirmations, remembering that it is you who controls your mind. It is not in control of you.
- Continue to actively avoid any negative inputs, be it from people you know or the forms of information you are 'absorbing' from the outside world.
- Try to surround yourself with more positive-minded people; their positivity will rub off on you.
- Be aware of what it is that you are eating and drinking as these can have negative or positive effects on your mind.
- Lastly, ignore what people think of you. You are doing great, you are amazing and you are not here to appease or befriend the entire world. You are unique and you are loved, so, please, love yourself more.

While I agree that it is important for our sanity to let off some steam and rant a bit every now and again as we are all human, I also think it is important not to stay with this negativity; let it out of your system. There is a way to do this in order to guarantee that you get positive results at the end. If you have a dream or an ambition that you want and need to achieve then what better way to release this frustration than venting it on building up your determination to succeed. Do not bottle up this frustration or anger as that is the most self-destructive thing that can be done. You can either use it to your advantage as described above or allow yourself to feel it and then release it by repeating to yourself positive affirmations that your situation will improve, and then work on improving it.

I used to walk into a room that was instantly and recognisably full of toxic-minded people. The people there would be critical and moaning about their situations. Everything they would say was issued with such venomous negative energy. This energy was draining to me. I found that I was being surrounded by people just swimming around in their same negative existence day in and day out without recognising that they had the ability to pull themselves out of it but maybe they just did not want to. They then wondered why everything stayed the same for them. I would find myself thinking, 'Are these people really happy with that mentality?' To me, that was no way to live. Nowadays, however, I can walk into a room full of positive and genuine people. They give off this positive energy that I yearn for. I can feel the joy and excitement in the room, I feel involved in this joy and a part of this excitement, and I honestly feel on top of the world. Since I have surrounded myself with those positive people, I have felt much better, both physically and mentally. Again, and I cannot highlight enough the importance of this, if the people around you are not making you feel good then you need to walk away. If these are people that you cannot walk away from because they are family friends or even family then limit your time with them, if possible. Remain positive-minded and make sure you look after yourself. You are doing great.

I have found, as obvious as this may sound, that when you look after your physical presentation it can have dramatic effects on your mindset and so I began attending a local salon at a young age to get waxed and beautified. The other women who also attended the salon got to know me and I would go there by myself and have the help and support that I required. I would get many treatments done over the years. I love getting my hair done up nicely as it boosts my self-confidence and is pleasurable. I then require assistance keeping my new hair style lasting over the days following my visit to the salon. I may not wear make-up except for occasional nights out but I still respect and love myself enough to get pampered. This, in my opinion, is another vital tip that I can pass on, despite its blatant obviousness. If you look after yourself on the outside, you will be looking after yourself on the inside too.

Dance to your own beat

It is also very important for your mental happiness to celebrate and express your individuality and to avoid conforming in any way, shape, or form. There was a song released a number of years ago by a well-known band at that time. In it, they had borrowed and modified a line written by an American author, which when closely examined discusses a person's inability to act as an individual and 'dance' to their own beat as opposed to society's. The question I present to you is this, are you human or are you a dancer?

Defy perceived 'logic' and take that 'one small step'

A great example of how our mindset limit and control our potential would be the following: In 1865, a writer by the name of Jules Verne wrote a fictional book that was perceived by the readers of that time as being extremely far-fetched and beyond human possibility. Almost 105 years after that book was published, this far-fetched idea was achieved through a combination of determination, motivation, and the idea that anything is possible with the right mindset. On 20 July 1969, a man by the name of Neil Armstrong walked on the moon. Do not let your negative thoughts dictate to you what you can or cannot achieve. We are the masters of our own universe. Self-assurance is an important thing.

"Always strive at achieving your dreams. Aim for the stars.
If you remain calm and positive while taking your shot, you cannot miss"
– Tracey Ellen Maria

Chapter 8
Patrick

"Love bears all things, believes all things, hopes all things, endures all things" - Corinthians 13:7

For nearly three decades Berlin was split by a wall that divided the city. Loved ones and families were separated for a total of twenty-seven years, and killed on the spot for attempting to cross this concrete barrier. However, on 9 November 1989, thanks to the support of many from around the world, the wall was finally demolished. Once again, love proved itself more powerful than presumed; it has the immense power to '*tear down*' walls.

Searching for my Prince Charming

I always visualised myself meeting a good, caring man who would not mind how I was or see me as a burden. He would fall in love with the person I am and see my abilities, not my disability. He would admire my strengths and my determination to keep on going. He would be proud of all the things at which I've tried my hand. He would see the fighter in me. The main thing I wanted was someone who would laugh with me about the stupid things that happen in life. We would keep each other going, through good and bad times; we would make a terrific team, have a complete understanding of one another and have a great, adventurous life together. I knew eventually he would come. How or when, though, I had no idea as my social life was non-existent for most of my late teens. I just knew I had to keep believing that I deserved to find someone and would when the time was right. I had no delusions of a happy-ever-after story that my man would come along on his white steed, sweep me off my feet, and rescue me from my misery. That only happens in Hollywood or Disney movies and I knew it.

Patrick Hogan

Patrick John Hogan was born on 16 June 1985. It was Father's day and Bloomsday all in one. He was born to Eithne and Patrick Hogan Sr who, along with the doctors present at the time of his birth, noticed something that made him entirely different from other newborns. He was not crying. He was breathing but did not make a sound. The doctors almost immediately began carrying out tests to see what the cause of this uncharacteristic behaviour was. It turned out that Patrick was born with a congenital heart defect known as a singular ventricle, which basically meant that his blood did not get thinned out properly. He also had complications with his lungs hence the reason he did not cry at birth. The early part of Patrick's life was to be tough on his mam, but no more so than on his first birthday when she discovered him in his cot looking rather awkward. She immediately brought him down to her own mam and dad. Her mam gave her theory as to what had happened and advised her to go to the hospital straight away with him. The doctors carried out their tests again and told his mam what had happened. Patrick's nanny was correct in her theory...Patrick had suffered a stroke. The after-effects of this were that Patrick had right-side hemiplegia, meaning that the right side of his body was weaker than the left and somewhat contorted.

Patrick's life from that day onward proved to be a daily uphill struggle for both himself and his mother. His parents split up when Patrick was four and his father's family asked to remain in Patrick's and his sibling's lives. His mother agreed knowing that they were not the cause of the events that led to the breakup.

His early life was always made difficult by the constant abuse he got from the neighbouring children over his disability. Patrick is the second-oldest child and has five siblings. He formed a particularly close bond with one of his sisters, Lesley-Anne, who is three years younger than him. This bond was due to the closeness in age coupled with joint interests in particular types of music, etc.

Patrick attended a special needs school in Clondalkin called Scoil Mochua. While at that school, his best friend at the time was seeing another girl who was only recently disabled due to a tragic life-altering disease. Her name was Jennifer McCann.

How we first met 'Love on the dance floor'

One day after school, I had an appointment at the Central Remedial Clinic (CRC) with the Occupational Therapist (OT). Mam had heard about a group that met once a month to attend a disco, which was held in the centre around the corner from the CRC. It was for special needs teenagers and children and was organised by the IWA. While I was seeing the OT, Mam went into the centre to get information about it and see if it would benefit me in any way.

My daily routine consisted of going to school happy and full of life. As soon as school had ended I would come home and just sit around the house being miserable due to the lack of friends or activities I could do. Mam knew I needed something; she thought it would be good for me to mix with people with different disabilities as they would have an understanding of the loneliness I was feeling. She had heard that my cousins Jenny and Michael went there every month. I really wanted to meet up with Jenny again as I had not seen her in a long time but had seen her on TV and in newspapers. The dystonia had really affected her so much so that she was wheelchair-bound and her face was extremely tense. She had a little bit of upper-body control but did not have the ability to speak anymore. She tried her best to enjoy what she had and live life to its fullest. When I came out of my appointment with the OT, Mam had a leaflet she had picked up while in the IWA centre. It was about the group that met every month for the discos and they were called The Spirit Group. The discos took place on the last Thursday of the month. I felt a boost. We both did. A new exciting beginning for me finally after years of isolation. I would be making new friends who would completely understand all the hardships and struggles that being disabled brings; they would accept me for who I was, not what I had wrong with me. Finally, I would have a social life and make friends, without any prejudgement. The disco happened to fall on the Thursday of that week. Mam came with me and stayed in another room with other parents and carers having a cup of tea and a chat. She wanted me to take that step on my own without her by my side. Naturally enough I was nervous going into this new world, which I never thought I would ever have to engage in. I was introduced to a guy called Stephen who was a nice, smiley, friendly guy. Then I met a girl called Olivia who was a lovely, friendly, blonde girl, and she collected my entrance fee. Then I went into the disco hall but it was still early and the lights were still on; no one had even arrived yet. There were buses that collected people from all over Dublin and brought them to the disco. I was introduced to my cousin Michael from my father's side who I had never met before. He had developed dystonia in his late teens and his speech, hands, and legs were affected. He used a walker to get around and his mobile phone to communicate. I sat at a table with him and took out my phone to have a chat with him.

I was very excited about meeting up with my cousin Jenny again after a number of years. I had heard lots of positive things about her. While waiting for her arrival, I was informed that her bus was delayed. It felt like the disco was over and all I was doing was waiting for so long. I remember thinking, "I wish this bus would just arrive so I can meet my cousin, relax and enjoy the rest of the night with her." Eventually, she arrived and I finally got to have a much-welcome conversation with my cousin. During our chat, I was introduced to her boyfriend, and then her boyfriend's mate, Patrick Hogan. Our story, which has spanned a decade, started on that night.

Patrick's shyness

Patrick and I were never straightforward. It took a number of years for us to be together properly. When we started off all those years ago, I kept thinking about how we could have a relationship. He lived on the south side of Dublin and I lived on the north side. Also, at the time of us getting together the first time, I was still in secondary school with two years left until my graduation. The girls in my class all had boyfriends and, as such, I felt delighted with myself when I told them about Patrick. They never met him, but gave him the nickname 'Paddy one ball'. I do not know where that came from but I suppose it had a certain ring to it. However, I would be upset anytime they referred to him by it. I would be laughing asking them to stop. I was afraid it would spread and everyone would think that the nickname was a true statement about him and that somehow Patrick would find out and that would be it. Maybe they came up with that because he did not have the courage to make it happen with me during that time. Our relationship was going so slow. I felt that I was only wasting my time even thinking about him, as we were going nowhere.

The discos would always finish in June and restart at the beginning of September. They were a great way to catch up with friends. This was also the time when Patrick and I were getting to know each other. June soon approached and I could still feel this apprehension from him. I knew he really liked me and I was falling for him too, but he was taking ages to ask me out. Considering we'd met back in November, after which he texted me saying he liked me but then we didn't text up to the December disco. He was very hot and cold with me, which nowadays he puts down to him being very nervous at that time. I was very excited about going to the disco for my second time as now I knew I had an admirer. When Patrick arrived he was very stand-offish. I was wondering what had happened. At the January disco, he was the same. I just accepted this and moved on. The main reason I went to the discos was to make friends and catch up with my cousin. It would have been a bonus if I'd got a boyfriend along the way but if not then so be it. I started getting to know the others who attended the disco, some from Patrick's school and others from the

CRC, and I was having a great laugh with them all. I always felt Patrick staring at me. I wondered if he liked me. Maybe this was how all relationships started. Not knowing where you stand with the other person. If so, then this could drive you mad and be way too much hassle. Patrick and his friend use to do DJ at these discos as he had plenty of confidence doing that.

In February, my birthday was approaching and during the disco that month he was still very stand-offish. He casually wished me "Happy Birthday", and then left me alone for the remainder of the night. I sought out my friends for a laugh. That night he announced my birthday on the microphone and got everyone to sing Happy Birthday to me. Patrick sang it above everyone else. He got my attention and was staring at me across the room. I was sitting at the back and I could feel his eyes glaring at me and could tell there were sparks flying from them. He came over when the disco had finished and spoke to me properly. I felt the vibe off him that he liked me. Then, Patrick finally got the courage to ask me to go see a film with him. He said he was sorry for how he had been acting around me and that he liked me. Then he kissed me on the forehead and said "Goodbye" and that he would text me to arrange our date. He did text me when I arrived home that night, which delighted me, and I went to bed on a high. He texted me after school the next day to arrange meeting up that following weekend. I know the cinema is not an ideal place for a first date, but given the age we were, me seventeen and him nineteen, it seemed the norm, plus it was more of a way to see how we felt around each other, being both very shy and awkward around one another. I knew we had to ease our way into it.

Our first date

That Saturday afternoon, we met up and arranged to see a film called *Hide and Seek*. I had arranged for Mam to bring me to the cinema with my aunty driving us. I sat in the back seat and my stomach was turning. We arrived outside and parked in the car park. Patrick texted me to say he was running late and that pigs would fly if he made it on time. The waiting was the hardest. Then, we saw him. Panic over. I needed a minute to relax. Plus I did not want to seem too keen. Mam and my aunty were laughing and commenting at how grown up I had become. Mam walked over with me as I was too shy to walk over by myself. I needed her to break the awkwardness but, I pre-warned her not to say anything embarrassing. As we walked over I could see him standing inside the glass hall, his back facing us, and I think he was too terrified to look around. We walked in and both Patrick and I had a look of terror on our faces as if we were going to get slaughtered. Mam ignored my pre-warnings and began teasing us. Then she went off to do some shopping saying that she would collect me later. Patrick wore a coat that had fur on the hood and a piece missing from its shoulder. He said, "Don't mind my coat, it's my mate's."

Because we were both late we had missed the film, so we randomly chose another, *Meet the Parents*. Patrick was complaining because he hates Ben Stiller but sucked it up and we went in. We were early for that one and were the only ones sitting there in the darkness, with light music on in the background. This was understandably very awkward for me. Patrick attempted to make a conversation and I got out my phone so he did not feel that he was doing all the work. I did really enjoy his company. He was very pleasant and I could tell that he was very ambitious. He wanted to get the most out of life and I liked that about him. I could also tell that he had a great sense of humour underneath his shyness. I felt that we just needed to get to know each other in order to be able to feel at ease. When the movie began, I was expecting that at any moment he would put his arm around me. I was trying to relax and be comfortable because I did not want him to be put off me if I got tense. It would be like hugging a plank of wood. We both enjoyed the movie and we laughed together, but the moment I was anticipating had passed and we hardly rubbed shoulders. Then it came time to go. I felt a bit disheartened at that moment and thought, "Maybe there will be a next time." We waited in the hall of the cinema for Mam to arrive, standing there, again, in our joint awkwardness. When she arrived she allowed us time to say goodbye. Patrick kissed me on the forehead, and then we parted. I felt it went well. As we drove home Mam and my aunty asked me how the date went. I was just giggling away to myself.

Our on and off relationship

Patrick and I had a drawn-out relationship for so long. It was on one minute and then off the next. After the first and second breakup, I had found it very difficult to live life without him. This was due to me missing the social environment that I had become accustomed to while with Patrick. I did say to him after one of the breakups that we should just be friends and I honestly believed that it could work. I know it can vary from couple to couple but I believed that we could become 'just friends'. The fact remained that I was drawn to his group of friends; at the time I had missed them more. I was craving feeling a part of any group of friends so much. Over time, however, the way they socialised became a bit repetitive, with the same routine, which was mainly drinking till all hours over the weekends. I do not want to come across as boring, but that type of repetition makes me feel worse. In saying that, nobody had a gun to my head but I did feel I had to continue with their way of socialising. It was my choice as I was afraid of completely cutting ties and feared being alone again and missing out on the 'normal' thing to do at that age. I continued to go back to them all, thinking in my head that Patrick and I were just friends. Of course, it did not end well. Patrick would completely blank me the whole time. I am certain that it looked weird as to why I was still hanging around him and putting myself through that situation. It was not healthy and was dragging me down. I knew it was time for me to stop being so needy and cut ties completely. I did not need to be tormenting myself, and I knew deep down that I would be ok. We went our separate ways and met other people but none felt right to either of us.

Lesley-Anne Hogan

Patrick has a great relationship with his younger sister, Lesley-Anne. They looked out for each other growing up and hung around with the same group of friends. His mam moved down to the country a few years ago with his other younger siblings. During this time, Lesley-Anne and Patrick lived together. I really got to know Lesley-Anne over the years. She reminded me so much of a female version of Patrick as they shared not only friends and hobbies but also had the same caring and considerate nature. I will say this, however; because she is a woman she has a much better understanding of my needs and struggles than her brother. Men are from Mars and women are from Venus, as the saying goes. I grew very fond of Lesley-Anne who is a lovely caring person who did not over help and was not always ready to just jump in. Instead, she gave me the space to do things by myself, until she saw that I was really struggling and then she would step in. She is very down to earth. She would tease the life out of me, which was done in a more humorous way, to break any tension, which I loved. One year, for my birthday, when I was turning twenty she had got me a granny's birthday card which said, "Hi Granny" and had a picture of a granny on the front of it. She wrote a list of funny things on the inside about what to expect now that you're old, which included slight baldness, brittle bones, and no weekend clubbing, etc. I did not mind. I am only a month older than her but she still had ammunition to mock me with, which I found hilarious. Lesley-Anne was always so good to me. She never had any problem assisting me with my hair or doing my make up if we all were going out somewhere. We spent a lot of time together, especially on Saturdays if Patrick was at work. She wanted to understand my way of communicating as her brother had. She was great at picking up on this. I felt that I could talk to her and open up without feeling judged. It was brilliant being around a woman my age that accepted me.

As part of a college course I was taking, I had to get work experience. It did not matter what I would be doing, I just needed to do some form of work. At the time, Lesley-Anne was working in a high-end retail company in Dublin and she got me in there every Wednesday for eight weeks. I could see she was delighted that she could help me. She also made me feel welcome and introduced me to everyone. I was a bit overwhelmed with being involved in the employment scene. She showed me around and could tell that I was nervous on escalators so she suggested using the regular stairs. What happened? I fell up them! I was rolling around on the ground and she was looking at me as though I was weird. I got up as quickly as I could and tried to contain my laughter. What a first day. There was too much excitement! It was a really great experience and there was obviously plenty of teasing from Lesley-Anne. During my time there I would always be found giggling away to myself in the corner, trying to work. One time I heard the other girls say, "Isn't Tracey always laughing? I wish I could be that happy." I think I was just overwhelmed with joy at being involved in the working environment and I could not contain it. I would just randomly giggle to myself. Lesley-Anne and I would go out for lunch together during my time there. That truly was a great moment for me.

The past five years with Patrick

The relationship Patrick and I have has been on and off and spanned more than a decade. As I write this book we have been together for five years this time and have done more together during those years than we had ever done any of the numerous other times we attempted "giving it a go together". There was a long gap where Patrick and I had no contact at all during one of those 'off' times in the relationship. It felt weird as usually, we'd had some form of communication with each other. I was starting to let him go completely and began to get my life together without him but no matter what was going on in my life though he would always enter my mind. The story of our relationship is very similar to the movie *When Harry met Sally.* We always bumped into each other at various stages over the ten year period and would "give it a go" again, and this would generally end in tears. That was the norm for a while until five years ago when Patrick made a decision that he wanted to 'grow up' and cut down on socialising in pubs with his friends (his words, not mine). He wanted to make it work this time as he really wanted to be with me. He claims he always knew that he wanted to spend the rest of his life with me, and because of what he has done for me the past five years I believe him.

Patrick and I have a very unique relationship and we appreciate the small things in life. However, we collectively long for, seek out, and actively participate in huge adventures together. An example of the finer things we enjoy doing include making a picnic and planning to go somewhere like a local beach, park, or up to the mountains in Wicklow, which has lovely spots such as Sally's Gap and Glendalough. I love nature. I always have since I was a little girl. Thanks to my family always bringing us to these fabulous locations, it is now natural for me to want to share these experiences with my man.

I now feel part of his wonderful family too. I adored his nanny because she always treated me like a granddaughter; I would always visit her and listen to her stories. She loved the company and would talk the ears off me. She always made me smile. She had nothing but praise for Patrick and me. A number of years ago I even managed to get her up to Mam's, to drop in and say hi, which was great fun. Mam gave her a great compliment by telling her that she looked like the queen. She laughed at this and began to wave like her royal highness!

Patrick has four sisters and I am delighted to be accepted into the family as I never had any female siblings myself. They are all amazing, and they all have a lovely sibling bond. He also has a brother who is the same age as Dean. Patrick's siblings are very supportive of me. They do not look down on me and think that I cannot achieve what it is that I am aiming to achieve. There were times, a number of years ago, when I had felt that I did not belong in his tight-knit family. I now realise that that was due to my own self-doubts. I can act shy and awkward around them, even to this day. But, they accept me for me, which is great. I now enjoy getting to know his friends too as they have all grown up and have their own lives. They are all great people. I now feel part of both Patrick's family and his group of friends. I admire them all for their own individual achievements and know also that they admire me in return. Also, I have recently taken the massive step of speaking vocally to them all, which is something I would not have felt comfortable doing a number of years ago. They are all encouraging and supportive of this and, like Patrick, are patient with me, which is something that I am extremely grateful to them for. I now have a group of friends who I have known the same length of time that I have known Patrick, who are just as good natured and caring as him. The sense of belonging is a very important thing to have.

How Patrick makes me feel

Patrick makes me feel like no other person can. It is very important in life to have a special person you can turn to at any given moment, someone to give you that time, who wants to know how your day went or how you feel about something. When you are apart from each other you miss each other's presence and company. They keep you going through moments of self-doubt or self-pity and you look forward to seeing them, which can make you feel excited. We all need someone like that, someone who laughs about absolute nonsense with you. Someone who understands you and completely gets the person you are and accepts your flaws. To me, Patrick would tick all of those boxes, and I know he feels the exact same about me. He makes me feel like I am the only person that matters. Due to the joint feeling of defiance we have regarding our supposed limitations, we can do anything and everything in both our shared and individual lives because we give each other the strength, belief, and encouragement needed. We push each other every step. Patrick is my rock and I know I am his. The connection between us is so strong, so unique, and it is incredible. He makes me feel so loved and wanted, makes me believe in myself and in the idea that I have a purpose here, and that I will touch so many people with the strength of the messages given in this book and in my future ventures. He admires me because he knows my true inner strength. Patrick would literally do anything for me. I know some men that would not go to the extent that he does. He does everything out of pure love and does it without complaining. He just loves supporting me and making sure I get where I want in life because he knows how much it means to me. He understands how important it is for me to be somebody who makes a difference.

We have both gone through different challenges in our lives, and we cannot be positive and give off the impression we are great all the time. It is only human to have up and down days even in our relationships. The person closest to us can pick up straight away on this, which can affect them too. What makes a couple strong is when they have the capabilities to overcome moments of conflict and realise that they are stronger together.

Daily life with Patrick

Anytime we are out and about we always bring food with us because I have an incredible appetite. I love my food, especially healthy food because I know how beneficial it is in every aspect. We bring packed lunches with us and enjoy the food out in the open in each other's company. We generally carry our food in one of the many shopping bags we have stored in a cupboard in the apartment. If we are going away for a weekend down the country to stay in a nice hotel, Patrick always tries to use these bags to put his clothes in until I stop him saying that we cannot bring shopping bags into a fancy hotel as we will stick out like sore thumbs! He concedes and packs our clothes into a small suitcase.

If someone were to ask me about Patrick's hobbies, I would know straight away what the most accurate answer was: he loves two things other than me, Manchester United and movies! Patrick is a bit of a weirdo with regard to his knowledge of movies, actors, actresses, directors, etc. He knows the most random facts about movies and, for some strange reason, knows how actors are connected to one another through the films they were in. He puts this knowledge down to a game he claims to have mastered a number of years ago when he had far too much time on his hands called Six Degrees of Kevin Bacon in which he can apparently link more or less any actor or actress to Kevin Bacon, his favourite actor, in no more than six moves, by the movies they were in. A little obsessive I know but believe me this is a real game. An example would be the following: Let's say someone said Robert Downey Jr., Patrick is able to work out that Robert Downey Jr. was in a movie called *Heart and Souls* with Kyra Sedgwick who was in two movies with and is married to Kevin Bacon. The movies they appeared in together are *The Woodsman* and *Murder in the First.* That is a rather easy example but you get the picture as to how obsessed he is with this. There is good to this obsessive behaviour, however. Patrick told me that, a number of years ago, he worked out a connection between Kevin Bacon and my cousin Jenny. He had worked this out shortly after her passing away. In 2004, Jenny appeared as an extra in a movie about two men with physical disabilities struggling to be accepted in society. The movie was called *Inside I'm Dancing* and starred James McAvoy who also starred in *X-Men: First Class* alongside Kevin Bacon. Patrick found great comfort in the fact that he was able to work that one out. It eased the pain of loss that he felt for his friend and my cousin.

Patrick and I can communicate fairly quickly because of the time we have spent together and his understanding of me. This is incredibly rare as not a lot of people understand me with such ease. Even still, I generally have to say a sentence slowly and one word at a time. Something he finds great amusement in is when I am asking him a question starting with "How—" he would immediately say "How now brown cow". He is a funny character and I do not know where I got him from. He does not take life too seriously. He makes me laugh like no other person I have met, which is wonderful. Laughter is a very important thing.

How we support one another

Patrick and I are an amazing support for each other. We care and look out for one another. We want the best for each other and to help one another grow and get everything out of our lives, both together and separately. We are always there for one another. If either of us is sad or worried we help by making one another happy again or with finding a solution to our respective problems. We do not add to it with stupid, non-productive questions like, "What are you going to do?" Sometimes Patrick can do that, but I give out to him and ask him to offer a solution or some positive input at least. He has eventually learnt and has a much more positive outlook now. He now equally hates it when people sympathise with him, instead of offering him some form of positive input. Ever since Patrick and I have been heavily involved in participated in quite a number of 'positive attitude' talks he has been a different person. He is still as supportive as ever, but now more aware of what he says, and how and when he says it. Now, everything he says is positive, constructive, and supportive, which I really love as his new-found attitude makes me feel happier and safer.

If I was to define what type of personality type Patrick falls into, then, I would say that he is an analyst. Analysts, by their very definition, are quiet, deep thinkers and are very good at coming up with solutions to problems. The problem with analysts is the following, however: they can, at times, take too long to think about solutions as opposed to getting to the work at hand. Patrick is one of these individuals, which means that he is a great analytical thinker and will come up with some fantastic solutions. However, it can be frustrating waiting on him to make a final decision, and there is no spontaneity with him. Even though this can be tedious, I appreciate that we are all different. I am also grateful with the knowledge that when we go to do something adventurous, that I am safe. Patrick has over-analysed every potential situation, be it good or bad, in advance.

Patrick is such a kind-hearted giver, and people can forget to give back. He holds no resentment towards the people who have given him grief throughout his life. He is a decent person who just wants everyone

to be happy. If only there were more people like Patrick. Despite the many years of drama that our relationship has endured, I know that I am extremely lucky to have him in my life. To me, our relationship demonstrates the enduring love two people can have for one another and if they are meant to be, even through all the ups and downs, love will always shine through and keep us together. We both always knew deep down that we were meant to be together. It was all about the correct timing for us. I am glad that we did not give up on each other.

Patrick is my partner, my soul mate, my best friend and my travelling companion all wrapped into one. Love conquers all.

Our united nickname

Due to our love of exploring the world and our participation in things that other people in our situation would not dream off, we have been recently dubbed The Limitless Couple. I believe that this is rather fitting as both Patrick and I constantly throw ourselves into doing things that others would not dream of. We have been to fourteen countries in the past five years alone. We have also done abseiling, speed boating, helicopter rides, swimming with dolphins, and zip-lining across alligators. We have done all of this, not to prove anything to anyone, but because to us life is meant to be lived, and we are intent on living ours to the fullest.

On a side note, I often see this couple on the bus who both have a mental disability. This is extremely apparent the moment you see them. The man cannot hold a conversation as it is impossible to understand him and yet he yaps away to himself. The woman seems more mentally advanced. However, despite their separate complications, they manage to understand each other and always get around independently. The love they have for each other is also very apparent and always makes me smile every time I see the pair. I also often see other people with both mental and physical disabilities out on their own. I truly admire them and can fully relate to their need to get out and let nothing hold them back.

These people are living proof, and shining examples of the fact that when facing adversity and obstacles, unity is a very important thing.

"There are no limitations to our potential.
There is, however, great potential within us,
to surpass our limitations." – Patrick Hogan

Chapter 9
Living life

"To live is the rarest thing in the world. Most people just exist" – Oscar Wilde

Allow me to explain the type of person that I am now. Even though I have always had this burning desire in the pit of my stomach, this optimistic determination that I could literally do anything and everything that I had set my heart on, I was still full of self-pity. I hated feeling I was not living my life to the full, and that my life was being wasted. I am a risk-taker so my attitude now is that I only have one life, so why merely dream of my desires when I can see them flourish into accomplishments that I could be proud of. I took my control back and now live each day as if it were my last. One of the biggest and most controlling frustrations I had from the earlier years of my life was that I was extremely eager to do everything all at once. However, I felt at the time that I was being held back from being my true self because I was trapped inside my head. I could not just explore life in an unsafe manner like some people do. I tried making friends with people who had the same interests, however, I felt people had their own things going on and that I was a bit of burden on them. Then when Patrick came back into my life a number of years ago and he proved to me that he was fully committed after years of making me play second fiddle to drinking with his friends, I knew it was for real this time. With that in mind, I grabbed life and Patrick by the hand and together we are unstoppable, living life to its full. We are now both expanding our 'global maps' and seeing new parts of the world.

I have visited many countries and achieved many things in the past twenty-nine years of my life. The following are a few short examples of some of the most memorable of these achievements with Patrick, and the journey taken by both of us in seeing our goals accomplished. For me, when I look back over my life at all that I have achieved, the end is only justifiable by the means. In other words, the journey has always been of more importance to me than the destination.

"It is not about taking pride in transforming our dreams into achievements. Pride should only be taken from the actions taken in making these transformations possible." – Tracey Ellen Maria

Australia, New Zealand and Malaysia – February 2014

I had always longed to travel the world as freely as other people. However, the most desired place that I wanted to visit was always Australia. My uncle Andrew who lived in my nanny's has lived over there for a number of years and is married to an Australian woman. He had always invited my family to come over and visit the wonderful country that he lives in, and in which he works as a lecturer. He knew that I wanted to go places and to see the world. He told me once that when you see a country and then move onto another, this is making your map bigger. He also said that a lot of people's maps are really small and they're happy enough with that, but there are others who crave to create a larger map, to see different ways of living, experience different cultures and have a different sense of adventure each time. My brother Alan took Andrew up on his offer a number of years ago and visited with his girlfriend. He came back telling us all of his amazing experience, and that hammered it home for me. I had to go. Shortly after Patrick and I got back together almost five years ago, I asked him if he had ever wanted to go to Australia and when he replied yes in a casual manner that was all I needed to hear. The next day I got a bus into town and headed straight for the travel agent. I booked the flights for Patrick and me to head to Australia a few months from that day. I had used the money that I had saved over the years to book it. We had spoken about it and we were both interested. But what is the point about carrying on talking about something? It becomes boring. Why not just book it and worry about it later? I had taken that leap. I left the travel agent with a huge smile on my face. I couldn't believe it. "Yes! It is finally happening." I sent a message to Patrick straight after and he was in shock but delighted. What I had booked and paid for were the flights, which included a three-day stop off in Malaysia on the outbound and return journeys. All we needed to book then was the hotel in Malaysia as we had accommodation in Australia. We would stay with my uncle.

I will admit, I was nervous enough telling Patrick that I had booked it in case he would say no for some reason, but deep down I knew he would not refuse this great experience. I was equally as nervous telling my family. When I did there were the obvious concerns over our safety but a few people had the cheek to advise Mam to go to the travel agent and cancel it and that she should not let me go. My stepdad intervened wondering why they were suddenly concerned about my well-being. He rightly informed them that they did not feel the need to concern themselves with me when I was at my lowest, why get involved when I am at my highest? They had no business interfering and their input was not required.

Needless to say, a few months later, Patrick and I were on a flight bound for Malaysia. It was a long flight but when we arrived there we were amazed at our new surroundings, and the heat. We stayed in a five-star hotel while there and took the opportunity to relax ourselves for the journey ahead. We went on a day excursion, which we had booked, and it was incredible. We saw fireflies and free-roaming monkeys. The following day we went to visit the Petronas Towers, which were amazing. After our three-day stop off in Kuala Lumpur, Malaysia, we found ourselves bound for Sydney, Australia.

Upon our arrival at Sydney Airport, Patrick had all his paperwork prepared and ready for inspection. He had gathered together a letter from his job proving that he was in full-time employment in Ireland and letters from his doctor confirming that he required the medication he was carrying in his luggage. He was, however, disappointed that he did not need to present any of these as he assumed he would have to. The only thing they were concerned with was that we had the correct visas and where we were going to be staying during our time in Australia. He had watched too much TV before we left Ireland and assumed that there would be some form of proof required that we were just two disabled travellers, exploring the world together. After we successfully made it through Australian customs and entered the arrivals hall I saw my uncle Andrew waving at us. He was delighted that we had come all that way and during our entire time spent with him made us feel so welcome. Patrick and I spent a month in Australia, during which time we visited plenty of tourist sites such as Bondi Beach, a wildlife petting zoo located in the beautifully scenic Blue Mountains and, of course, the Sydney Opera House. We had arranged to meet up with Patrick's two sisters who were living in Sydney at that time. It was class. We also took a short flight over to Christ Church in New Zealand for four days, which was a gorgeous place to visit with its amazing scenery. While there, we took a day trip to do some whale watching, which we had the luxury of doing on a seaplane. The whole experience was surreal and when Patrick and I arrived back in Ireland we felt like invincible travellers. There was nowhere on this planet that we could not visit, and no one to tell us that we could not.

USA – Summer 2015

After the achievement of going to Malaysia, Australia, and New Zealand, Patrick and I began to feel a buzz of excitement at our potential next big adventure. We had caught the travelling bug and we loved it. One evening, Patrick met me after work and we took a stroll through Dublin city centre. Our attention was immediately drawn to a poster in a travel agent window, which featured a couple sharing a pool, with a dolphin, in the warm sun. We decided in that moment on our next adventure and went in to get a quote. Just as rapidly as I made the decision with Australia I decided in that moment to place a deposit on our trip to America. We did not even know if we could afford it, but we gave ourselves plenty of time to save the money. We had booked five days in New York City and two weeks in Orlando, Florida. We hired a car for Florida as Patrick felt fairly confident about driving over there and sorted everything out financially and logistically for this trip within the months building up to it. We knew, just like with Australia, that we were ready.

When we arrived in JFK airport, we were instantly hit with, again, the heat. Winter in New York may be full of snow and wintery bliss but the summer there is one of sticky, humid heat. Being Irish, however, I loved it. We stayed in yet another five-star hotel in the middle of Time Square, which was lovely. All the staff in the hotel were extremely nice and we had no problem getting someone to help me with my hair in the morning. A kind-hearted lady who worked in the restaurant had no objections in offering us this assistance. Her name was Vivienne. Even though we were only in New York for five days, we managed to fit in a lot of sightseeing. We visited the new World Trade Centre, took the Staten Island ferry and a bus tour, which visited all the famous shots that were featured in movies such as Ghostbusters and programmes such as Friends. We also took a helicopter tour down the Hudson River, which enabled us to get a view of the world's most famous city that most people do not get. The whole experience had in New York was so incredible that I am not surprised it is referred to as 'the city that never sleeps'.

Florida is not known as 'the sunshine state' for nothing, as it honestly lives up to its name, and anyone who has been there will vouch for that. When Patrick and I arrived in Orlando after our short flight from JFK, we immediately made our way towards the car hire desk where Patrick got the keys to his new vehicle for the following two weeks. He was a little apprehensive for two reasons. Firstly, he had never driven in the USA before or any other country for that matter, and secondly, he had only ever driven a Nissan Micra and was not fully aware as to what 'monster car' would be awaiting him. In the end, he had hired a Chevrolet Impala, which is a saloon style car that was huge in comparison to his own little Micra. All his fretting was, however, for nothing in the end as he proudly discovered that he was more than capable of handling both the vehicle and the road. We had booked an apartment in Orlando, which was in a lovely quiet estate and was bigger than my own apartment. We felt at home during our two weeks there.

While in Florida, both Patrick and I took part in many fun activities, aside from visiting all the incredible theme parks that they have there. We had arranged to parasail on a lake that was based within the Disney theme park, and that was an experience. We decided to do something crazy and really adventurous one of the days – having seen a poster for a park that enabled us to zip line across lakes, which were all full of alligators. I remember I turned to Patrick and he said, "Do you want to?" to which I replied, "You only live once!" We also made sure that we took part in the thing that attracted us to Florida in the first place – to swim with the dolphins.

Patrick has family living in Florida and wanted to go down to visit them, and for them to meet me. We arranged this and made our way down from Orlando to West Palm Beach, which was a two-and-a-half-hour drive. I was very privileged to meet Patrick's two aunties and his two cousins as they were all extremely welcoming and proud that Patrick and I had made all the journeys that we had. That recognition was important to me but not as important as it was to Patrick, as he wanted to prove how much his life had developed, to people who he admired and respected. In all, our trip to America was met with so much happiness and so many funny moments. Again, we felt invincible.

Iceland - January 2016

We met a colleague of Patrick's, Scott Watson and his partner, at Penny's in Swords. They had just bought a lot of winter clothing such as thermals, etc., as they were off to Finland and were going to do many adventurous things while there like ride huskies and try to see the Northern Lights. This got me thinking that I would love to do that, so Patrick and I discussed where we would go next before we even went on the trip that we had planned. We always jump ahead and keep planning our next big adventure. After we got back from America, Patrick asked Scott about Finland and he recommended we go to see Iceland first, as it is a cool little country, expensive, but worth it. Scott has travelled to lots of cool places so we took his advice. We started to get the ball rolling. It would be a completely different holiday from our usual trips to hot sunny places. Patrick was a bit apprehensive at first as due to his heart condition and the medication he is on it means he feels the cold a lot more than most. He had visions of himself turning into an instant ice sculpture like that scene in *The day after tomorrow*! We booked a five-day trip in June 2015 for the following January. We booked it in the winter because it is the optimum time to go as there is a higher probability of seeing the Northern Lights. But it was still a matter of luck as to whether we would see them or not. Over the coming months, we saved like crazy and booked our flights, hotel, and day excursions as we wanted to make the most of our five-day trip.

When the day came to finally set off, we had to get an early flight to London Heathrow first. We did not sleep well the previous night as we were too excited. We were like zombies on the plane due to our night of insomnia and even though our flight time was only an hour from Dublin to Heathrow we were in a constant daydream. On arrival in London, we made our way to our connecting flight to Reykjavik. As soon as we landed in Iceland, I felt butterflies as I did not know what to expect. We got off the plane to be greeted by this massive queue at arrivals to get through airport security and customs. The queue was moving so swiftly that Patrick and I ended up having to go to two separate security checks. Our carry-on items went through the X-ray machine, I went into one queue, and Patrick was told go to the next queue. I put my big, padded coat up to be scanned and when I collected my coat on the other side I thought it felt somewhat lighter like something was missing. I waited for Patrick to get through the security wondering what it is that was missing. Then "Bang!" I remembered. It was like that scene out of *Home Alone* when the mother cannot remember what she forgot only to quickly realise it was her son. I had left my bag under the seat on the plane. I thought to myself,

"Hang on. Before I panic, was there anything in it that I needed?" I was making a list in my head of everything that I had in my bag. There was my mobile phone, my fob for my apartment, my travel pass, Patrick's car keys and my bank cards. "Damn, I am screwed!" I saw Patrick gathering together his stuff from the conveyor belt so I ran over to him panicking, saying I had no handbag, that I had left it on the plane. We immediately reported it. After we reported it we assumed that the cleaners would stumble across it and this would be resolved in a matter of minutes. We waited around for a bit but there was no sign of it being discovered. We were eventually informed that the plane had taken off and my bag was not discovered by any of the cleaners but once the flight arrived at its final destination it would be searched again and if found would be sent to our hotel in Iceland. Needless to say, however, this did not happen, and my handbag was not returned to me until almost one year later. It was discovered by a lady on her way home to Mexico on the same plane that I left it on. My handbag had been to parts of the world that I had not!

Iceland is an amazingly beautiful country, and as much as I and Patrick assumed it would be, it is not that cold a place to visit. We were there for a total of five days, and again, managed to fit in a great number of excursions in that time. We had booked horse riding on Icelandic horses, which allowed us to admire the beautiful picturesque views of the snowy mountains as our horses fearlessly trotted through the snow and across frozen lakes. The following day, we took a day relaxing in an outdoor lagoon that rested on top of a dormant geyser and created a pool of naturally warmed water. We also had the privilege, as not many have, of seeing the aurora borealis, commonly known as the northern lights. This took a great deal of waiting around on a boat and staring up at the sky in hopeful prayer, only to see in absolute astonishment the true beauty of this natural phenomenon. All in all, Iceland was the most eye-opening of all our trips as to the sheer beauty of our little blue planet.

Panama – New Year's 2016

For as long as I can remember, I have always wanted to spend New Year's in a foreign country. To be able to say that I have experienced 'ringing in the New Year' in a different part of the world was always a dream of mine. It was not until following a typical Irish New Year's in 2015, that I decided to pursue this 'dream' and see it successfully accomplished. Patrick and I were determined to go somewhere, and one evening while I was doing some research on the internet I stumbled across the most random of places, Panama. Once again, Patrick and I began making the preparations for our trip. We had given ourselves the best part of a year to prepare, and, on 26 December 2016, we found ourselves bound for Panama.

We spared no expense in our preparations, and while there, we stayed in a five-star hotel and took part in plenty of excursions. We visited natives, and a 'small' catchment of archipelagos, 365 islands to be exact. We also went to a place known as Monkey Island, which was an island inhabited by free-roaming and 'wild' monkeys. Of course, we made it our business to visit the Miraflores locks, which makes up a small part of the world famous Panama Canal. At the end of it all, I achieved what I had always dreamt of, to spend New Year's in a different country, and on a different continent. What a way to ring in the New Year!

Switzerland – my twenty-ninth birthday

On 10 February 2017, I turned twenty-nine, and Patrick splashed out big time on my birthday present. He had told me that he had booked a holiday abroad for us but would not tell me where we were going. In truth, I did not want to know anyway as I wanted to be surprised. It was not until we reached Dublin Airport on the day of our departure that I found out. We were walking through the departure hall past a number of check-in desks and Patrick finally stopped, turned to me and asked, "Where do you think we are going?" As I scanned the check-in desk we had stopped at, the first thing that I saw was Zurich. I was amazed as I knew that Patrick does not like cold countries, even though we had been to and thoroughly enjoyed Iceland. When we boarded our plane destined for Zurich I was nervously excited at what lay ahead.

We spent a total of four days in a nice hotel in the middle of Zurich. As we had gone in February, which, was still technically winter we had expected it to be extremely cold but again as with Iceland, it was not. While we were there we took our first day venturing around the beautiful city that is Zurich, and we were astonished by the city's beauty and the surrounding scenic landscape. On one of our days there, Patrick had organised a day trip for us to visit a place called Mount Titlis, which is a mountain belonging to the Alps mountain range. We had to get a cable car up to the top of the mountain; not that we minded as that was a new experience for both of us. When we reached the summit we were in awe at the sheer beauty of what we were viewing, as everywhere we turned we were met with gorgeous views of the vastness of the snowy Alps. That was a view that is scorched into my memory for the remainder of my days.

Other achievements

All the achievements detailed above, have been shared with Patrick. There have been many other accomplishments that I have made solo, making everyone who knows me very proud, even as small child as when I first started going on the bus by myself, which I now do on a daily basis and look forward to seeing the friendly faces of the bus drivers that I have come accustomed to. All those achievements, even the small ones, have proved to me and everyone who knows me, that there are no limitations to my potential and they have acted as an inspiration to all, to see the same within themselves.

New York

Even though I went to New York City with Patrick in 2015 that was not my first time there, as when I was nineteen, I was picked to go there and participate in a sports event for the physically challenged, which was for fifteen days. I was in a relationship with Patrick at that time and we were going well. When I went I will admit that it did feel strange going off and not seeing him during that time, but absence makes the heart grow fonder, as they say. I had gone over with a lovely group of people. We all had our own PAs while we were there. They were great and it helped that they were all around our age and did not treat us any differently. My PA's name was Maeve and she was very down-to-earth, classy, funny and good hearted, and we clicked straight away. Maeve made me feel relaxed and did not 'baby' me the whole time, which I appreciated a great deal. I felt that I could have my own space to relax in the environment and not feel pressured.

I am the worst packer as I either pack too much or too little and not enough of what I really need. For that America trip, I honestly do not know what I was thinking when I packed. I found a random old book about love in my suitcase and I knew Patrick would not be that romantic to pack it. He had bought me a notebook so I could record my journey on paper, which was a lovely idea. Maeve helped me to record my days and experiences there, and it turned out to be a very funny journal. For some reason, I had packed the equivalent of a suitcase full of G-strings. Maeve could not help but tease the life out of me as everyone found out about it. It was both hilarious and embarrassing all in one. The event itself was set in Long Bay and was an experience that I will never forget.

I absolutely loved the group of assistants and my fellow disabled participants as they were all really sound. One of the participants in particular that I had made good friends with was Lee and we got on really well. He was always cracking jokes and was a great laugh. I did my races while there and did really well in them. Lee's PA whose name was Ross gave me the nickname "lucky underpants", which we all found hilarious. One night, while messing around, Lee and Ross tried to sneak into my room to find the G-strings. The laugh we all had at my expense. Another night, we were all out and there was a raffle taking place. I saw a chocolate cake and almost immediately 'pigged' out on it. I had assumed that I would not win in the raffle and would be given the time required to enjoy my cake. However, I quickly learnt that it is never right to assume anything as my name was called. I refused to go on to the stage as I was covered in chocolate, but, I was forced to go up and collect my prize. I found myself on the stage with chocolate everywhere, and the stage lights blaring down on me, feeling like such a 'waffle'. I was definitely out of my comfort zone, but, I was also loving my life.

Abseil in Croke Park

One day, while doing some random browsing online a few years ago, I stumbled across something that almost immediately appealed to me. It was a sponsored abseil within Croke Park stadium, for motor neuron disease. I asked Patrick to ring up the organisation that was arranging this and enquire about the possibility of my participating. When Patrick rang them and explained my situation they were excited about the prospect of my taking part.

On the day itself, Mam, Stepdad, Patrick, my brother Alan and I made our way to Croke Park. Billy from boxercise came along also to offer me his support and he assisted me all the way along. It was great having him there as extra support. The abseil was actually easier than I imagined; the difficult part was walking along the roof of the stadium itself and then down the narrow and awkward ladder to reach the point where I was due to abseil from. When I eventually made it down, thanks to the assistance of Billy, I was ready. I was to release myself from the side of the large TV screen within the stadium, which is a couple of hundred feet above the pitch. Thankfully, I do not have much of a fear of heights, because as I was preparing to 'launch' myself I took a brief look down and was in awe at the distance between myself and the pitch. It was bit of struggle letting go and as I was preparing to I was instantly hit with a sudden rush of adrenaline. Maybe it was the excitement, maybe it was nerves, or maybe it was both. Then came the moment of truth. All the adrenaline in the build-up helped me to finally let go of any worries about the situation that I had voluntarily put myself in, and it helped me to let go of my 'safety net', which was the bar that I was holding onto. Within less than a few seconds, I was hanging off the roof of the stadium, being slowly lowered down towards the pitch while I laughed my head off. There were no sudden thoughts of any dreaded incidents occurring and there were no screams from me either. I was just enjoying the moment as I was slowly being lowered back towards the earth, and feeling the success of yet another achievement. I felt happy in that moment when I saw my family cheering me on from the stands. As proud as I was at what I had achieved, I was more proud of the funds that I had raised for a worthy charity. Afterwards, all my family and friends gathered in a local pub to celebrate and congratulate me on my achievement. Patrick had bought me a chain that had an Asian symbol on it meaning 'strength'. He and everyone were all extremely proud of me, and I was extremely proud of myself too.

Women's mini marathon

In 2017, I registered to take part in the women's mini marathon, which is a ten kilometre run within Dublin city centre. As part of the registration for this, I was required to select a charity that I wished to run on behalf of. I could only think of one and it was one that I held closest to my heart. A number of years before her death, my cousin

Jenny had wanted to run the mini marathon. She'd said that one day she would. The charity I chose to represent was Enable Ireland, which Jenny had attended. While there, Jenny had taken part in many educational opportunities in an attempt to equip her with an independence to some degree. She had a keen interest in journalism as she loved creative writing and had written many articles while in school, one of which detailed her own dramatic life prior to and after her developing dystonia. She wanted to eventually pursue this love into a field of employment. She was able to follow that dream thanks to Enable Ireland so I registered to run on their behalf and in memory of my cousin Jenny.

For the mini marathon itself, I aimed to jog. I had not fully trained at jogging for ten kilometres before but was determined to achieve this regardless. In the weeks building up to the marathon, I did laps around the local park, during which I would be half dead but I was determined as jogging it was another one of my goals. How I would manage this I did not know but what I did know with absolute certainty was that I would give it 100 per cent and try my best, and when it came to it, that is exactly what I did. My friend Sandra also registered to take part in it with me as she is an avid 'lady of fitness'. On the day of the marathon itself, I pushed myself the whole way. I jogged over five kilometres, which was mostly uphill. When I got to the halfway point I went to the water station and got a woman there to assist me in refreshing myself. She kindly gave me some water and even dampened the back of my neck. During the second part of the marathon, it began raining, which was welcoming to not only myself but the thousands of other tired and excessively overheated women taking part. The last five kilometres were a bit torturous, but once I made it across the finish line and gathered my thoughts I realised all that I had achieved, coming from where I was when I was first diagnosed with dystonia, locked in a spasm and unable to do a great deal of things, to a woman who had just finished a ten kilometre marathon. I felt pride in that moment and I know that wherever she was that day, Jenny felt it too.

I had lost Sandra after the first kilometre but we met again at the finish line. She, Patrick, a few other friends and I all went to get food together in celebration.

Travelling to Budapest

I am now a member of a travel group whose members are all avid travellers like me and with whom I travelled to Budapest with. This was another occasion that I travelled abroad without Patrick, but I was not alone. I went off with a fantastic group who were constantly positive and encouraging towards me and they all made the whole experience great fun. I did not have to worry about anything while there as every single person gave me a hand. I was not made to feel like a burden because of my need of that extra support as they all help each other in the same manner anyway. We created some lovely memories together. It was for five days and was all in aid of a personal development event.

I went over there a few days before the start of the event with another member, who is a wonderfully supportive and caring person by nature. While there, we all had such a laugh together and everyone was fabulous towards me the entire time. Going abroad with a group of like-minded and energetic people has always been a goal of mine and I am so grateful to them for making this happen. A beautiful couple called Bronagh and Karl, who I'd met via other friends, had got me involved with this brilliant group. The group has opened up so many more doors for me. It is not just a travel group but, it is about connecting with the right people and socialising on a daily basis. Developing and growing together, while making lasting friendships. Over the past two years, the people who I have come to know as friends are constantly supportive and encouraging towards me achieving one of my most challenging ambitions, which is to do public speaking in aid of assisting others to overcome their own obstacles and see their dreams achieved. It means a lot to have this support from a group of friends who I truly appreciate. If I had tried my hand at this a number of years ago, I know I would have failed. Timing is everything.

Kayaking

I had wanted to participate in kayaking as it has always looked like great fun. However, when I was in sixth year in secondary school we went on a school trip up to Wicklow for some outdoor activities. I love being outside. We did some treks and then we were to do some kayaking on the Glendalough Lake. I had never done it before and was excited about it. When the instructor explained what would be involved, however, I immediately got this nervous feeling in my stomach and thoughts of the boat toppling over sent shivers down my body. I have a major fear of water because I cannot swim. Even still, though, I was not going to say no, not without giving it a go first. I went onto the kayak boat with my sixth-class mates and positioned myself in the middle. The moment the kayak was in the lake I felt very uneasy and I began screaming at the top of my lungs as I was petrified. One of my friends who sat in front of me turned and said to me "Tracey, you're grand. Relax." I then tried relaxing, but it reached a stage where I knew that I needed to get out of the boat. It was far too shaky and I had this fear of it turning over, and again I screamed intently. There was a big commotion and when I was asked if I wanted to get out, I leapt at the chance. When I got out I was extremely relieved to be on dry land again, and soon after I got out, the boat I was in toppled over. Thank God I decided to get out, I thought.

Fast forward to present day and while recently attending a hen's weekend I discovered that, among numerous outdoor activities, we were to do kayaking. When I found out I decided to just go with it and try to face my fear. I was around a good group of people and an instructor who I knew would look out for me as I kept telling myself. "You will not die!" The seating arrangements were the same as the first time I had attempted this, with me in the middle of the boat. I knew it would be over as quickly as it started but I began to panic again. I lasted a bit longer than the first time in fairness. Eventually, after everyone saw how panicked I was, I was given the option to join the instructor in a speedboat, which I chose. Looking back on it now, I am glad I made that choice but at the time, I did not know if it really was 'the safest option'. The instructor was flying in the speed boat, trying to catch the girls off guard, and give them a little scare. Meanwhile, I was in the back of the speed boat bopping all around, and I had to use my whole body in order to keep my balance and prevent myself from falling out. In fairness, it was immense fun. While on the speed boat we went over to a group of caves inside of which was a waterfall. The instructor got the girls to come along individually while he held their heads under the lashing waterfall for five seconds. I definitely wanted to give it a try; I did not want to be too left out. After our 'baptism by waterfall,' we got back on our boats. In my case, I got back onto the speed boat and began hanging on for dear life again. He then brought us all to a wooden platform in the middle of the lake, from which we could all jump in the water. I wanted to jump in, knowing that I would be safe. I honestly did try everything, but even still, the kayaking turned out to be a disaster. It did not deter me, however; I will still try it again in the future.

Recently, Patrick and I went on a big hike in Howth with the travel group. It was a challenge for us both but equally, an achievement too. Everybody there was much faster at the walk but Patrick and I decided to do it at our own pace, and we managed to complete this struggling trek, together. I definitely want to take up hiking as a hobby after that wonderful experience.

Darkness into Light

I had always wanted to do the Darkness into Light run since first hearing about it a number of years ago. It is for a very worthy cause and attracts a large crowd that is growing annually. However, I was waiting to meet the right person to take part with me. When my new-found friend Sandra came into my life, we realised we were in the same boat. We both wanted to experience life and take part in fun activities that were run in aid of charities. We quickly realised that we both had a great deal in common. I find that my time with Sandra is always full of laughter; proper belly laughs, which are amazingly uplifting for both of us, and so, without any hesitation, we signed up to do the Darkness into Light run. We were both very excited about this and counted down the days in eager anticipation.

On the night of the event itself, Sandra stayed at my apartment. I was getting a bit worried because she was taking her time to arrive and I knew that I needed a good sleep as we were due to get up at 2:15am. She eventually arrived at 9.30pm and I was relieved. Patrick and I were aiming to go to bed for 9:00pm, which obviously did not happen, but I was just relieved that she had not let me down. As soon as I saw Sandra I felt a positive energy from both her and myself. She instantly made me laugh, not even saying anything funny. It was just her being her naturally positive self. We all went to bed shortly after her arrival. I had never got up so early, not even for Christmas. I managed to get up at 2.15am and have my shower and some cereal. The laughter at that time of morning, from start to finish, was so amazing that we could write a book on the whole thing.

I had wanted to take part in this great event for so long. I finally found the right person to do it with, and it turned out to be an experience that I will never forget. The image of the sunrise while I was surrounded by a few thousand other people as we walked towards this bright glow will stay in my mind for the rest of my life. It was incredible. The air was so crisp even if it was a bit windy when we got up hill and had no surrounding trees to protect us. I was very proud of myself when I reached the finish line. Afterwards, Sandra and I walked to a local hotel and we rewarded ourselves with a buffet breakfast. I kept asking Sandra to get me more food. I love to make a pig of myself, especially when the food is there for the taking. Then, as if that was not enough, I got Sandra to hide some cakes in my handbag to smuggle home. In fairness, though, I was thinking of Patrick as he had got up with us that morning and brought us to the event in his car. I felt that I had to include him by bringing him home some cakes. Patrick is great and is very supportive of me.

When I got home I was exhausted and I, like so many others, cannot function properly without adequate sleep. A few hours later, I felt brand new again, and able to sit back and analyse yet another achievement accomplished. As much as I love being around great people and doing amazing things in the process, I still enjoy time to myself. This is important as it gives me time to reflect. I love sitting in my mam's garden, relaxing, and stepping back out of the beauty of the world, feeling proud about all that I have achieved so far, and planning my next move.

Conclusion

To me, living life is trying my hand at anything and experiencing new things. I love travelling and connecting with new people. My motto is "What is the point in travelling to the other side of the world and not attempting to connect with at least one new person?" To me, that is what makes travelling so exciting.

I now know that as long I visualise a great life for myself, it will happen, because I will remain focused on seeing it through. It is now all happening for me. I used to be fed up living the life that I had and feeling that I wanted and deserved more, and so I stopped at nothing to get it. If anything, this should prove to you that you can do whatever you desire in life. Stop dreaming, wake up, and go make it happen. Nobody else can do it for you, and nobody else should be expected to.

Even though Patrick and I have our own separate physical disabilities we also have a combined determination that makes us unstoppable, even in the face of our apparent obstacles. When we set a goal for ourselves, we will achieve it. Patrick puts this down to my 'get-go' attitude, and I put it down to his amazing organisational skills. It is through the combination of these two characteristics that we are the "limitless couple". I may have recommenced my own life, and saved myself from a dire mental state but Patrick has told me that I have also saved him from suffering the demons of negativity that he had previously faced. We are now unstoppable and are both living the lives that we want to live, not the ones that people expect us to. If the past couple of years are anything to go by, the future will be full of more adventures and achievements. This I know, with absolute certainty.

"While your past may be written, and possibly full of darkness,
your future is within your control, and can, if you want,
be full of light" – Patrick Hogan

Chapter 10
The Future

"Have a vision of tomorrow's results that can be shaped by today's actions, and not defined by yesterday's mistakes."

– Tracey Ellen Maria

Thinking back over my life, and everything that I have been through, both good and bad, I honestly would not change a thing. The dramatic, life-changing disability that struck me at the age of eight, combined with my strong family support and my even stronger motivation to live my life by my terms, has shaped me into the person that I am today. When I decided to take back my power all those years ago, I knew from that moment that I needed to begin planning the life that I wanted to live and then go about making it happen by taking action. With all that in mind, I will now share my final bits of information with you that assisted me in making all these changes. My first piece of advice for you going forward from today is that you must create a future plan, no matter how far-fetched it seems even to you; just put it down, and then get to work.

The importance of creating a future plan

Even though it is important to set goals for yourself, and remain focused on them to prevent getting side-tracked in achieving those goals, it is also very important for you to have a plan in place which is not too far into the future. Change your thinking of the concept of your goals to something that is used within any development life cycle. Instead, think of goals as milestones. Each time you hit one of your milestones, you move onto the next and the next and so on. Also bear in mind that, as humans, we are never completely happy, and as such you will constantly be setting new milestones as you continue on your life's journey. Your goals may change as the years progress and you mature, but one thing that should never change is the level of motivated action that you take when building towards the achievement of each milestone. People often get asked in interviews, "Where do you see yourself in five years' time?" Frankly, I think five years is too long to plan for because when we start looking that far ahead we subconsciously think of those dreams as being unachievable as they are too far away from our current reality. Not only that but we miss out on the moment. I recommend setting your life plan with more of a realistic timeframe in mind. How do you see yourself in three months? Six months? Next year? It is far easier to focus on the coming months and hitting your milestones one at a time as opposed to being purely focused on a five, ten, or even twenty-year plan that can, and possibly will change. Do not waste time missing out on the now and acknowledging all the milestones that you have hit so far, as this present moment is the one thing that we can never get back. Live in the moment and take action in the moment to work towards your future.

Here is my own future plan, which, while contradicting what I have said above with regards to the timeframe, is simply an example.

My future plan

- Write more books
- Travel to South America
- Partake in plenty of motivational speaking events
- See Antarctica by cruise ship
- Become well known
- Teach in different countries for a few weeks or months
- Improve on myself more
- Volunteer in a third world country
- Drive a little car, getting me from A to B
- Volunteer at home in Ireland with kids
- Continue travelling the world and experiencing the sheer beauty of this planet
- Trek across Machu Picchu in Peru with a lovely, friendly group who will look after one another
- Participate in a mud obstacle run

- Have my own children
- Walk under the sea in a scuba diving suit
- Look after Patrick and my family

Looking at my future plan can give you the impression that I am an over-ambitious person. This may be true. However, I know with absolute certainty that I can achieve all of the above through doing what I have done the most of my life, i.e. taking action.

"Action has always been required in order to achieve anything that has ever been achieved. Sitting around just conceiving and believing in a dream does not guarantee results. A result, be it positive or negative is only achieved by taking the necessary action." – Tracey Ellen Maria

Achieving our goals gives our lives meaning

Since the dawn of time, human beings have sought to find the 'meaning of life'. To me, the answer to this question, that has left many searching heaven and earth for the answer, seems so apparent. When we set goals for ourselves, put in the necessary work required, and then achieve these goals, this gives us a feeling of fulfilment, happiness, pride, and self-empowerment. These feelings, to me, are the true meaning to life.

I strongly believe we all need to give ourselves a reason to exist. We can, of course, all just sail through our lives, get up every day, and do the same routines. Some people, me included, actually get bored of that monotonous existence and some people are used to that form of living day by day and just existing. To each their own, I suppose. They are comfortable with their routines so much so that they are not prepared to make any changes. What I would say to people like that is this: whatever they feel that they are not capable of doing or if they feel that the life they live presently is the only life that they can or deserve to have, whatever their situation is, they have the power to change it, if they truly want to. For me, the importance of having a reason behind reaching our target each day is this: when we complete targets, even the simple ones, like going to the shop and getting food, going out and seeking employment, or booking a holiday these give us a sense of achievement. For some people, tasks such as these can be a big deal and they can often make excuses. However, it is through taking a leap of action in fulfilling these seemingly easy tasks that you will be prepared for your next challenge, whatever life throws your way. Also, it is that action that will give you a feeling of self-worth, a feel-good factor, independence, and pride in yourself. However, if you did not take the action you would miss out on all these positive feelings, and you would not develop as a person. You would not learn your true purpose or reason, so I implore you all to take the leap. The world is out there waiting for you to explore, any way that you see fit.

Asking why & saying yes

"He who has a why to live can bear almost any how"
- Friedrich Nietzsche

Whatever goal it is that you desire, it is important to keep in mind your 'why'. An example of this would be not to just go around saying random things like "I want to be rich". You must focus on what benefits you would get from becoming rich. With this example in mind, you could change what you are saying to, "I want more money so that every day is not a struggle. I can provide better for my family and do nice things like take nice holidays." It is important also to keep in mind what it is, when you achieve these goals, you can do to help others. Life is like a big game of 'trust falls' The more you show an eagerness to be there and 'catch' others, the more that they will do the same for you in return.

It is important also to become a "yes" person. Say yes to every opportunity that is presented to you as saying yes creates an internal mental wellness and makes people aware that you are open to anything. Also, it opens the door to new opportunities and new experiences that could work in your favour and which you may have overlooked by instantly turning them down. Do not shut things down instantly with a clear "no". With that in mind, however, there is a massive difference to saying no to people who constantly take advantage of you and offer you nothing in return. You are an adult and you know how to look after yourself but, at times, a lot of us get overcautious and presume that we know someone's true intentions. Too many great opportunities have been turned down due to people making incorrect presumptions.

Motivation > Limitation

Out of the many life lessons that I have learnt over the years, the most important is this. Even though I have a physical disability, even though initially I did not want it, and even though at times I still get moments of depression because of my situation, I am not automatically entitled to the same things as an able-bodied person. I realised this as I was growing up with my disability. I may be entitled to the same human rights and protection as per my country's constitution but not other things like employment, participation in local groups, or a social life full of great friends. I, along with many other disabled people like Patrick, know that it takes strong determination to actively seek out ways to reach our targets. The lives that Patrick and I now have were not handed to us on a plate, we went out and made our memories, and shaped our lives all by ourselves, and we will continue to do so, confident in the knowledge that we **will** succeed. We have this knowledge due to the following simple fact: our motivation is greater than our limitations. If you are reading this and are able-bodied with no real restrictions other than the ones you have made up in your head from listening to too many pessimists over the years, then you have no excuse. Change your mindset, and then change your results.

"Our inner world creates our outer world"

Keeping motivated

One of the most dangerous words in the English dictionary with regard to staying motivated towards reaching our goals is the word 'wish'. In my honest view, wishful thinking is extremely dangerous, as it takes away a person's ability to use positive motivated action. It enables the speaker of the phrase to think that what they want to achieve will only ever be accomplished through some form of miracle and immediately hinders any movement by that individual towards achieving whatever it is that they desire. Do not spend your life saying, "I wish". Instead, change your thinking and say, "I will". Then begin putting the required actions into achieving your desired goal. Keeping motivated is the ***most important*** thing you can do.

Change your world

Mahatma Gandhi once famously said, "Be the change you want to see in the world". However, for the purposes of this book and the message that I am trying to deliver in it allow me to add my own version...*Be the change you want to see in* ***YOUR*** *world.* You and you alone are the only person who can and should make any necessary change. Ultimately, no one wants or deserves to be spending their days in a room on their own ***staring out the window...watching their lives pass them by***.

"To live a happy life is not something that is reserved for the minority in this world; it is within all of our capabilities to live happily. All that is required of us is to take baby steps on a daily basis towards reaching our happiness. Remain positive and patient, because life is a marathon, not a sprint." – Tracey Ellen Maria

Notes

---

[i] http://www.webmd.com/brain/dystonia-causes-types-symptoms-and-treatments#1

[ii] https://www.dystonia-foundation.org/what-is-dystonia/frequently-asked-questions/frequently-asked-questions-symptoms

[iii] https://www.dystonia-foundation.org/what-is- dystonia/frequently-asked-questions/frequently-asked-questions-symptoms